The support of the BGTHA executive committee is acknowledged
in publication of this book

Dedicated to my wife Valerie for her support
and tolerance, and for the artwork

TRAVEL & HEALTH:
The Management of the Older Patient

I B McIntosh BA(Hons) MBChB DGMRCP DRCOG FFTMRCPS(Glas)

Copyright

Reserved by author

IMCI Publications and Research

2013

All rights not specifically granted are retained by the author and the right of integrity is maintained. No alterations are to be made to the script without the author's consent.

The author retains the electronic rights to book contents. The right of paternity is asserted but brief excerpts may be published with attribution of credit to the author.

The author and publisher have made every effort to ensure that information is accurate and as up-to-date as possible. However, they are unable to accept responsibility for any loss, injury or inconvenience sustained by any person, caused by errors or omissions or as a result of the advice and information given in this book.

All rights reserved. Non-commercial use of this material is encouraged as long as acknowledgement is made to the copyright holder. ©IMCI

Published by Dr Iain McIntosh.

Preface

Providing care and advice for the older traveller often seems to be a neglected aspect of travel medicine. There is very little literature specifically on this topic. It is surprising that more is not written since international travel by the older people is now very common and increasing. Every GP, practice nurse and pharmacist involved in giving travel health advice will know this all too well and will see older patients regularly. This may be because the issues involved overlap a variety of professional specialties. All the usual concerns apply such as determining appropriate vaccinations schedules and malaria prevention.

However, many – probably most – older patients have a background history of present or past medical problems that need be taken into account when they are planning their trips quite apart from the issues arising, for example, out of the normal physiological and mobility changes associated with ageing. Sometimes experience helps the older traveller to avoid risky situations but this is not always the case. A large number of older people are on multiple medications and availability may be an important issue to address. Side-effects may occur while they are away in unfamiliar environmental surroundings or undertaking unusual activities. Some are on drugs that need blood-test monitoring, such as anticoagulants.

Medical care abroad and health insurance may be difficult to obtain or very expensive. All these factors explain the need for more training and professional support for those advising the older traveller; this book has been a leading resource on the subject for many years.

It has recently been updated and can be strongly recommended as an important and reliable reference on the subject as well as being an enjoyable read.

Eric Walker MBChB DSc (Hon Madras) FRCP FFTM(Glas)
Past Dean Faculty Travel Medicine RCPSG(Glas)
Past President British Global and Travel Health Association

Promoting Education and Networking in Travel & Global Health

The British Global & Travel Health Association
www.bgtha.org

Promoting Education and Networking in Travel & Global Health

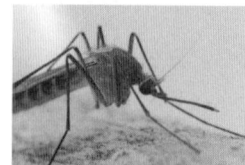

British Global and Travel Health Association

The author was co-founder and later president of the British Global and Travel Health Association, a charity that, for many years, has been dedicated to the education of all health professionals working in the discipline of travel-related medicine. It is very active in promoting conferences, educational courses, bursaries and literary publications of practical value for members, doctors, nurses and pharmacists working in this expansive clinical field. It encourages health risk assessment of international travellers, identification of potential hazards, sound counselling, prophylaxis and prevention of disease and disorder. The association publishes a scientific journal, newsletters, broadsheets and reviews to increase awareness of travel related medical topics.

The support of the BGTHA and input from executive committee members is acknowledged in publication of the earlier edition of this book, which is available to all members of the association online at www.bgtha.org.

All those working in travel health and in clinics and medical practices are encouraged to apply for membership of the organisation, which is committed to advancing good practice in an expanding field of preventive and clinical medicine.

About the Author

Iain B. McIntosh

BA(Hons) MBCHB DRCOG DGMRCP FFTMRCPS(Glas) FBSMDH

Former GP, GP trainer and hospital practitioner (geriatrics)

Author of several books and many research and general publications on travel related medicine. Former columnist for *Pulse* and *GP* newspapers; former editor of *Glasgow Medicine*, *Scottish Medicine* and *Rostrum*; editor in chief of BGTHA's journal and *TravelWise*; and editorial board member of *Geriatric Medicine*.

Co-founder and president of the British Global and Travel Health Association and fellow of the British Global and Travel Health Association. Established one of the first Scottish travel health-related clinics and British national travel medicine conferences.

Current travel health consultant and international lecturer to the public and professionals on travel health topics.

Extensive travel experience in over seven continents as expedition doctor and air repatriation physician.

Acknowledgements

Sincere thanks to Julie Gallagher, Larry Goodyer, George Kassianos, Mike Townend, Eric Walker and executive committee members of the British Global and Travel Health Association for their support and input with this project, and to Susan Olley for assistance in writing the chapter on psychological problems encountered in world travel.

The help of Norgine Pharmaceuticals in ensuring a wide professional readership is also appreciated.

Illustrations: Valerie McIntosh

Contents

Preface   5
About the British Global and Travel Health Association   7
About the Author   8

1   Ageing Effects on the Traveller   11

2   Risk Assessment   19

3   Travel Related Infection, Illness and Trauma   35

4   Air Travel and Associated Illness   45

5   Land and Sea Travel and Associated Illness   61

6   Travel Induced Disorders   75

7   Infection and Disease   87

8   Psychological Problems   109

9   Heart and Diabetic Problems   123

10   Frail and Disabled Travellers   135

11   The Older Adventurer   157

12   Medications   169

13   Travel Health Insurance and Medical Tourism   175

14   Emergency Healthcare Overseas   191

Index   225

1

Ageing Effects on the Traveller

The older traveller

The older population
Older people make up an increasing proportion of the UK European and North American populations. Many lead active and healthy lives for many years over the age of 65. With increasing life expectancy there will be many more of them, motivated to expand personal horizons and fit to embark on travel. Living longer, they can anticipate years of international travel after retirement from work.

In Britain the number of older people is increasing steadily each year. It increased from 15% in 1984 to 16% in 2009 – an increase of 1.7 million people. Twenty per cent of the UK population will soon be 65 years of age, with a considerable increase in those over 75 years anticipated in coming years.[1]

The most numerous five-year age groups at the 2001 census comprised those born in the years 1946–51 and 1966–71 (the largest group of all). The first group has reached retirement and, at the end of 2011, pensioners outnumbered children for the first time. In 2010, 11.3 million drew a state pension. By 2031 there will be 15 million pensioners, even though the pension age will have increased to 66 years for men and women.[2]

Although health expectancy has not improved at the same rate as life expectancy, older people can currently look forward to better health in old age than those of previous generations.[3]

Life expectancy
Life expectancy at age 65 in the UK has reached its highest level ever for both men and women. Men aged 65 can expect to live a further 18.2 years and women a further 20.8 years if mortality rates remain the same. The majority of the recently retired population are physically fit and in good health. They have time on their hands, relative affluence and past experience of travel in near Europe. A large number are now seizing the opportunity for extensive travel abroad. Budget and no-frills air travel encourages them to make long-anticipated global journeys of a

lifetime, to meet loved ones, satisfy a thirst to see the world's wonders and enjoy international adventure before passing years bring declining health. There is a window of opportunity for people aged between 65 and 85 years to travel to the far corners of the earth and many now do so regularly. The majority of older people make the pilgrimage to distant family and fulfil world travel dreams to remote objectives without mishap. With women having a longer life expectancy than men, they will travel into more senior years and, once widowed, many choose to travel on their own.

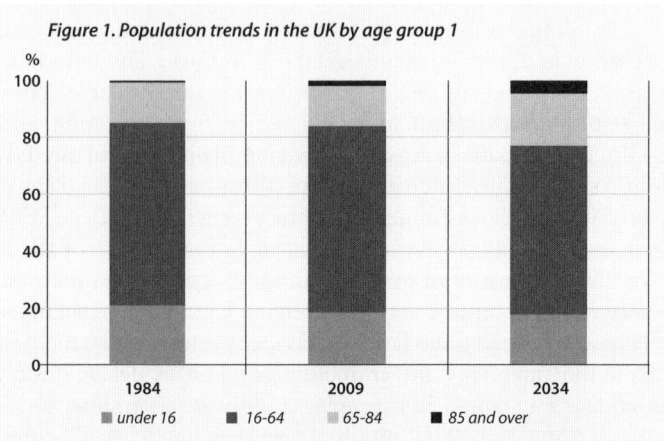

Figure 1. Population trends in the UK by age group 1

Table 1. Life expectancy in UK population, aged over 65 years
Source: *Office for National Statistics, Government Actuary's Department*[2]

Year	Life expectancy (years)	
	Women	Men
2008	20.1	17.4
2009	20.3	17.6
2010	20.4	17.8
2011	20.6	18.0
2012	20.8	18.2
2013	20.9	18.3
2014	21.1	18.5
2015	21.2	18.6

Not only can older people expect to live longer, many can also assume that they will remain physically fit for much of this time. The majority will remain healthy enough to undertake global travel to the farthest reaches of the planet for at least 10 years after state retirement age.

The healthy and not so well depart from Britain on vacation and intercontinental journeys, often with scant concern or consideration for risk to health that world travel can bring. They travel to destinations in developing countries and to remote parts, where conventional medical support in emergency is not available. They venture forth undeterred by pre-existing and chronic illness, on medication, and can put their lives at risk. Few consider the availability and quality of local medical resources and repatriation possibilities when embarking on eagerly awaited holidays.

Many depend on travel medical insurance for protection in times of need. This cover may be illusory however, limited to the best available in the locale, dependent upon environmental factors and may not match needs in an emergency. Insurers are becoming more selective in accepting senior citizens as clients and some older people are now travelling with limited or no health insurance protection. If a medical emergency arises while they are away and immediate first aid is delayed, local resources can be inadequate, evacuation protracted and hospitalisation suboptimal. This may have a serious impact on the individual and their recovery. Chronic morbidity and mortality is a possibility and, in the absence of adequate health insurance protection, financial demands for treatment and repatriation may prove penal.

Case history
An unfortunate cruise ship experience

A 72 year old man who had previously had a myocardial infarction and transient ischaemic attacks was determined to continue his winter cruise ship voyages in the Caribbean Sea. He was unable to obtain travel health insurance cover for his cardiac condition and stroke disease and opted to travel uninsured. He made one trip without medical mishap and on the next voyage suffered a severe stroke on board ship. He was disembarked at the next port of call on the island of St Thomas and ultimately transferred to hospital in the United States. His medical and nursing care fees were exorbitant and meeting them bankrupted the family. The endeavour to meet fees and care for her husband precipitated depressive and physical illness in the spouse, who required hospitalisation herself when the patient finally returned to the UK. Many older travellers conditioned to NHS care do not appreciate the high cost of health support overseas.

Physical and clinical fitness

A large number of older people remain fit and well into their 80s and can indulge in international visits and holidays with impunity. Many retain car driving ability into advanced old age – a measure of their independence and capability.

Community surveys have shown that 80% of 75 year olds are fit enough to travel from home unassisted and considerable numbers now indulge in international travel.[3] In a community study of people aged over 65, 33% had travelled out of the UK within the previous year and 35% of 75–80 year olds had participated in foreign travel in the preceding three-year period.[3] Many older people set off from the security of their homes and the protective net of the NHS and reciprocal European Union health provisions on long foreign journeys, ignorant of the health risks that accompany global travel.[4] Seeking winter sun and relaxation, they embark on world sea cruises and the increasing popularity of fly/cruising and adventure holidays is testimony to their commitment to long-distance travel.

In Britain, many now take early retirement, or leave employment aged 65, assuming they will retain good health until well through their seventh decade. Statistically, many can anticipate healthy global wanderings until their mid-70s with serenity.[5]

Thereafter, increasing age and chronic disease begins to take an inevitable toll and may make long-distance travel a more hazardous undertaking. The stereotyped view of the older person as confused, disabled and dependent is outdated and one finds older people exploring in the Amazon, visiting polar regions, climbing to high altitude and adventuring into remote parts of the world. They are also more likely to indulge in active leisure time activities while abroad and participate in white water rafting, paragliding, snorkelling and horse riding, intent on making up for lack of opportunity when young.

Mild and moderate physical impairment does not deprive the right of older people to venture afar or indulge in active sports, but they should do so with careful consideration of potential additional risk to wellbeing. It is the responsibility of the health professional and the travel agent to apprise them of likely health hazards they may encounter when far from home. They should endeavour to minimise the risk and optimise protection. Family doctors, surgery nurses and practice travel clinic pre-travel encounters with those intending to travel are ideal opportunities to meet this challenge.

Ageism and age discrimination are still dominant attitudes in Britain. Many cultures value their older people but Britain has yet to come to terms with its older population and value its contribution to society. There is often an assumption that advancing years alone rob the individual of physical and mental prowess, and steal independence. Compensatory mechanisms, the accrued wisdom of years and sound medical advice can, however, ensure that most older global holidaymakers will travel in good health. Realistic recognition of the wear and tear effects that come with advancing age is a prerequisite for enlightened risk assessment of foreign travel in senior citizens. The fittest and most healthy older traveller has not the physical integrity or endurance of those in the prime of life.

A reduction in immune, renal, cardiac and pulmonary function, as well as declining glucose tolerance with physiological stress, can place older people at higher risk of succumbing to travel-induced illness. Pre-existing disease, plus the effects of senescence, can make senior citizens very vulnerable to ill health during international travel. Mild mental and memory impairment can precipitate confusion in stressful travel situations. As a cohort they are also more likely to have an impediment of physical disability that must be considered in travel abroad.

Health status and the traveller

In terms of health risk, the potential older traveller is likely to fall into one of three categories:[3]
1. **The low-risk group** – 'young' older people, including those travelling to low-risk destinations, those on short-haul journeys, travellers free from any pre-disposing illness
2. **The medium-risk group** – group 1, where travel involves environmental extremes or tropical countries, older people who are frail, and those with pre-existing illness
3. **The high-risk group** – those with terminal illness, people with pre-existing illness, those travelling to high-risk countries, visiting areas with environmental extremes, visiting the tropics,[4] visiting malarious areas.

Aeroplanes, cruise ships and tourist resorts have their complement of older people in all of these categories, who will enjoy their vacation and return home in sound health. A minority will however become ill abroad and require local medical services, evacuation and repatriation.[5] Some will never return to good health after acquiring travel-induced illness and the experience will prove physically and psychologically traumatic. This critical event may adversely also affect the travelling companion and spouse.

Effects of the ageing process

The 65+ age group of people shows differences from the general population and younger cohorts that can have an effect on the outcome of global travel. These are:
- heterogeneity of health status
- age-related physiological changes
- increased incidence of co-morbidity
- atypical disease presentations.

Other effects of the ageing process are:
- increased incidence of iatrogenic illness
- higher need of social support

- increasing functional disability (this is closely associated with chronic disease[6]).

Pre-existing or chronic illness is likely to affect this group and has to be considered by travel health professionals when members of this group travel far from Britain. Long-term illness and disability affects an increasing number of people with advancing longevity.

Table 2. Long-term illness or disability that restricts daily activities, by sex and age

	Great Britain (%)	
Age	Men	Women
50-64	27.02	26.44
65-84	47.22	47.57
85 and over	67.10	73.79

Limiting long-term illness: calculated from a 'yes' response to the question 'Do you have any long-term illness, health problem or disability that limits your activities or the work you can do?' This includes problems due to old age.[5]

Many people in the older age group are, however, healthy, health conscious and follow active fitness programmes. They still wish to travel and they should be encouraged to do so as long as it is practical; however the impact of relocation, international transit and environmental factors en route and at the destination require consideration. The medical risk factors of transit mode, destination, itinerary, local environment and the medical facilities at the locale require the attention of a knowledgeable doctor or nurse. This requires pre-travel health consultation when clinical assessment, risk, precautions and prophylaxis can be discussed. Age in years is not the arbiter of fitness to travel abroad, however a fit 90 year old will have a pulmonary function of only half of that of a 30 year old[7] – a serious consideration when the individual can be exposed to reduced partial pressure of oxygen in an aircraft or at high terrestrial altitude.

Effects of the ageing process impacting on the world traveller[8]
Changes occur in:
- renal function
- water and sodium regulation
- temperature regulation
- cardio-pulmonary function
- gastrointestinal function

- cell-mediated immune response
- neurological function
- metabolic response.[8]

The physiological baseline in the older individual should be considered by health professional and travel organisers so advice can be given on health risks likely to impact on their travels.

Physiological function effects
Renal function
A 60% loss in renal function by the age of 65 years leads to increased cardiac load and decreased:
- sodium conservation
- ability to conserve water
- sweating ability
- pulmonary function
- ventilatory response to hypoxia.[6-8]

Psychological factors also require consideration in the long distance international traveller. The effects of stress in airports and transit stations and congestion on the roads and public concourses can be marked in the general public and have deleterious health effects in older people. Transit through airport lounges has been shown to have marked physiological and psychological effects on travellers[9] and may be sufficient to tip the vulnerable older person into cardiac failure or arrest.[6]

When the potential adverse effects of over-exposure to the sun, tropical infection, high altitude and environmental effects are also considered, it is obvious that there can be disadvantageous effects on global travellers' health status. Many of these can be neutralised by careful advance planning by traveller, travel health professional and travel agent organiser.[10]

Following chapters

The following chapters in this book consider:
- risk assessment
- travel-related health hazards
- prophylaxis and precautions
- effects of differing transportation modes
- adverse environmental extremes and adventurous travel
- pre-existing illness in world travellers

Assessment procedures, vaccination schedules and therapeutic procedures are presented with emphasis on the practical handling of potential older travellers in travel health consultation and the travel health clinic. Chapters on sea, air and adventure travel identify risk and offer recommendations to minimise hazard. The diabetic, cardio and pulmonary, and immuno-compromised traveller is dealt with in depth.

This medical handbook is a comprehensive aid, which should assist all involved in travel-related health care of older travellers. Its advice and recommendations can ensure that older people who seek a pre-travel health consultation will travel aware of risk and take appropriate measures to reduce it; this should ensure they travel and return in sound health.

References

1 www.statistics.gov.uk. Accessed 01/04/2012
2 Office for National Statistics (2007) Govt Actuaries Department
2 McIntosh IB (1992) Travel and Health in the Elderly. Lancaster: Quay Publications
3 Cossar J, Reid D et al (1990) Cumulative review of studies on travellers. *J Infect* 21: 27-42
4 McIntosh I (1991) Travel induced illness. *Scot Med* 11: 4,14-15
5 Census, April 2001, Office for National Statistics General Register Office, Scotland
6 Cameron J (1991) Functions in the elderly. *Ger Med* 29-34
7 Villar P, Wiggins J et al (1991) Structure and function of the ageing lung. *Care of the Elderly* 3: 129
8 Abrams W, Berror R (1990) *Manual of Geriatrics*. New Jersey: Merck & Co
9 McIntosh IB (2008) Psychological features of travel. *Brit Trav Health Assoc J* 11: 34-37
10 McIntosh (2012) Caring for the vulnerable elderly global traveller. *Ger Med* 42: 14-19

2

Risk Assessment

PRE-TRAVEL HEALTH RISK ASSESSMENT

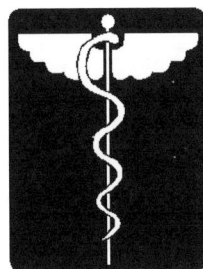

The pre-travel health consultation provides an opportunity to gather general and health data from potential travellers, to identify factors that may impact on their health status while abroad and initiate measures to minimise or prevent adverse effects. Creation of a personalised database is essential. Management requires consideration of potential hazards – untoward events that may occur – and risk, which relates to the degree of chance that an event will occur. Many factors are involved. For instance, disease hazard in a country depends not only on its presence, but also on other elements such as climate, sanitation, water supply, disease vectors and carriers, with level of health risk determined by personal immunity, vaccination and exposure to infection.[1]

Those with pre-existing disease have the added disadvantage of physical constraints relating to the condition. They are less able to compensate for the demands of a hostile environment and are more likely to succumb to travel-induced illness and disease.

Factors that influence health risk

Age effects
Each consultation with an older potential traveller should consider the impact of the ageing process on the individual. Ageing organs gradually, but progressively, lose function and there is a decrease in maximum functioning capacity. This often goes unnoticed by the individual as organs have a reserve ability to function beyond routine needs, but travel can bring additional physiological demands.

The heart of a 20-year-old is capable of pumping 10 times the amount that is actually needed to preserve life. After age 30, about 1% of this reserve is lost annually. With advanced years, the organ, when worked harder than usual, may not be able to increase reserve function – e.g. sudden heart failure can develop. Body stressors, e.g. disease, life changes such as an energetic vacation, suddenly increased physical

Table 1. Identifying the risk

Data to be acquired	Considerations
Age and gender	Older, very old
Regional destination	Developing country
Season	Monsoon
Journey duration	Short haul, long haul
Holiday type	Visit to relatives, city tours, safari, up-country, adventure, sporting
Climate	Climatic extremes
Altitude	High altitude
Latitude	High latitude, low latitude
Transportation mode	Air, sea, land
Itinerary	Touring, static
Holiday activities	Sporting, adventure
Vaccination status	
Smoking status	
Current physical status	Functional ability
Psychological status	Personality, travel phobia, confusional, anxiety state
Past medical history	
Current health status	
Pre-existing chronic disease	
Health facilities at destination	Quality, proximity
Travel health insurance status	Adequacy, exclusions

demands on the body from change in physical activity and exposure to high altitude can produce extra cardiac load. The effects of ageing on the heart, lungs, kidney and brain can make older world travellers more vulnerable to travel-related disease and trauma than younger people.[2]

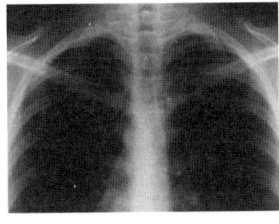

Ageing heart
Heart functions slow down with age. The ageing process reduces heart-muscle strength so pumping power declines and maximal heart rate also decreases. When the amount of blood pumped by the heart per minute declines, systolic blood pressure tends to rise. Ageing of the heart is associated with a number of disease-independent changes associated with a reduction in function including:
- a fall in the number of myocytes and cells within the conduction tissue
- development of cardiac fibrosis
- reduction in calcium transport across membranes
- lower capillary density
- decrease in the intracellular response to beta-adrenergic stimulation.

There is a steady increase in heart size and thickness of ventricular walls with age, with the cardiovascular system becoming more susceptible to diseases including high blood pressure and atherosclerosis. Nearly 40% of all deaths, among those in people aged 65 years and older, are due to heart problems.

By 80 years, men are nine times and women 11 times more likely to die of chronic heart failure than they were at age 50.

The older heart – even in the very fit – is no match for a younger one during exercise or stress. During physical activity the heart must pump more blood to working muscles. In the young, it increases the heart rate and squeezing harder during contractions, sends out more blood with each beat. The response differs with ageing: the heart rate still rises, but not as high.

In 20 year olds, maximum rate is 190–200 beats per minute; by age 80, this has diminished to 145 beats. There is a substantial decline in the peak rate at which the older heart can beat. The force of contraction during vigorous exercise increases, but this does not occur as much in older people as in the young and cardiovascular reserve diminishes.

A 20 year old can increase cardiac output during exercise to 3–4 times over resting levels, but an 80 year old can only muster about two times. The Frank-Starling mechanism compensates in part for this shortfall; however, during vigorous exercise, the older heart still pumps less blood overall because it cannot beat as fast as a young heart. This adaptation helps the heart meet immediate needs of the exercising older body, but it increases heart load and forces it to work harder. Ventricles do not fully relax between beats, causing end diastolic left ventricular pressure to increase and left atrial pressure to rise. This pressure increase is transmitted to lungs and, as pressure rises, oxygenated blood struggles to get from the lungs into the left side of heart to be pumped out to the body. The person then exhibits dyspnoea with effort.[2]

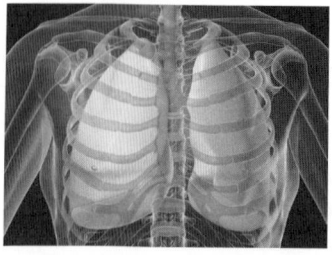

Ageing lungs
Abnormalities occur in the ageing human lung, which include:
- decreased mucociliary function
- dilatation of airspaces
- loss of elastic recoil
- loss of elastin fibres
- diminished diffusion capacity.

These changes explain the progressive decline of pulmonary function,[3] which gradually occurs after age 20. In the absence of respiratory insults (e.g. smoking, environmental toxins, prior respiratory infections), most older people have sufficient respiratory reserve to avoid symptoms. Reduction of respiratory reserve with ageing, however, often increases the risk and severity of pulmonary infections. After age 20, the number of alveoli and lung capillaries gradually begins to decrease, although lung volumes, airflow, diffusing capacity and purely age-related changes of lung function do not lead to clinically significant symptoms in non-smokers. In smokers and former smokers, injury due to inflammation is superimposed on, and accelerates, the effects of ageing, resulting in dyspnoea.

Changes in lung and chest-wall compliance are primarily responsible for age-related decreases in ventilation and the corresponding decreases in gas distribution that result from the collapse of small airways. After age 30, there is decrease in number and elasticity of parenchymal elastic fibres, which causes gradual loss of elastic recoil of the lungs. Airway size also decreases.

After age 55 years, respiratory muscles begin to weaken and the chest wall gradually becomes stiffer (decreasing compliance). The increased outward pull of the stiffer chest wall, combined with the reduced ability of the lung to pull inward, result in a small increase in functional residual capacity and residual volume.

Diffusing capacity peaks in people in their early 20s and then declines. From middle age onward, it declines at a rate of about 17% per decade in men and at a rate of about 15% in women. Loss of alveolar-capillary surface area decreases venous blood oxygenation, particularly under conditions of high pulmonary blood flow (e.g. exercise).

Partial pressure of arterial oxygen (PaO2) declines linearly with ageing (at a rate of about 0.3% per year) until age 75, at which time it stabilises at about 80mmHg in healthy non-smokers.[4]

Autonomic response in ageing

Heart rate and ventilatory responses to hypoxia and hypercapnia diminish with ageing because peripheral and central chemoreceptor responses diminish. Ageing also decreases neural output to respiratory muscles and lowers chest-wall and lung mechanical efficiency. *As a result, ventilatory response to hypoxia is reduced by 51% in healthy men aged 64–73 years compared with healthy men aged 22–30; ventilatory response to hypercapnia is reduced by 41%.* After age 40, decreases in FEV1 and FVC occur due to ageing itself. There are also superimposed cumulative effects of inflammatory injury from respiratory illness, smoking and exposure to environmental toxins.[5]

Blood and circulation changes

Ageing causes a reduction in total body water so there is less fluid in the bloodstream, with decreased blood volume. The number of red blood cells is reduced, which contributes to fatigue. Blood vessels become less elastic with average blood pressure increasing from 120/70mmHg to 150/90mmHg. Blood vessels lose elasticity and respond more slowly to changes in body position, with resultant postural hypotension, dizziness and falls.[2]

Other systemic deterioration

Body temperature changes

Body temperature does not change significantly with advanced years, but temperature regulation is more difficult. Loss of subcutaneous fat makes it harder to maintain body heat. Skin changes result in the reduced ability to sweat. Older people find it more difficult to tell when they are becoming overheated and are at greater risk from hyperthermia or heatstroke. They are also affected by dangerous drops in body temperature (hypothermia).[6]

Immunity change

There is a decline in immunity associated with increased vulnerability to infectious agents, with several causes of immunosenescence. The progressive atrophy of the thymus gland occurring with ageing, affects the ability to generate a cell-mediated immune response. The thymus gland is where T-lymphocyte (T-cell) immune cells mature. The thymus begins to atrophy and by middle age is about 15% of its maximum size at adolescence; although the number of T-cells does not decrease with ageing, T-cell function decreases, causing a weakening of the parts of the immune system controlled by these them. *Older people produce fewer helper T-cells and the ones they do have are often less effective than they were earlier in life.*

These changes bring a slow, steady decrease in immunity after young adulthood. When the body is exposed to bacteria or micro-organisms by actual exposure or by immunisation, fewer protective antibodies may be formed or they form slower.

Diminution of cell-mediated immune response with age, leads to a progressive reduction in antigen-driven lymphocyte proliferation – a common deficit in older individuals. Antibody responses to some vaccines (e.g. pneumococcal, influenza) that can decrease the risk of pneumonia decline with increased age. *Cellular immunity also declines with age.* Influenza immunisation and other immunisations may be less effective and protection may not last as long as expected. The immune system also becomes less able to detect foreign particles and infection risk is greater.

Other factors related to ageing also increase the risk of infections; these include sensation and skin change, which increase the risk of injury and permit bacterial skin entry. Ageing also affects inflammation – an immune response – and wound healing, which proceeds more slowly.[7]

Ageing kidney

The ageing process has several effects on the kidney:
- decline in glomerular filtration rate
- decreased urinary concentration
- decrease in diluting ability
- diminished urinary acidification
- impaired potassium clearance
- proneness to drug toxicity.

There is also impairment of fluid and electrolyte imbalance, especially when dehydrated. Dehydration can occur more readily in older people who frequently have less sense of thirst.

Kidneys have a built-in extra capacity but decreased efficiency occurs when they are under increased workload from illness, medications and dehydration. Renal changes may affect the ability to concentrate urine and hold onto water, and response to fluids and electrolyte intake is slowed.

Ageing increases the risk for urinary disorders including acute and chronic renal failure. By the age of 75, 10% of older people will have sufficient loss of kidney function to be categorised in level 3A of chronic kidney disease.

Ageing bladder, pelvic floor and prostate gland

The bladder wall changes with age: elastic tissue is replaced by tough fibrous tissue and the organ becomes less distensible.[8-10] Muscles weaken and the bladder may not empty completely when urinating with resultant continence problems.[10] Loss of pelvic floor tone in older women may be associated with a measure of prolapse. In older men, the prostate tends to enlarge with resultant hyperprostatism and obstruction to urinary flow. (*See Chapter 3 for incontinence problems.*)

Ageing skin

Thinning of the skin occurs as the rate of cell production slows in the epidermis.

The dermis may also become thinner, more 'papery'. Less elastin fibres are produced, causing sagging and drooping. Melanocytes tend to increase in certain areas – such as the backs of hands – forming age or liver spots. Older skin has fewer sweat and oil glands, resulting in the older individual having a reduced ability to sweat. Loss of subcutaneous fat makes it harder to maintain body heat. Older people also often find it more difficult to tell when they are becoming overheated and their skin is more susceptible to sun damage.

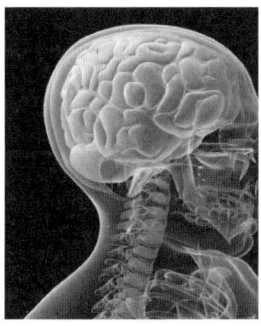

Ageing brain

As people get older, there is a decrease in brain weight and brain volume, a widening of the grooves on the surface of the brain and enlargement of the ventricular system, probably due to loss of cells surrounding the ventricles. Decrease in brain weight and brain volume are probably due to loss of neurons and extra cellular fluid. *A person may have a 20% reduction in brain weight between the ages of 45 and 85* and, with ageing, a loss of 30,000–50,000 neurons a day from the brain and nervous system.

Two thirds of older people eventually experience significant loss of mental lucidity and independence as a result of ageing. Individuals aged 60 years and older, often experience cognitive decline including:
- impairment in memory
- loss of concentration
- decreased clarity of thought
- impairment in focus and judgment.

The way the brain processes information is slowed, affecting the rate that people can put new information, especially that which is factual, into permanent memory. With ageing, delayed recall occurs – i.e. not being able to remember a familiar name or word – and it becomes harder to pay attention to more than one thing at a time. Common factors that impair normal memory function are stress, alcohol use, lack of sleep – all of which are elementsthat are associated with international travel.[6]

Bone changes

In early life, a careful balance exists between bone formation by osteoblasts and bone resorption by osteoclasts. With ageing, the process of coupled bone formation is affected by the reduction of osteoblast differentiation, activity and life span, which is further potentiated in the peri-menopausal years with hormone deprivation and increased osteoclast activity. Resultant osteoporosis can bring fracture from minor falls.[11]

Sensorial change

At age 70, 30% of people have impairment of vision and hearing. At 81 years, 6% have low vision and moderate-to-severe hearing loss, and only 10% have normal vision and hearing. At 88 years, 8–13% have low vision and moderate-to-severe hearing loss, and no men and less than a tenth of women have normal vision and hearing.[12]

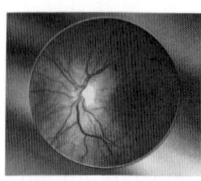

Sight
With change in vision there is loss of accommodation and focusing. The extent to which the pupil can dilate decreases with age. The light-adapted eye at 20 years of age gets six times greater light to the eye than at 80 years. The 20 year old dark-adapted eye gets 16 times greater light to the retina than its 80 year old counterpart. There is an age-related delay in dark adaptation. Failing visual acuity with advancing years creates difficulties in reading instructions and locomotion, with older people becoming particularly vulnerable in low-light situations.[12]

Hearing
Older people develop presbycusis, with as many as half those over 75 years having hearing loss. As a person ages, cochlear hair cells may become damaged. This results in a high-frequency hearing loss that can start as early as middle age, with males more affected over the age of 40. The middle ear also ages, going through physical changes that make it more difficult for a person to discriminate sound. Hearing loss is most pronounced at higher frequencies for both sexes. Loss of auditory acuity makes for difficulty hearing public-address systems.[13]

Environmental stress and ageing

Stress – the physical or psychological condition elicited by a situation – can be perceived as an external danger, hazard, threat or challenge. It places demands on the person who responds with coping mechanisms and adaptation.[14]

Relocation and international travel are stressors. Older people with more rigid thought processes can be slow to adapt and coping strategies may be less confrontational. They may be less likely to 'stand up for their rights' and have slower reaction times in emergency situations.[15-17]

Effects of existing disease

Illness, or recent surgery and trauma, can further weaken the ageing immune system, making the ageing body more susceptible to subsequent infections. Diabetes, more prevalent with age, can lead to decreased immunity. Reductions

in ventilatory response increases the risks of developing hypoxia and hypercapnia if older people acquire disorders that produce low O_2 levels (e.g. pneumonia, COPD, obstructive sleep apnoea).
Chronically low oxygen levels in older people result in:
- reduced tolerance to illness
- decreased exercise tolerance
- abnormal breathing patterns, including apnoea
- increased risk of lung infections such as pneumonia, bronchitis and diseases caused by tobacco damage such as emphysema.

Additional factors for cardiovascular decline in function are disease insults such as diabetes, hypertension, hyperlipidaemia and the habit of smoking.[7]

Bladder infections and other urinary tract infections are more common in seniors, in part related to incomplete bladder emptying. Urinary retention is more common as is urinary incontinence and frequency of micturition. The ageing kidney is constantly exposed to the effects of a variety of potential toxic processes, i.e. drugs and chronic illnesses including hypertension, diabetes and atherosclerotic disease.[8]

Renal changes that occur with ageing also consist of impairment in the ability to concentrate urine and to conserve sodium, as well as the ability to concentrate urine and to conserve sodium and water. These physiological changes increase the risks of volume depletion and pre-renal type of acute renal failure.[8] In men, the urethra may become blocked by an enlarged prostate gland; in women, weakened muscles can allow the bladder or vagina to prolapse, also causing blockage and urinary difficulties. With often-restricted access to toilets in world travel these are serious considerations for older travellers.[8-10]

Medication
Long-term medication can also add to health risk with potential effect on prophylaxis and travel-related health threats and failed compliance, which is common in travellers (*see Chapter 12*).

Age effects on bodily function that can increase the risks of world travel
- Decreased heart capacity decreases the ability to cope with travel-related stresses such dehydration, high altitude or physical exertion.
- Decreased lung capacity means less reserve to deal with reduced oxygen at altitude or from chest infection.
- Weakened immune system makes infection more likely.
- Deteriorating kidney function increases the likelihood that dehydration will lead to kidney failure and diminishes the ability for the kidneys to cope with salt loss when diarrhoea occurs.
- Deteriorating brain function can cause confusion in stressful situations and some older people find it difficult to cope with new situations and

- have a lower anxiety threshold.
- Decline in visual and auditory senses can cause accidents or failure to see or hear public announcements in airports, rail stations and on ships.
- Poor balance and slow reaction time can increase the risk of fall and make walking more perilous.
- Poorer circulation and wound healing results in slower healing of scratches, bites and injuries.
- Thinning bones from osteoporosis increases the risk of fractures with falls.
- Reduced stomach acid increases the risk of food poisoning and problems from contaminated food and water.[6]

Increased vulnerability during travel can be due to:
- high temperatures and heatstroke
- environmental extremes
- deep vein thrombosis
- hypothermia
- hypoxaemia
- fatigue and exhaustion.

EXTERNAL FACTORS AFFECTING TRAVELLERS

Destination
Certain regions of the world, primarily developing countries, present higher health risks due to the risk of infection and road traffic accidents.

Season
Travelling outside of the tourist season, in monsoons, or in extreme heat or cold can be hazardous for the traveller.

Transportation
Air travel of over 8 hours' duration, as well as prolonged coach and car travel, can create a risk of travellers' thrombosis.

Holiday type. Visitors to friends and relatives in Africa and Asia can be at higher risk of infection as they assume immunity and do not acquire appropriate vaccinations.

Climate extremes of heat or cold can result in travellers suffering heatstroke, dehydration, hyperthermia and hypothermia.

Local medical facilities. In emergencies, local medical and nursing aid may be substandard, inadequate and distant, with prolonged evacuation being a disadvantage to the ill or injured traveller.

Assessment and management planning

Management plan
1. Identify health hazards using a questionnaire.
2. Analyse the risk.
3. Advise patients of health hazards in the proposed travel itinerary.
4. Advise on factors that can be altered to decrease risk.
5. Negotiate a management plan and programme with the client.
6. Provide adequate prophylaxis and vaccination.
7. Provide appropriate advice regarding precautions to be taken en route, at the destination and on return.
8. Counsel on appropriate changes in drug medication, e.g. with diabetes, and how to deal with alterations in circadian rhythm.
9. Advise on minimising the effects of pre-existing disease during travel and on holiday.
10. Provide appropriate certificates and referral letters.
11. Complete certificates required by transport authorities or tour operators.
12. Advise clients on sources of useful information, e.g. booklets, websites.
13. Provide clinical valuation for the high risk, very frail old, and those with pre-existing disease that may exclude them from travel. Much of the assessment can be carried out by members of the care team, i.e. practice or travel-clinic nurse.[18]

Data acquisition
Acquisition of the data from one-to-one consultation, or from a questionnaire presented to the patient on arrival at the pre-travel interview, will provide the necessary information for the health professional to make an informed risk assessment of the health hazards likely to confront the person on international travel. Analysis of data will identify the traveller at higher risk and permit the creation of a customised management plan to minimise or negate potential challenges to health. The client can be apprised of risks, encouraged to recognise them and advised on appropriate prophylaxis and prevention. Creating a customised management plan for the individual, to minimise the risks of global travel, is recommended.

Risk appraisal

Advanced age makes world travellers more vulnerable to trauma and infection, but other key factors affecting a sojourn abroad must also be considered. It can help to sort travellers into low, medium and high-risk categories using a scoring tool that is based on a questionnaire.

A risk-scoring tool[18]

		Low	Medium	High
Age	65–74	•		
	75–84		•	
	85+			•
Destination	Northern Europe, Canada, America, Australia, New Zealand	•		
	Eastern Europe, Former Soviet bloc, Mediterranean littoral		•	
	Tropics, SE Asia, India, Africa, developing countries			•
Season	Favourable	•		
	Monsoon, out of season		•	
Transportation	Air, long haul		•	
	Sea, land	•		
Climate	Moderate, low altitude	•		
Environment	Extreme, high altitude			•
Smoking status	Non-smoker	•	•	
	Smoker			
Physiological function	Functional, visual, hearing, continence defect		•	
Psychological state	Travel phobia, anxiety/confusional state		•	
Medical status	Current illness, pre-existing and chronic illness, terminal illness		•	
	Recent stroke, myocardial infarction, insulin dependent diabetes, COAD <50%			•
Medications	Multiple		•	
Vaccination status	Unprotected, immuno-suppressed			•
Other	Predisposition to severe motion sickness		•	
	Travelling alone			•
	Medical facilities at destination poor, distant			•
	Travel insurance – absent, inadequate		•	

Summating the score in predominantly medium- and high-risk categories will help to identify those who should have a comprehensive health screen before departure.[18]

Figure 1 provides a rough guide to risk per month of travel.[19]

Figure 1. Risk per month of travel (from Steffen et al, 1997)

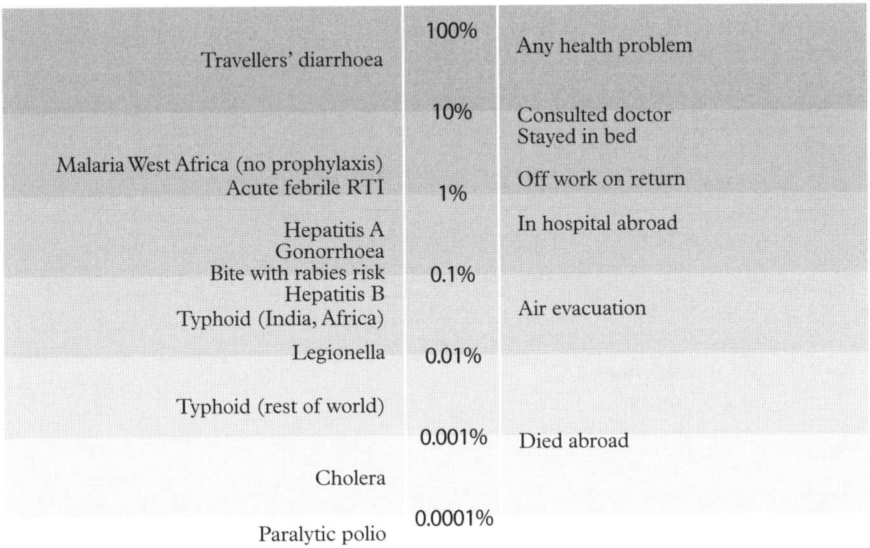

Travellers' diarrhoea	100%	Any health problem
	10%	Consulted doctor / Stayed in bed
Malaria West Africa (no prophylaxis) / Acute febrile RTI	1%	Off work on return
Hepatitis A / Gonorrhoea / Bite with rabies risk / Hepatitis B / Typhoid (India, Africa)	0.1%	In hospital abroad / Air evacuation
Legionella	0.01%	
Typhoid (rest of world)		
	0.001%	Died abroad
Cholera		
Paralytic polio	0.0001%	

This is a logarithmic chart. Each graduation represents a 10-fold difference in risk. 100% would imply that all travellers would be likely to develop the problem, 1% that 1 in 100 travellers would likely to develop it and 0.0001 that 1 in 1 million would be likely to develop it.

Destinations in developing countries, the tropics, environmental and latitude extremes, and more distant countries in the former eastern bloc, may present high risk. Travel in the monsoon season, on safari, up-country and for adventure and sport are also likely to be riskier health undertakings. Prolonged travel by air or coach can present health hazards and people visiting family and friends often risk disease by failing to take appropriate vaccinations. Smokers, the unvaccinated and those with predisposing or chronic disease, have to be regarded as potentially higher-risk travellers.

Infection risk

The risk of the traveller succumbing to infection while overseas has to be gauged. This is an important determinant of advice and vaccinations.[15]

Summary

Increased vulnerability in people who are old is due to:
- increased infection risk
- decreased ability to fight diseases
- slowed wound healing
- change in gait
- imbalance
- poor temperature control
- decreased immunity
- increased health risk accompanying heavy exercise, high altitude, environmental extremes, physical and psychological stress
- renal changes
- decreased cardiovascular efficiency
- ventilatory changes
- skin thinning
- cognitive impairment
- less ability to cope with psychological stressors
- pre-existing illness
- medications.[19]

References

1 McIntosh I (ed) (2010) *Travel and Health in Older People.* Peterborough: Fast Print Publishing
2 Roffe C (1998) Ageing of the heart. *Br J Biomed Sci* 55: 2, 136-48
3 Signola AM, Bousquet J (2001) *The Ageing Lung.* Current Allergy Reports, 1, 1-2 Current Science Inc.
4 Cameron J (1991) Functions in the elderly. *Ger Med* 29-34
5 Villar P, Wiggins J et al (1991) Structure and function of the ageing lung. *Care of the Elderly* 3, 129
6 Abrams W, Berror R (1990) *Manual of Geriatrics.* New Jersey: Merck & Co
7 Overstall PW (1994) In: Souhami R, Moxham J (eds) *Medicine.* Edinburgh: Churchill Livingstone
8 Zhou XJ, Saxena R, Liu Z et al (2008) Renal senescence in 2008: progress and challenges. *Int Urol Nephrol* 40: 3, 823-39 EPub
9 Muhlberg W, Platt D (1999) Age dependent changes of the kidneys, pharmacological implications. *Gerontology*
10 Meyer BR, Bellucci A (1986) Renal function in the elderly. *Cardiol Clin* 4: 2, 227-34
11 Chan G, Duque G (2002) Age-related bone loss: old bone, new facts. *Internat J Exptl Clin Behave and Tech Gerontology* 48, 2
12 Bergman B, Rosenhall U (2001) Vision and hearing in old age. *Scand Audiol* 3, 255-63
13 Pedersen K, Rosenhall U, Muller M (1989) Changes in pure tone thresholds. *Audiology* 28: 4, 194-204

14 Simonton KN (1955) Presbycusis, hearing loss of old age. *Geriatrics* 10: 7, 337-38
15 Costa P, McRae A (1990) *Ageing Stress and Health*. Chichester: Wiley
16 McIntosh I, Power K et al (1996) Prevalence, and intensity of travel related stressors. *J Trav Med* 3: 2, 96-102
17 McIntosh I, Power K et al (1998) Anxiety and health problems related to air travel. *J Trav Med* 5, 198-204
18 McIntosh I (1992) *Travel and Health in the Elderly: A Medical Handbook*. Lancaster: Quay Publishing
19 Townend M (2008) Risk assessment. *Brit Trav Health Assoc J* 12

3

Travel Related Infection, Illness and Trauma

All travellers are exposed to a range of health risks during a trip overseas. Health professionals need to be aware of these, how they affect older people, how to prevent them, and must provide best advice in pre-travel consultation.

Older travellers may be more vulnerable to these risks and, if they are affected, may be more adversely disturbed. Lowered immunity makes it more likely they may become infected and secondary effects of infection such as fever, dehydration and electrolyte imbalance can prove a greater health threat than in younger people. They are at greater risk of having a road traffic accident while abroad. The effects of trauma with fracture, and of disability, may have greater impact on seniors with slower wound healing and complicating chronic medical problems.

Risk can be categorised, with actual risk to the individual being dependent upon prevalence of the condition at destination, or en route. Travel destination is associated with the probability of contact with certain diseases. Significant trends are based on regional differences:

Infectious health risk

- dengue fever
- diphtheria
- hepatitis A, B, C, D, E
- HIV and sexually transmitted infections
- influenza
- Japanese encephalitis
- Legionnaires' disease
- leishmaniasis
- leptospirosis
- Lyme disease
- malaria
- meningococcal meningitis
- poliomyelitis

- rabies
- Rickettsial disease
- schistosomiasis
- tetanus
- tick-borne encephalitis
- travellers' diarrhoea
- trypanosomiasis
- tuberculosis
- typhoid and paratyphoid
- West Nile virus
- yellow fever.

It is estimated that only 5% of travel-related infectious disease is vaccine preventable.[1]

Non-infectious environmental health risk

- altitude illness
- insect and animal bites
- ultraviolet light radiation
- traumatic accident
- travel-related deep vein thrombosis.

In returning travellers
- Fever with only generalised symptoms occurs disproportionately among those returning from sub-Saharan Africa or Southeast Asia.
- Acute diarrhoea occurs most frequently in those returning from south central Asia.
- Dermatological problems are primarily present in those returning from the Caribbean, or Central or South America.
- Malaria is one of the three most frequent causes of systemic fever-related illness among travellers from every region.
- Travellers from every region except sub-Saharan Africa and Central America have confirmed or probable dengue more frequently than malaria.
- Travellers from all regions except Southeast Asia present with parasite-induced diarrhoea more often than with bacterial diarrhoea.

Travel-related illness

The risk for infections is high during travel and visits to many developing countries.[2] However, disease causes just 9% of deaths in overseas travellers. To determine the incidence of travel-related illness in a typical urban population in Scotland, 1,568 patients presenting to a GP within a one-year period were studied and morbidity rates investigated. Forty-two per cent of travellers became ill while abroad, with 48% of ill travellers returning to consult their family doctor. Travellers to Africa and Asia were shown to have the highest rates of illness.[3] People who consulted a doctor were likely to be older, in poorer health and taking regular medication. Gastro intestinal is common.[4]

In a sample of ill, returned travellers, the male-to-female ratio was 1.6; 70.9% were returning from sub-Saharan Africa and the median time from return of travel to hospitalisation was 13 days (IQR: 7-21). Malaria was the most frequent diagnosis (49.1%), which was especially encountered in patients returning from sub-Saharan Africa (95.6%), without adequate chemoprophylaxis (78.2%).[5]

Adventure travel puts travellers at added health risk from environmental hazards, which are important causes of morbidity and potential mortality among travellers. Injuries are common among adventure travellers (6.1%).[6,7]

Travellers' diarrhoea

Case history

A couple in their mid–70s were travelling in a group on a conventional tourist trip along the old Silk Road to Samarkand. They both unwisely enjoyed an ice cream from a roadside vendor in Tashkent. Through the next night the wife became ill with vomiting, profuse diarrhoea, fever and prostration. The hospital doctor arranged admission to the local infectious disease unit and for the husband to remain in the hotel until the return of the group a week later.

The wife was treated with magnesium trisilicate and fluids in the district hospital, which had few resources. She slowly returned to health. The husband was left isolated, in his own care, in an environment with no English speakers. He soon fell ill with travellers' diarrhoea. The local water supply was contaminated and he did not replace his fluid loss as bottled water was expensive. At the end of the week when the main party returned, he was found to be ill, confused, extremely dehydrated and suffering watery diarrhoea. Hospitalised, he received the same treatment as his wife and made a partial recovery. Flown back to the UK with an accompanying nurse, he was readmitted to hospital in Britain with gross electrolyte imbalance and renal failure; he died shortly afterwards. His death was untimely, travel related, potentially avoidable and the outcome not inevitable if treatment had been prompt and adequate.

Travellers' diarrhoea is the predominant problem in global travel, in terms of frequency, and personal and economic impact.[5] It can have deleterious effects on older tourists if there is marked fluid loss with electrolyte imbalance. It merits mention in pre-travel health consultations with advice on avoidance, prophylaxis and treatment. Self-medication shortens the duration of the illness[8-10] (see Chapters 6 and 7).

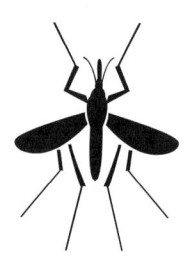

Malaria

Malaria is one of the most prevalent human infections and the world's second biggest killer disease after tuberculosis. It is present in over 100 countries, the majority affected by drug-resistant strains. Over 90% of cases occur in Africa, most caused by *P. falciparum*; 90% of deaths occur in sub-Saharan Africa. It is the tropical disease most imported into UK. Non-immune people, such as travellers, are at highest risk of severe disease. In developed countries, malaria occurs mainly in people who have returned from endemic regions. Personal protective measures and appropriate chemoprophylaxis can significantly reduce risk of infection in international travellers. Prophylaxis, early treatment and standby emergency treatment (SBET) can reduce morbidity.

Malaria is not endemic in the UK but nearly 2,000 cases occur annually in travellers returning to Britain from malaria-endemic countries. Older people are often more seriously affected if infected. Malaria is a preventable disease transmitted by the female *anopheles* mosquito. The types that affect humans are *plasmodium falciparum* (causing most deaths), *vivax, ovale,* and *malariae* resulting in 1 million deaths per year worldwide.

Analysis of people travelling abroad in 2007 showed 18% were visiting friends and relatives with a significant number of them travelling to countries with a high prevalence of malaria, typhoid, paratyphoid and hepatitis A; these inlcuded India, Pakistan and Bangladesh in particular. Many did not seek travel health advice before the trip and the majority did not take malaria prophylaxis. Many of these travellers are first-generation immigrants returning to former homelands and those in the first wave of post-war immigration are now of senior years. They assume they have infection immunity from their previous residence abroad but this is illusory and they need antimalarials or other protection.[11]

Treatment depends on the infecting plasmodia species, geographic area of acquisition (related to drug resistance) and severity of infection. Increasing resistance has brought new preventative drugs, all with potential serious side-effects. Adverse effects and contraindications to antimalarial medications are common and can be serious in older people. A high degree of suspicion and rapid diagnosis of malaria are essential to optimise therapeutic outcome. The possibility should be considered in all cases of unexplained fever starting in a visitor spending seven days in an endemic area.

Guidelines recommend malaria chemoprophylaxis for travellers; however, the relevance of this prescription for older people may be questioned, especially for those on multiple medications making very transient visits to an endemic area such as a cruise-ship day visit. Drug prophylaxis to prevent chloroquine-resistant *P. falciparum* malaria, can induce adverse effects and it may be better to avoid chemoprophylaxis if not absolutely necessary. For instance, in many tropical and subtropical countries, malaria does not occur at all; in others, the level of transmission is insignificant or low. Travel without chemoprophylaxis to an area with malarial transmission, even at minimal level, requires rigorous antivector protection however. Malaria must be considered with unexpected febrile illness, and medical treatment sought urgently or immediate recourse made to have treatment on standby.

The Advisory Committee on Malaria Prevention for UK Travellers (ACMP) has produced guidelines of essential information on malaria prevention for healthcare workers advising travellers, entitled *Guidelines for Malaria Prevention in Travellers from the United Kingdom*. The risks of malaria need to be balanced against the risks of the preventive measures.

Road traffic accident

Travellers often are involved in a road traffic accident at the start or end of their travels while travelling to the airport or port. The UK national estimate for road accidents while travelling and touring was 48,066 in 2007. Statistics show that the chance of being involved in a car accident in mainland Europe, however, doubles – and it almost triples in Greece and Portugal.[11] Accidents cause 20% of all deaths among overseas travellers – the second most common cause after heart disease (68%).[12]

Accidental injury can occur through road traffic accidents or personal violence. It is a serious travel-related risk accounting for about 25% of all deaths of travellers while abroad.[13,14] Accidents kill and injure many travellers, with 28% of accidental deaths due to road traffic tragedies. Developing countries have 20 times more traffic accidents per road miles than developed countries. Particularly high-risk road activities are travelling in unsafe vehicles, by motor scooter or on overcrowded buses.[15] Older drivers have a higher crash risk per mile driven than other adults. The higher risk of their dying in a crash is probably attributable to the frailty of older drivers rather than the functional limitations that accompany ageing. Research literature indicates that older drivers are not a risk to other road-user age groups, but primarily to themselves. It is the older driver and their vehicle's occupants who are at higher risk of dying when in a crash.[16]

Accidents in vehicles or on the road are one of the riskiest aspects of travel abroad. They are far more of a risk abroad than other sources of danger, such as terrorism or exotic diseases, which travellers often fear.

Environmental accidental injury

In the UK there are 2 million accidents and 6,000 deaths each year in the home. Unfamiliar surroundings in a foreign environment will increase these risks. Falls are a common cause of injury and are often associated with alcohol. They are particularly likely in older adults, due to poor vision, imbalance and postural hypotension. The common habit on holiday of walking barefoot or in sandals increases the risk of falls and foot injuries.

Personal violence

Most violence occurs through resisted muggings, or theft.

Altitude illness

High altitude – above 5,000m – is associated with decreasing partial pressure of oxygen and can expose the traveller to acute mountain sickness. This can be related to an individual climbing too fast, too high and too far on a day of travel in high mountains. Older people are perhaps less likely than the young to exhibit this behaviour and are no more likely than other adults to succumb to the condition. However, their lungs and heart have not the performance of younger climbers and lower PO_2 can push older people into cardiac and respiratory failure, with those with underlying cardio/pulmonary disease at greatest risk.[7] The majority of older people exposed to high altitude will be travelling to destinations in South America where cities like La Paz and Cusco have airports at high altitiude (approximately 4,000m and 3,300m above sea level respectively). Many people arriving here are unaware of the risk until they find themselves with laboured breathing and anoxia or angina in the rarefied atmosphere (*see Chapter 14*).

Pre-travel preparation

In anticipation of distant foreign travel, older people should consider a travel health consultation so that a doctor/nurse can appraise the health risk and consider prevention and protection. The traveller should seek appropriate vaccination and malaria prophylaxis. The need for mechanical protection against mosquito bites has to be emphasised and repellents should be used in conjunction with prophylactic medication.[17] GP and commercial travel health clinic staff can then provide a customised action plan.

Travel health clinics significantly reduce the morbidity of illness for travellers and the burden on general practices can be reduced with pre-travel advice and prophylaxis. Travel-clinic attendees are more likely to be travelling to high-risk destinations but are better prepared, experiencing a significantly lower rate of illness during travel (22%). Clinic attendees are also less likely to consult their doctor regarding travel related illness on return home.[6]

The Cochrane Collaboration Database of Systematic Reviews and meta-analyses was searched for studies relevant to family physicians; at the time of the search there were no randomised control trials on prevention of accidents and travel abroad.

Patient information leaflets
Avoidance of injuries from 'natural hazards'
- Foot injuries in those unfamiliar with wearing sandals, or when going barefoot, are common. Sensible footwear should be worn. Sea creatures (e.g. fish, eels, molluscs) and caterpillars may be unexpectedly venomous, causing rashes or more serious illnesses. Wear protective footwear when entering unfamiliar water.
- Dogs and cats in many countries run wild, are often hungry and may respond aggressively when approached. Avoid handling them.
- Do some homework and be aware of where the nearest emergency facilities are situated at the holiday destination.

Avoiding road accidents
- Be aware that driving custom may be on the opposite side of the road to the UK.
- Reliable cars should be used. Examine the car carefully to ensure it is roadworthy and has seat belts – use them.
- Avoid driving in poor light and at night.
- Strictly observe speed limits, traffic lights and other road signs.
- Never drink and drive.
- Be very careful on potholed and non-sealed gravel roads, which can become corrugated.
- Avoid overcrowded buses.
- Hiring scooters and motor bicycles is risky; ensure safety helmets are used.
- Segway transportation is unwise if balance and reactions are poor.

Ensuring personal safety (mugging, theft, violence)
- Most authorities say that, to avoid injury, travellers should not resist if mugged.

Prevention of diarrhoea
Where food and water is concerned, 'boil, cook, peel or avoid it' is good advice. Systematic reviews on preventing diarrhoea confirm that bismuth subsalicylate, doxycycline, ciprofloxacin and trimethoprim/sulfamethoxazole are useful prophylactics.[18]

The second generation prebiotic food supplement B-GOS, taken immediately prior to and during travel, may be of value in preventing or diminishing the impact of travel-related diarrhoea[19].

Prevention of malaria

The **ABCD** approach to prevention recognises four points that are essential to minimise the risk of infection:[12,20]
- **A**wareness: know about the risk of malaria
- **B**ites by mosquitoes: prevent or avoid
- **C**ompliance with appropriate chemoprophylaxis
- **D**iagnose: breakthrough malaria swiftly and obtain treatment promptly.

Guidelines now give greater emphasis to the importance of balancing the risk of malaria and the risk of adverse reactions to antimalarials. This depends upon:
- place to be visited
- duration of the visit
- degree of exposure
- level of drug resistance
- type of traveller

All these factors affect the risk of getting malaria. Most adverse reactions to antimalarials occur with the first few doses, but the cumulative risk of contracting malaria is proportional to the length of stay in a malarious area. The longer the stay, the more important it is to implement a regimen with a high protective efficacy[12]

Prevention of altitude sickness

Use of acetazolamide as a prophylactic may be recommended. The risk/benefit of the prescription has to be considered if the traveller has concomitant disease and is on routine medication, e.g. diuretics[21] *(see Chapter 14)*.

Information sources

National Travel Health Network and Centre (NaTHNaC), London: 020 7380 9234
Scottish Centre for Infection and Environmental Health (SCIEH), Glasgow. For Travax users only, 2-4pm: 0141 300 1130
Birmingham Heartlands Hospital (Infectious Disease Unit): 0121 424 0357
Liverpool School of Tropical Medicine: 0151 708 9393
Northwick Park Hospital, London: 020 8864 3232

References

1 National Travel Health Network and Centre. Vaccine preventable illness 2007 report .London
2 Wilson E. Hospitalisation for Travel-Related Illness. Journal Watch Infectious Diseases July 8, 2005
3 McIntosh I. Elderly travellers and fitness to travel in travel Medicine and migrant health. Ed. Lockie C. Walker E. et al 2000. Churchhill Livingstone. London
4 Evans R. Thomas A. Howard J. Domestic and travel-related food borne gastrointestinal illness in

a population health survey. 2006 Epidemiology and Infection 134:4:686-693
5 Leroy H. Arvieux C et al A retrospective study of 230 consecutive patients hospitalised for travel related illness. Eur.J. Clin. Microbiol.Infect. Disease. 2008 (11) 1137-40
6 Reed JM. McIntosh I.B Power K Travel Illness and the Family Practitioner: A Retrospective Assessment of Travel-Induced Illness in General Practice and the Effect of a Travel Illness Clinic.J.Trav. Med.1. 192–198.
7 Boggild AK,Costiniuk C, Kain KC, Pandey P. Environmental hazards in Nepal: altitude illness, environmental exposure, injuries, and bites in travellers and expatriates. J Travel Med. 2007 Nov-Dec;14(6):361-8
8 Peltola HP. Gorbach LS Travellers diarrhoea in Textbook of travellers' health .ed. Dupont. Steffen 1997 Decker. Canada
9 Zeichner LO Ericson CD Travellers diarrhoea in Principles and practice of travel medicine. 2001 ed. Zuckerman Wiley Chichester.
Office Nat Stats. Internat. passenger survey 2007/8)
10 The Centres for Disease Control and Prevention (CDC) 2007 report. Atlanta
11 Office Nat.Stats.Internat. Passenger Survey. 2007/8 London
12 Health Protection Agency. Foreign travel associated illness –a focus on those visiting friends and relatives – 2008.London
13 Paisao MT. Cossar J. Read D. Mortality amongst overseas travellers from Scotland First Internat Cong Trav. Med. 1988 London
14 Hargarten S Baker T Guptil K Fatalities of American Travellers Proceedings. First Internat Conf Trav. Med. 1988 London
15 Eberhard J Older drivers. 2008 Traffic Inj. Prev Aug. 9 284-90
16 Petridou E Askitopolou H et al epidemiology of road accidents during pleasure travelling Accid. Anal. Prev. 1997 687-93
17 Thomas RE preparing patients to travel abroad safely 2000.Can.Fam. Physician 46 1634-8
18 The Cochrane Database of Systematic Reviews and The Cochrane Library 2003 London
19 Drakoularakou A,Tzortzis G, Rastall RA et al. A double-blind, placebo-controlled, randomized human study assessing the capacity of a novel galacto-oligosaccharide mixture in reducing travellers' diarrhoea. Eur J Clin Nutr 2009; 1-7.
20 The Advisory Committee on Malaria Prevention for UK Travellers (ACMP) Public Health Lab. Service 2008
21 Green A. Kerr A. McIntosh I. 1981 Acetazolamide in prevention of acute mountain sickness. Brit. Med. J. 283 .11

4

Air Travel and Associated Illness

About 2 billion people travel aboard scheduled aircraft annually.[1] One in five international air journeys originates from Britain and traffic flow through UK airports involves about 150 million passengers each year.[2] A substantial number of them are senior citizens; they and travel healthcare professionals should be aware of the potential health risks associated with air travel. Environmental and physiological changes occurring during routine commercial flights can lead to mild hypoxia and gas expansion, which can exacerbate chronic medical conditions and precipitate acute in-flight medical occurrences. The latter are increasing in frequency. With ageing of national populations, a growing number of individuals are older and have pre-existing medical conditions. They are vulnerable to venous thromboembolism (VTE), cosmic-radiation exposure and jet lag, as well as healthcare issues related to cabin air quality and psychological stress.[2]

Air transport is the favoured long-haul mode for protracted travel. Up to 5% of airline passengers suffer from chronic illness, with many of these older people conforming to 'invalid passenger' status. As individuals are responsible for reporting incapacity to air carriers, this may be an underestimate. Ninety-five per cent of people with health problems who have to travel by air desire more medical advice from their physicians about its effects.[3]

Many older passengers instigate mid-air emergencies. About 72 people, many of advanced years, die annually while airborne, with sudden cardiac crisis the cause of death in one group studied; only 34% of these individuals had reported health problems prior to travel.[4] Air carriers are not obliged to report in-flight medical

45

events, but limited data report an incidence of one in 10,000–40,000 passengers, suggesting about 50–100 in-flight medical events per day, with US airlines.[5]

British Airways carried 17 million people and recorded 1,328 medical incidents to airborne passengers a gross attack rate of 1:13,000, in one report. The ratio narrowed to 1:350 passengers, many of whom were old and infirm, who notified themselves as less than fit beforehand. The same airline reported 31,200 medical incidents aboard its aircraft during 2007, with 3,000 being deemed serious.[6] Most recoded in-flight medical events are, however, minor in severity and often are panic attacks.[7] The effects of pre-existing disease resulting in chronic pulmonary, cardiac, renal, hepatic and physical dysfunction can place older people at higher risk from physiological and physical stressors that are inseparable from modern air travel. The air traveller mainly faces problems stemming from:
- pressure of the air in the aircraft cabin
- amount of oxygen in the air
- quality of air.

The first two are related. Although modern aircraft are pressurised, they are not pressurised to sea-level air pressure but to approximately two-thirds of this. This is equivalent to the atmospheric pressure on the summit of a 2,700m-high mountain, which has two consequences:

- The concentration of oxygen remains unchanged, so the actual partial pressure of oxygen must also be reduced to about two-thirds of that at sea level.
- The reduced pressure causes gases to expand by about 30%, according to Boyle's law.

Cabin air at high altitude

Tolerance to thin air experienced at altitude may be poor in passengers suffering from chronic illness such as hypercapnia, which is associated with severe anaemia, active cerebrovascular and cardiovascular disease. Cardiac, neurological and respiratory complaints are the most serious in-flight medical events, with cardiac and neurological complaints accounting for most diversions. Passengers aged over 70 years have highest rates of in-flight medical events.[8] Individuals may cope in day-to-day living at ground level but exhibit fatigue, cardiac arrhythmia or vague symptoms due to anoxia, when exposed to moderate degrees of high altitude, as occurs in high-flying aircraft.

Regulatory authorities require compensated cabin altitude to not exceed 2,438m.[2,9] Healthy passengers tolerate the hypoxaemia induced by the lower than normal oxygen pressure. The arterial oxygen partial pressure (PaO_2) drops to about

8kPa (two-thirds of normal) but the shape of the oxyhaemoglobin dissociation curve ensures that saturation only falls by 5–6%.[8] In passengers with respiratory disease, however, the changes can be more challenging. Many passengers with pre-existing cardiac, pulmonary and haematological conditions have a reduced baseline PaO_2, so reduced cabin pressure leads to further reduction of oxygen saturation, which lowers further with increasing flight times.[8,9] However, in adult volunteers simulating 20-hour flight conditions, frequency of reported complaints such as fatigue, headache, lightheadedness and nausea increased with increasing altitude. Symptoms peaked at an altitude of 2,438m, with most symptoms apparent after 3–9 hours of exposure.[10]

Cabin pressurisation to an altitude of 2,438m reduces atmospheric pressure in the cabin, resulting in a concomitant decrease of PaO_2 from 95mmHg to 60mmHg.[11] The decreased oxygen saturation can exacerbate medical conditions.[11-14] Eighteen per cent of passengers with chronic obstructive pulmonary disease have at least mild respiratory distress during a flight. Continuous supplemental oxygen should be provided for all passengers whose saturation will fall below 85% (or PO_2 below 6.2kPa) when exposed to the maximum permitted altitude.[13] New aircraft, such as the Airbus A380 and Boeing 787, are designed to operate at cabin altitude of 1,829m, which should reduce hypoxic effects but older passenger aircraft are likely to fly around the world for decades to come.

Adverse effects of air travel

Commercial flights usually cruise at altitudes of 7,010–12,498m above sea level, with passenger cabin pressurised to an altitude of 1,524–2,438m.[2] Cabin pressures equivalent to an altitude of 2,000–2,500m create a hazard of hypoxia for older travellers and place at risk those with little cardiac, cerebrovascular or respiratory reserves. Aircraft control systems maintain a pressure differential of about 9psi between cabin and the exterior environment. At 13,300m the cabin is pressurised to about 2,333m and the need to fly higher to circumvent bad weather leads to a further drop in pressure. Arterial PO_2 at sea level is around 9mmHg but, at 2,600m, this falls to 60mmHg in healthy young adults.

Healthy passengers normally respond to pressure changes with hyperventilation and tachycardia. Those with pre-existing lung disease may not compensate adequately for the changes in atmospheric pressure in aircraft cabins. If PaO_2 levels fall to 30–40mmHg, light exercise such as arm movements and walking may lead to dyspnoea, fatigue, lightheadedness and dizziness.

Quality of cabin air
Aviation techniques have changed over 50 years of commercial flying, but currently

most passengers and crew breathe air directed from the engines. When commercial flights began, passengers breathed in air supplied directly from the atmosphere using compressors. In 1962 a system was installed to draw air from the heart of the engines. 'Bleed' air is drawn out of the compression section of the engine and cooled. It then enters the cabin, mixes with recirculated air passed through filters to remove bacteria and viruses. These recirculated air filters do not remove fumes or vapours from the engine and, with a leak of hydraulic fluid or engine oil, contamination of cabin air can theoretically occur. Most jet aircraft systems recirculate 50% of the air and top it up with fresh air. In many current aircraft the purest air often goes to the first-class section and the poorest to the rear.

Nearly all types of aircraft have been reported as affected by contaminated air, but Civil Aviation Authority (CAA) records show that British Aerospace 146, Boeing 757, Airbus A319 and the Embraer 145 aeroplanes seem to be particularly susceptible. The CAA denies there is a health issue, or that incidents involving fumes are not being reported. In the United States, the Federal Aviation Administration, however, noted in 2006 a serious worry about under-reporting. The government insists there was no information cover-up, that only one in 2,000 flights are affected by "fume events" and the number of people who reported feeling unwell as a consequence is very small. The Department of Transport is undertaking research on contaminated air in aircraft cabins.[15]

Until the last few years about $0.57m^3$ of fresh air was provided per passenger per minute. Recently this has been halved, approximately, and more air is recirculated raising further concern about cabin contaminants, particularly carbon dioxide (CO_2) and ozone. CO_2 is produced by passengers and the quantity of it is determined by their number and the amount of ventilation. The percentage of occupied seats, therefore, has a significant effect as the ventilation system is relatively limited in efficacy.

With the reduction of fresh air entering the cabin, CO_2 levels have risen and, although within safety limits, may be above levels associated with comfort on some flights. Distribution of cabin air is not uniform, with ventilation rates in older aircraft sometimes two or three times higher in better-class accommodation than in the economy section where the majority of people sit. Passenger and crew complaints of dry eyes, stuffy nose, skin irritation, headaches, lightheadedness and confusion have been associated with cabin air quality. Chemical compounds, the result of vaporised jet oils that can mix with air, have been blamed. Controlled studies on the effect of vaporised organic compounds, such as tricresyl phosphate are in progress.[16] Episodic lightheadedness, headache and confusion are not uncommon occurrences in older people, especially those on medication; this make this area a difficult field to research in older travellers, who may also be less tolerant of contaminated air supply.[17,18]

New Boeing 787 Dreamliners entering service in 2013 use a different system to ventilate the cabin; they pump fresh air into the cabin from a source away from the engines, which ought to reduce the risk from toxic chemicals entering the oxygen supply.

Infection in aircraft

Atmospheric recycling within the aircraft may also theoretically increase the infectivity of certain bacteria and viruses carried by travellers, e.g. influenza. This effect is made worse if closed aircraft spend long periods on the ground during delays. Infections from serious diseases have been reported aboard commercial airlines, including influenza,[19-21] severe acute respiratory syndrome (SARS),[22,23] tuberculosis[24,25] food poisoning and enteritis.[26-28]

Air travellers travelling from San Francisco to Denver during winter months showed an upper respiratory tract infection frequency of 3–20%. However travellers may acquire their viruses before, rather than during, the flight.[29] Congestion in airport lounges and security areas may present higher exposure to infection than time spent in an aircraft where at least some of the infective factors are filtered out. Risk of on-board transmission of infection is mainly restricted to individuals with close personal contact or those who are seated within two rows of an infected passenger.[2] The risk of infection for vulnerable older people emphasises the wisdom of pre-travel influenza and pneumococcal vaccination.[18]

Air humidity and expansion of gases

In most aircraft, fresh air is brought in from the outside, cooled and delivered to the cabin without humidification and cabin humidity can be as low as 5%. In the new Boeing 787, this will usually be 15–20%. Low figures may cause voice and throat problems, and dehydration effects on long flights. Many older people take diuretics and may already be dehydrated, compounding the effect. Over-indulgence in alcohol on the journey may further add to dehydration. Air in body cavities at ground level increases by 30% at an altitude of 1,830m, causing gastric distension and sinus problems. These changes can adversely affect the older traveller, who has undergone recent surgery, gastrointestinal haemorrhage or ear operations.

Pre-existing illness

The highest attack rates of travellers' illness are recorded in those who set off with pre-existing illness.[1,30] One in two 60 year olds have evidence of severe coronary arterial narrowing, although only half will have clinical signs and symptoms. Age-related myocardial changes tend to present as dyspnoea rather than chest pain; a sudden breathless attack in the older traveller is likely to have a cardiac cause. Older travellers with hypertension may slip into cardiac failure if stressed. Cardiac patients frequently omit or forget to take mediation during travel, and stress and strain associated with transit often results in anginal attacks and arterial occlusion. There is also a tendency for patients to avoid diuretic therapy on long journeys, which precipitates cardiac failure on prolonged flights.[18]

In-flight deaths are relatively uncommon worldwide, but a considerable number of people of advanced years succumb to travel-induced illness in transit or immediately after air travel. Unexpected cardiac events (myocardial infarction and ischaemia) on international flights caused 56% of in-flight fatalities in 2000.[31] One passenger in 7 million dies en route, but many are found to be seriously ill in transit airports.[32] Data collation from hospitals adjacent to international airports is poor. The myocardial insufficiency in 25 people with cardiovascular problems, who had collapsed in a London airport, was found to have primarily occurred on the ground. Airport stress and exhaustion was considered to be as important a predisposing factor as in-flight hypoxia. Noise, poor communications, unexpected delays, unfamiliar melee, and uncertainties of airport transit through customs, security and check-in can all dispose older travellers to confusion.[33,34]

Travellers can also find themselves exposed to extremes of heat or cold at flight destinations or in unscheduled transit situations, resulting from adverse weather or delay. They can also arrive at airports situated at high altitude, such as La Paz and Lhasa, and be exposed to low partial pressures of environmental oxygen and suffer from hypoxia. Many older patients omit to take drugs on the day of the journey or forget to carry routine medications with them; failure to pack regularly required drugs in hand luggage could precipitate cardiac and respiratory crisis in mid-air or in an airport.

Psychological stressors

Air travel cannot be divorced from physical and psychological stressors associated with the journey to the airport, security and customs clearance, baggage handling and boarding and transfers. For many it is an anxious and even phobic experience with fears of crash, explosion and terrorist event prominent in their minds. Older travellers are less capable than younger people of coping with the associated transit of long walkways, physical baggage handling and the angst of delays. They become confused, fatigued and stressed, with the less fit experiencing angina and breathlessness, precipitating a cardiac event. [34,35]

In-flight immobility

Many older people rarely leave the security of their seats while on board an aircraft. This immobility results in an accumulation of fluid in the lower limbs. Gross peripheral oedema is often experienced by older passengers during prolonged air travel. Physical constraints and immobility bring the risk of deep venous thrombosis and pulmonary embolism (PE).[36] Senescent and arthritic patients with stiff hips or fixed knees are at particular disadvantage when restricted to the narrow confines of aircraft.

Air travel and risk of VTE

The relation between long-haul flights (more than eight hours) and increased risk of VTE remains controversial. Studies show an association between VTE and long-haul air travel, with risk being up to four-fold.[36,37] Risk peaks after more than eight hours' flight time[38,39.] and starts to increase when a flight duration is more than four hours.[40] Cabin-class seating has no effect on VTE incidence[41] but the greatest frequency occurs in non-aisle seating, where passengers tend to move less.[42–46]

Prospective controlled cohort studies suggest a relative risk of 2.93 (95% confidence interval [CI] 1.5 to 5.58).[42,44] One – a study of 9,000 business travellers over four years – showed an absolute risk for VTE of one every 4,656 flights (incidence rate ratio 3.2, 95% CI 1.8 to 5.6).[33] Risk increases with increasing number of flights during the first two weeks after a flight and when other risk factors are present.

Incidence of venous thrombosis (deep vein thrombosis and pulmonary embolism) by age and sex

Rates are shown per 100,000 per year

■ Men
▓ Women

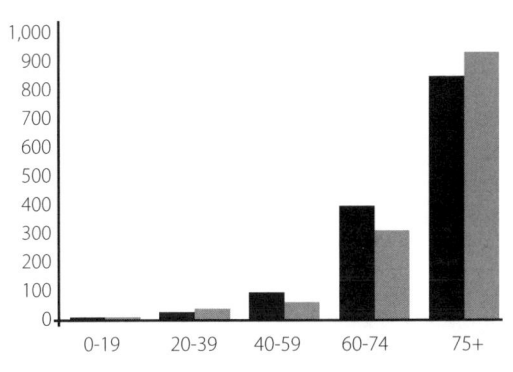

Factors increasing risk in association with air travel
- immobility in flight and airport
- advancing age
- dehydration
- hypobaric hypoxia in flight
- obesity
- malignancy
- recent surgery
- history of hyper-coagulable states.[42,44]

One of the strongest risk factors is age; incidence is many times higher in older people.

Additional causes of increased thrombosis in older people
- decreased mobility
- reduced muscular tone
- increased frequency of risk enhancing disease (e.g. malignancy)
- ageing tissues: vein walls, valves and subcutaneous tissues.

Immobilisation has been linked to 75% of air-travel cases of VTE. Dehydration can increase the risk of it due to haemo-concentration and hyperviscosity, potentially leading to hyper-coagulable states.[47] Use of graduated compression stockings, with an ankle pressure of 17–30mmHg can reduce risk during air travel. In a meta-analysis, only two of 1,237 people who wore compression stockings had VTE compared with 46 of 1,245 individuals who did not wear them.[48]

Anticoagulant thromboprophylaxis has been recommended but no formal guidelines exist. Aspirin for individuals at moderate risk of VTE is not recommended as the risk of side-effects is high and its value is unsupported by research evidence.[49,50] Randomised trials have shown the benefit of low-molecular-weight heparin for air travellers at moderate risk of VTE, who are not taking routine anticoagulant drugs.[51] Routine use should be for those at high risk and should be based on customised individual assessment.

Jet lag
Air travel may prove to be an endurance test for the fit, but time-zone changes and disturbance to circadian rhythm can have serious consequences for the less healthy. Time-zone changes – especially from west to east – and crossing three or more time zones can disturb mental alertness and cause disorientation, particularly in people who are old.

Jet lag is a temporary circadian-rhythm disorder that is associated with long-haul flights. It is due to desynchronisation between the body's internal clock mechanism, residing within the suprachiasmatic nucleus of the hypothalamus, and the new light–dark cycle caused by abrupt time-zone changes.[52-54] Symptoms are:
- daytime fatigue
- sleep–wake disturbances
- decreased appetite
- constipation
- reduced psychomotor coordination
- reduced cognitive skills.[52-54]

The degree and severity of jet lag is influenced by both flight direction and time zones crossed. Westward travel lengthens the day, causing a phase delay in circadian rhythm; eastward travel shortens the day and causes a phase advance. Travellers have greater difficulty falling asleep after eastward travel than after westward travel because of the internal clock's natural tendency to resist shortening the 24-hour day cycle.

Resynchronisation takes one day for every time zone crossed westward, or 1.5 days for every time zone crossed eastward.[54,55]

Limited toilet access

Older people have legitimate concerns about bladder function; these are often associated with bladder and uterine prolapse and urinary frequency in the case of women, and hyperprostatism and frequency in men. There can be limited toilet access in foreign airports and very limited access in aeroplanes. Queues to enter the toilet are standard on most long-haul flights in economy class, which adds to the anxiety relating to bladder relief.

Many seniors reduce fluid intake and miss out diuretic medication on the day of travel to try to reduce this problem, with resultant cardiac problems or peripheral oedema. Toileting problems seem likely to worsen if passengers are not allowed to access toilets in the hour before landing, which has happened recently for security reasons in aircraft landing in the United States.

Prostatic obstruction and urinary retention related to travel is not uncommon and is a worry for many older male travellers. Health professionals should be aware of these concerns and potential problems, and offer counselling and encourage routine uptake of diuretics during travel.

Advice for potential older air travellers

VTE avoidance

Low risk
Fit slim passengers with a flight time of less than eight hours, or a distance of less than 5,000km. The passengers should:
- avoid constrictive clothing
- avoid dehydration
- move about the cabin when possible
- do calf-stretching exercises.

Moderate risk
Passengers with a flight time of more than eight hours, or a distance of more than 5,000km who are obese, have large varicose veins, are undergoing hormone replacement therapy, use tobacco use or are relatively immobile should take note of the measures for passengers at low risk, and:

- wear properly fitted below-knee compression stockings providing 15–30mmHg of pressure at the ankle, ideally fitted before leaving home on the day of flight
- sit in the aisle.

High risk
Passengers who have a flight time more than eight hours or who are travelling a distance greater than 5,000km, who also have a history of previous VTE or hypercoagulable state (e.g. Factor V Leiden), have had major surgery in the six weeks before air travel (including hip or knee arthroplasty) or malignancy should take note of the measures for passengers at low and moderate risk, and:
- be injected with low-molecular0weight heparin before departure (in people not on warfarin).

Contraindications to commercial air travel

Total contraindications to flying on scheduled services are few and delays in departure dates may allow acceptance of those who are temporarily unfit. People must refrain from flying, however, if they suffer from a disease adversely affected by hypoxia or pressure changes produced by altitude. Those with little cardiac, cerebrovascular and respiratory reserves can meet with problems. In general, dyspnoea at rest is a contraindication to prolonged air travel. Patients with severe anaemia and within two weeks of myocardial infarction occurrence, cerebrovascular accident or in cardiac failure should not travel. Alternative routing, a different trip or even cancellation may be advisable.

Medical fitness for air travel

Airlines have the right to refuse to allow passengers on board, if they are unfit to fly for medical reasons.[6,56] Passengers should be able to walk a distance of 50m and climb one flight of stairs without angina or severe dyspnoea.[6] Airlines regulations exclude immediate travel for the following:

Cardiac conditions
- unstable angina
- myocardial infarction occurring 7–10 days before air travel
- uncontrolled dysrhythmia
- coronary artery bypass graft operation 10–14 days before air travel
- decompensated heart failure.

Respiratory conditions
- baseline, sea-level PaO_2 of <67–70mmHg without supplemental oxygen
- exacerbation of moderate obstructive/restrictive lung disease
- contagious pulmonary infections

- large pleural effusion
- pneumothorax three weeks before air travel.

Neurological disorders
- stroke within 5–10 days of travel
- uncontrolled seizures, or within 24 hours of a grand mal seizure.

Surgical interventions
- gastrointestinal; thoracic; ear, nose, and throat; and neurological surgical procedure
- 10–14 days before air travel
- laparoscopic surgery five days before air travel.

On-board medical assistance

In one in 50 international flights, medical help is requested. In three out of four in-flight emergencies, there is a physician on board when it occurs.[2] Commercial aircraft carry between one and four medical kits with at least one enhanced emergency medical kit, which is required by aviation regulatiosn. Most commercial flights also carry an automated external defibrillator.

Some commercial air carriers use on-ground telemedical assistance to medically assess passengers who seem unfit for travel at boarding. This service can provide medical advice during in-flight medical events, offering 24-hour ground-to-air medical support and advising the flight deck on the best diversion locations, as well as the availability of emergency personnel. Illness on an aircraft is an experience best avoided as attending doctors may have limited or unpractised emergency skills and are limited by resources and space in providing an optimum therapeutic response.

Pre-flight assessment

Many airlines consider that a passenger who is fit enough to walk up steps into the aircraft is fit to fly. Modern airport design means passengers seldom need to climb steps, but should be able to walk 50m on the flat without becoming breathless. There may still be doubt about the fitness to travel of some passengers who can only just manage to do this. More scientific assessment may require referral to a respiratory unit. If simple spirometry and blood gases are known and the patient has chronic obstructive airways disease, an idea of oxygenation at altitude can be obtained from a hypoxia challenge test.

The hypoxia challenge test involves the patient breathing 15% oxygen in nitrogen and measuring saturation. This gas mixture simulates the oxygen available in the aircraft cabin at maximum cruising altitude. If saturation falls below 85% during the test then in-flight oxygen will be required. This test also allows for the assessment of symptoms that may arise at a lesser degree of hypoxaemia, e.g. the patient with coronary artery disease who gets angina during the hypoxic challenge, even though the fall in saturation alone would not be regarded as severe enough to require oxygen. This patient too would require continuous in-flight oxygen to prevent angina during the flight.[57]

Oxygen supplementation is recommended for passengers with either a resting oxygen saturation of 92% or lower (PaO_2 of 67mmHg) or if the expected in-flight PaO_2 is <50–55mmHg.[9] The American Aerospace Medical Association recommends in-flight oxygen for individuals with a sea-level PaO_2 of 70mmHg or lower, or an expected in-flight PaO_2 of 55mmHg or lower.[10] Guidelines from the British Thoracic Society[13] suggest hypoxic-challenge testing in individuals with resting oxygen saturations of 92–95% at sea level, who have additional risk factors such as hypercapnia or abnormal spirometry.

Practical recommendations for all older air travellers

- Carry routine medications in hand luggage.
- Travel with spare medications.
- Take medications as normal, unless advised otherwise by a travel health counsellor.
- Carry a list of routine medications for information regarding emergency personnel.
- Maintain good hydration.
- Reduce alcohol and caffeine consumption en route.
- Walk in the cabin when possible and stroll about departure lounges.
- Periodically exercise calf muscles when sitting en route.
- Use compression stockings if at higher risk of VTE or prone to immobility, and put them on when recumbent before leaving home.
- If moderately breathless at rest, seek a pre-travel health assessment from a doctor.
- A passenger needing supplementary oxygen requires physician documentation stating their fitness to travel at an altitude of 2,438m.
- Passengers who have had surgery or a pneumothorax within two weeks should seek pre-travel medical advice as they are at risk of retained pockets of air expanding and causing problems.
- Passengers with colostomies are advised to use a large bag and to carry a spare.
- Advise the airline by using the medical information form of any potential medical or mobility problems before travel.
- Utilise wheelchairs, moving footways and invalid transport where at all possible in airports.
- Consider business-class travel if it is affordable; this will provide enhanced comfort on aeroplanes and in lounges.

Jet-lag precautions

Pre-flight sleep preparation
- **Westbound**
  - Go to sleep one hour later than usual.
  - Rise one hour later than usual three days before travelling.
- **Eastbound**
  - Go to sleep one hour earlier than usual.
  - Awake one hour earlier than usual on the three days before travelling
- **Exogenous melatonin**
  - Taken in the evening, melatonin phase advances the circadian clock.
  - Early-morning administration delays the circadian rhythm.
  - 0.5–5mg of melatonin taken at the desired destination bedtime is effective for reducing or preventing jet lag. (Cochrane meta-analysis)
- **Bright-light exposure**
  - Use bright-light exposure if crossing five or more time zones.
  - Use this if the traveller is going eastward history of has a history of jet-lag symptoms.
  - Caution is required in people with epilepsy or who are on warfarin.
- **Benzodiazepines**
  - Some reported efficacy in sleep quality (e.g. with temazepam) and other circadian-rhythm or sleep parameters. Sleeping medication increases the likelihood of immobility and may increase the risk of developing deep vein thrombosis.

References

1 British Airports Authority. Audit and development Annual report 2007.
2 Silverman D, Gendreau M .Medical issues associated with commercial flights www.thelancet.com Published online February 19, 2009 DOI:10.1016/S0140-6736(09)60209-9.
3 Cummings R. Chapman P. 1988 In-flight deaths during commercial air travel J. Amer. Med. Assoc. 259,13,1983-88
4 Woods D 1991 Medical hazards of flying Med. Monitor. 5.4
5 Cocks R, Liew M. Commercial aviation in-flight emergencies and the physician. Emerg Med Australas 2007; 19: 1–8.
6 Tonks A. Cabin fever. BMJ 2008; 336: 584–86
7 Gendreau MA, DeJohn C. Responding to medical events during commercial airline flights. N Engl J Med 2002; 346: 1067–73.
8 DeJohn CA, Wolbrink AM, Veronneau SJ, Larcher JG, Smith DW, Garrett JS. An evaluation of in-flight medical care in the U.S.
Aviat Space Environ Med 2002; 73: 580–86.
9 Cabin cruising altitudes for regular transport aircraft. Aviat Space Environ Med 2008; 79: 433–39.

10 Toff WD, Jones CI, Ford I, et al. Effect of hypobaric hypoxia, simulating conditions during long-haul air travel, on coagulation, fibrinolysis, platelet function, and endothelial activation. JAMA 2006; 295: 2251–61.
11 Seccombe LM, Peters MJ. Oxygen supplementation for chronic obstructive pulmonary disease patients during air travel. Curr Opin Pulm Med 2006; 12:140–44.
12 Burnett JC. Long – and short-haul travel by air: issues for people with diabetes on insulin J.Trav. Med. 2006.13.255-60
13 Managing passengers with respiratory disease planning air travel: British Thoracic Society recommendations. Thorax 2002;
57: 289–304.
14 Cabin cruising altitudes for regular transport aircraft..Aviat Space Environ Med 2008; 79: 433–39.
15 Air Travel and Health Report. House of Lords Select cttee. on Sc. and tech.201 HMSO
16 Humphreys S, Deyermond R, Bali I, Stevenson M, Fee JP. The effect of high altitude commercial air travel on oxygen saturation.
Anaesthesia 2005; 60:458–60.
17 McIntosh I Travel and Health in the elderly.1992 Quay Books Publishing. Lancaster
18 McIntosh I The vulnerable, older traveller 2009 CME Geriatric Med.11(3)118-22
19 Evans A, Finkelstein S, Singh J, Thibeault C. Pandemic influenza: a note on international planning to reduce the risk from air transport. Aviat Space Environ Med 2006; 77: 974–76.
20 Moser MR, Bender TR, Margolis HS, Noble GR, Kendal AP, Ritter DG. An outbreak of influenza aboard a commercial airliner.
Am J Epidemiol 1979; 110: 1–6.
21 Marsden AG. Outbreak of influenza-like illness related to air travel. Med J Aust 2003; 179: 172–73. 189 (suppl 1): S81–85.
22 Olsen SJ, Chang HL, Cheung TY, et al. Transmission of the severe acute respiratory syndrome on aircraft. N Engl J Med 2003;
349: 2416–22.
23 Wilder-Smith A, Leong HN. A case of in-flight transmission of severe acute respiratory syndrome (SARS): SARS serology positive.
J Travel Med 2004; 11: 130.
24 McFarland JW, Hickman C, Osterholm M, MacDonald KL .Exposure to Mycobacterium tuberculosis during air travel. Lancet
1993; 342: 112–13.
25 Exposure of passengers and flght crew to Mycobacterium tuberculosis on commercial aircraft, 1992–1995.MMWR Morb Mortal Wkly Rep 1995; 44: 137–40.
26 Tauxe RV, Tormey MP, Mascola L, Hargrett-Bean NT, Blake PA.Salmonellosis outbreak on transatlantic fl ights; foodborne illness on aircraft: 1947–1984. Am J Epidemiol 1987; 125: 150–57.
27 McMullan R, Edwards PJ, Kelly MJ, Millar BC, Rooney PJ, Moore JE. Food-poisoning and commercial air travel. Travel Med Infect Dis 2007; 5: 276–86.
28 Widdowson MA, Glass R, Monroe S, et al. Probable transmission of norovirus on an airplane. JAMA 2005; 293: 1859–60.
29 Zitter JN, Mazonson PD, Miller DP, Hulley SB, Balmes JR. Aircraft cabin air recirculation and

symptoms of the common cold. JAMA2002; 288: 483–86.
30 McIntosh I Travel Induced Illness Scot. Med. 1991.11. 14-15
31 Agostoni P, Cattadori G, Guazzi M, et al. Effects of simulated altitude-induced hypoxia on exercise capacity in patients with chronic heart failure. Am J Med 2000; 109: 450–55.
32 Erdmann J, Sun KT, Masar P, Niederhauser H. Effects of exposure to altitude on men with coronary artery disease and impaired left ventricular function. Am J Cardiol 1998; 81: 266–70.
33 McIntosh I 1990 The stress of modern travel Trav Med Internat.118 18-24
34 McIntosh I Power K. et al. Prevalence and intensity of travel related stressors J Trav Med. 1996 3(2)96-102
35 McIntosh I Power K Anxiety and Health problems related to air travel . J Trav Med.1998 12. 40-3
36 Becker NG, Sall M A, Kelman CW. Air travel and the risk of deep vein thrombosis. Aust NZ J Public Health 2006; 30: 5–9.
37 Schwarz T, Siegert G, Oettler W, et al. Venous thrombosis after long-haul flights. Arch Intern Med 2003; 163: 2759–64.
38 Hughes R, Heuser T, Hill S, et al. Recent air travel and venous thromboembolism (NZATT) study. Lancet 2003; 362: 2039–44.
39 Bartholomew JR, Schaffer JL, McCormick GF Air travel and venous thromboembolism: minimizing the risk. Cleve Clin J Med. 2011 Feb;78(2):111-20. doi: 10.3949/ccjm.78a.10138.
40 Cannegieter SC, Doggen CJ, van Houwelingen HC, Rosendaa l FR. Travel-related venous thrombosis: results from a large population-based case control study (MEGA study). PLoS Med 2006;
41 Jacobson BF, Munster M, Smith A, et al. The BEST study–a prospective study to compare business class versus economy class air travel as a cause of thrombosis. S Afr Med J 2003; 93:522–28.
42 Philbrick JT, Shumate R, Siadaty MS, Becker DM. Air travel and venous thromboembolism: a systematic review. J Gen Intern Med
2007; 22: 107–14.
43 Trujillo-Santos AJ, Jimenez-Puente A, Perea-Milla E. Association between long travel and venous thromboembolic disease: a systematic review and meta-analysis of case-control studies.
Ann Hematol 2008; 87: 79–86.
44 Aryal KR, Al-Khaff af H. Venous thromboembolic complications following air travel: what's the quantitative risk? A literature review.
Eur J Vasc Endovasc Surg 2006; 31: 187–99.
45 Kuipers S, Schreijer AJ, Cannegieter SC, Buller HR, Rosendaal FR,Middeldorp S. Travel and venous thrombosis: a systematic review.
46 Tasker A, Akinola O, Cohen AT. Review of venous thromboembolism associated with air travel. Travel Med Infect Dis
2004; 2:75–79.
47 Bendz B, Rostrup M, Sevre K, Andersen TO, Sandset PM .Association between acute hypobaric hypoxia and activation of coagulation in human beings. Lancet 2000; 356: 1657–58.
48 Hsieh HF, Lee FP. Graduated compression stockings as prophylaxis for flight-related venous thrombosis: systematic literature review.J Adv Nurs 2005; 51: 83–98.

49 Geerts WH, Bergqvist D, Pineo GF, et al. Prevention of venous thromboembolism: American College of Chest Physicians Evidence-Based Clinical Practice Guidelines (8th edn). Chest 2008; 133 (suppl): 381S–453S.
50 Watson HG, Chee YL. Aspirin and other antiplatelet drugs in the prevention of venous thromboembolism. Blood Rev 2008; 22: 107–16.
51 Chee YL, Watson HG. Air travel and thrombosis. Br J Haematol 2005; 130: 671–80
52 Sadun AA, Schaechter JD, Smith LE. A retino-hypothalamic pathway in man: light mediation of circadian rhythms. Brain Res 1984; 302: 371–77.
53 Saper CB, Lu J, Chou TC, Gooley J. The hypothalamic integrator for circadian rhythms. Trends Neurosci 2005; 28: 152–57.
54 Dubocovich ML. Melatonin receptors: role on sleep and circadian rhythm regulation. Sleep Med 2007; 8 (suppl 3): 34–42.
55 Sack RL, Auckley D, Auger RR, et al. Circadian rhythm sleep disorders: part I, basic principles, shift work and jet lag disorders.
An American Academy of Sleep Medicine review. Sleep 2007; 30: 1460–83.
56 Jorge A, Pombal R, Peixoto H, Lima M. Pre-flight medical clearance of ill and incapacitated passengers: 3-year retrospective study of experience with a European airline. J Travel Med 2005; 12:306–11.
57 Dine CJ, Kreider ME. Hypoxia altitude simulation test. Chest 2008;133:1002–05.

5

Land and Sea Travel, and Associated Illness

Sea travel

In the last decade there has been a huge increase in sea and river cruising. Fly-cruising has become very popular, with passengers flying from Britain to board vessels berthed in ports across the globe. Older passengers in particular have embraced sea cruising, attracted by its luxury, protected environment, access to far-flung destinations and 24-hour on-board medical attention. Cruise ships travel regularly to the Arctic, Antarctica, across the Pacific and Atlantic Oceans, and up the world's great rivers.

They disembark passengers in exotic ports; remote islands, unexplored gulfs, congested conurbations and disease-ridden destinations. Their human cargo pours into major cities with excellent medical facilities and into undeveloped areas, with poor health resources and scant emergency aid for foreign visitors. The voyager can be exposed to malaria, exotic disease, infected water, contaminated food and physical trauma.

Ships carry a large number of senior citizens, many in imperfect health. They travel with pre-existing illness, taking several medications, with scant knowledge of health risk, resources and facilities at ports visited en route. They are unaware of the limited facilities available to on-board medical staff and the inadequacies of healthcare and evacuation they might meet in emergency.

The majority indulge in maritime adventure and return home in good health. Some are not so fortunate – travel health insurance claims from older travellers continue to rise. Health insurance companies now reject applications from people over 65 years of age and exclude pre-existing illness from cover, resulting in more travellers going abroad without medical insurance protection. Travel health professionals need to be aware of the risks to which older travellers are exposed, precautions they should take before and during travel, and appropriate prophylaxis and vaccinations to reduce health risk.

Ever-bigger ships are being launched. Some can accommodate 5,000 passengers and they venture to more adventurous and exotic locations. Worldwide, over 12 million people cruise the high seas annually, visiting 2,000 ports. One million Britons cruised in 2005.[1] The Mediterranean and Caribbean Seas are the most popular destinations with cruises lasting an average of 7–14 days. World cruises can last months and many older people stay aboard for 6 weeks or more. The overall health and safety record is good, but ships are inherently unstable and operate in regions where there are hazards to health. The recent capsizing of the Concordia has drawn attention to cruise ships' sea worthiness. In addition, they are potential transmission sources and reservoirs for infection. Infection and injury befall cruise passengers, especially those who are frail and very old.[2,3]

Older passengers

Older people are the second largest group to visit long-haul destinations.[4] The type of itinerary affects passenger risk, with deep-sea, ocean, large river (e.g. Amazon/Orinoco), polar and adventure cruising expeditions presenting different health hazards. A cruise ship encompasses a global community, a closed, air-conditioned environment with the potential for disease exposure. Rapid movement between ports with varying sanitation standards and disease exposure can introduce communicable disease, with speedy spread of infection in a crowded vessel. Shipboard living may become a problem for older passengers if they have an exacerbation of chronic illness or an acute event.[5] A third of passengers are over 60 years age on many ships and, in some, three quarters are over 65. The majority are middle aged and above, and many have pre-existing medical disorders.[2]

Passenger morbidity
Warm-water cruising
Incidence of disease and medical intervention depends upon conditions of sea, climate, ship size, passenger age and sex.[6-8] Many passengers are injured ashore.

Data considered commercially sensitive is limited and often relates to single ships or cruises. On average, on a one-week cruise to the Caribbean, medical staff will be consulted by up to 55 passengers; 80–90% of infirmary visits will be for non-urgent conditions, 10–15% will be urgent, 5–10% will be for serious illness or injury requiring on-board hospitalisation or evacuation, and 1% of ship patients require emergency transfer to shore-based hospital.[3,9] One in every 250 passengers experiences a serious illness that requires in patient care.[10]

Cold-water cruises
In 1996, 9,322 tourists went to the Antarctic. Between 1998 and 2000, four ships carried 13,637 passengers on Antarctic cruises of 15 days and the number has increased over the last decade. The majority of passengers are 64–74 years old. Older passengers did not consult the ship doctor more frequently, but had more serious illnesses and injuries than younger travellers.

Photo. J.Davies

The spectrum of disease is similar in cruise ships to the Arctic and Antarctica, with a significant increase in seasickness in the Antarctic. The proportion of passengers consulting the doctor was similar for polar regions, but much less for warm-water cruises.[13] The consultation rate was 33.1 consultations per 1,000 passenger days in Antarctica, as opposed to 4.6 for warm-water cruises.[11] Five per cent of passengers consulted the doctor on polar cruises compared with 3.6% on warm-water ones.[12]

Over 60% of consultations in Antarctica were for seasickness. Respiratory illness was the second most common presentation in Arctic[13,14] and Antarctic cruises (5%) and most common in warm waters.[14,15] There was no significant additional medical risk for passengers cruising polar waters. Cold injury (1%) was uncommon in people cruising in Antarctica. Patients with illness and injury may have to remain on board for some time in heavy seas in polar waters.[16]

Passenger morbidity[14,17]

Condition	%
Respiratory	26–29
Injury related	12–18
Gastrointestinal	12–16
Cardiovascular	3–7
Skin	3–13

In 5,215 passenger presentations to ship doctors over 20 cruises, the most common presentations were respiratory (18%) and circulatory (13%) problems, and injury (12%);[18,19] one in three had seasickness. Seasickness, respiratory problems and injuries accounted for 72% of presentations.[20] Contusions, lacerations and burns were common injuries with lower limbs affected in passengers. Contusions were most frequent, representing a third of all injuries. In further studies, most frequent illnesses were respiratory, seasickness and gastrointestinal disease.[21,22] Medical intervention was requested for virus infection, hypertension, seasickness, injuries and chronic disease in older passengers.[23] On 35 cruises, 35 passengers were hospitalised, four with myocardial infarctiona and two with peptic ulcer perforations.[24]

Deaths aboard ship

In a six-year study of passenger mortality on two ships (comprising 88 passengers), 25 died, with an average of one death per six months per ship. More men than women died (P>0.05). Nine passengers died after up to 52 hours of intensive on-board care. Five passengers had cardiac problems.

Findings were similar on four larger ships studied over a year. In total, 7,147 passengers attended the ship's clinic over 1,537,298 passenger days with 2.6 versus 3.6 mortalities per 1,000 passengers per year. A total of 18% presented with injuries, with the precipitating event being a slip, fall or trip. Older women were the largest group to be hospitalised, 69.3% for medical conditions.

The most common diagnosis was respiratory infection.[21] Eleven per cent of passengers had a serious or life-threatening event. The spectrum of conditions was similar to hospital emergency departments with 12% related to injury, 88% to medical problems and 3% requiring emergency intervention.[22]

Emergency on-board care

Three cruise lines reported that one in 5,000 passengers suffers a serious medical crisis requiring evacuation. A ship physician, caring for 1,000 passengers, may expect potentially serious illness or injury and have to disembark people once a week.[12] People older than 64 years accounted for 51% of clinic attendees.[23] Similar results were obtained on a 103-day cruise with 3,033 passengers and 693 consultations. The average age was over 60 years, passengers accounted for 59% of doctor consultations, 27% of accidents to passengers occurred ashore, seven passengers were referred to shore specialists and seven were hospitalised on land. One died aboard.

A case comparison analysis of factors associated with injuries aboard ships resulting in the hospitalisation of residents and non-residents in Alaska showed that non-resident females aged over 65 were aboard cruise ships when injured. They were more likely to suffer fractures and serious injury, and experience post-injury disability.[24]

Small-boat and rigid, inflatable dinghy transfers add risk for older cruise passengers with ship-to-shore transfers from large ships to small boats inherently dangerous in cold, rough seas. Transfers involve a floating hull-side bridge with cross-deck transfer to a lifeboat or tender – a crossing fraught with peril for passengers using walking frames and walking sticks for support, and a challenge for the physically able as both boat and ship undulate with the sea swell.

Shore excursions require stamina and can challenge older people. They may last 12–13 hours and take passengers to remote spots, exposing them to infection, trauma, fatigue, immobility (for example, while in coaches) and morbidity, especially if people are travelling with pre-existing illness.[21,25,26]

Ocean cruising may be inappropriate for very old, frail, handicapped and mentally unprepared passengers.[27,28] Many ships now have designated cabins for handicapped persons but the inherently unstable, hazardous environment will pose a heightened risk for these people; they would be particularly challenged in a disaster situation.

Risks to health in cruise travel

- infection
- trauma
- exposure to ultraviolet light
- motion sickness
- air-transit problems.

Cruise infections
Infection can occur:
- *en route to embarkation.*
- *on board.* Bacteria and viruses introduced by crew, passengers and ship systems result in influenza and para-influenzal illness, diarrhoea, Legionnaires disease and Rubella – all of which can spread rapidly.
- *on shore excursions,* which expose passengers to local and exotic infection, malaria, dengue fever, food and water-borne infection, insect-borne disease and infection from bites.
- *on return home.* Risk of exposure to infectious disease is difficult to quantify because of the broad spectrum of cruise ships and itineraries, and the limited data on infectious diseases occurring on ships.[29] Cruise lines are loath to publicise data. Surveillance systems have identified cases of food poisoning.

Causes of infections
Legionella, influenza A and B infections, Norwalk virus, chicken pox and measles[12] are common cruise-ship related infections.

Legionella pneumophila can cause severe pneumonia and even death in people who are frail and very old. *Legionella* species enter ship potable systems. The organism needs poor water chlorination or temperature control to multiply.[30] Outbreaks have been associated with ship spas, fountains and showers, which generate aerosols necessary for the spread of disease.[12] In a case–control study, among 215 passengers to the North Cape, 45 were affected and one died. The source was prolonged exposure to the ship's spa pool.[31] Inhalation of aerosols contaminated with *Legionella* bacteria often occurs in the whirlpool spa area.[32] A prevalence study on nine cruise ships and ferries revealed 42% of water supplies were contaminated by *Legionella* species. *Legionella* is a ubiquitous organism that can survive in a ship's freshwater system.[33] In specimens from ship showers and washbasins *L.pneumophila* was isolated in 95.5% of samples.

Influenzal outbreaks have occurred on cruise ships worldwide. Although cruise ships were not the actual source, they became a reservoir of infection. There is recorded increased morbidity on cruise ships. There have been prolonged outbreaks of both influenza A and B with fatalities in the Caribbean, the Pacific, Alaska and the Mediterranean.[34-36]

Gastrointestinal illness

Gastrointestinal is common, comprising 5–10% of sick-bay visits. Some incidents are due to the ingestion of water and food partaken off the ship; half are due to Norwalk virus, and the rest to **Enterotoxigenic** *E. coli* (ETEC), *Salmonella*, *Shigella*, *Staphylococcus aureus* and *Campylobacter*.[37,38] Norovirus infection is difficult to eradicate in cruise ships where rapid transmission can occur between passengers. It is not usually serious, although older people can become dehydrated and require fluid replacement. Symptoms arise 24–48 hours after exposure and illness lasts 1–4 days. It is transmitted through contact with infected persons, poor hygiene or the handling of contaminated objects. Raw or undercooked shellfish and chilled foods, including salads and sandwiches, can become a source of infection.

In 2002, there was a sharp increase in norovirus-associated illness on ships and land.[39] In 14 laboratory confirmed outbreaks on ships,[12] 86% were attributed to caliciviruses with continuation on successive cruises, multiple methods of transmission and high attack rates (58%). The Centers for Disease Control and Prevention Atlanta recorded 21 outbreaks of acute gastroenteritis on 17 ships, nine associated with noroviruses, three to bacterial agents and nine of unknown aetiology.

In 2003, 600 passengers were infected on two ships; 2% of passengers and 7% of the crew had intestinal illness. Another vessel with 2,250 passengers was also affected with the same virus. Some 200 passengers were infected and confined to their cabins for four days. Three other ships and the world's largest liner were affected on Caribbean cruises that year.

Ship-board outbreaks of Norwalk infection have been caused by ice, shrimps and fresh fruit. Intensive ship cleaning does not always eradicate the infection.[12] In cruises of 3–15 days there are 1.4 outbreaks of diarrhoeal disease per 1,000 cruises or, 2.3 outbreaks per 10 million passenger days, or six outbreak-related illnesses per 100,000 passenger days. In a seven-year period, 5,278 passengers were affected. The most common source was undercooked scallops, eggs and food taken during shore excursions. Thorough cooking of seafood and use of pasteurised eggs would have reduced the infection by half.[40] ETEC infection has been sourced to the consumption of fresh-cut fruit and water bunkering in transit ports.[41]

In 2005 a report revealed poor hygiene practices and health hazards on random checks on 14 British cruise ships docking in British ports. There has been a call for Britain to follow the United States and publish cruise-ship hygiene reports by ports inspectors.[42]

Accidents and injuries

An agency offering ship physician assistance reported on 1,700 cases on 500 different ships; 65% were due to illness and 33% injury, which included musculoskeletal (21%) and skin trauma (15%) conditions. In total, 13% were eventually repatriated.

- Most frequent cause of ship accidents are steep stairways, gangways and slippery decks.
- Unfamiliar environment causes many accidents, especially in older people with poor balance, disturbed gait and locomotion difficulties.
- Sprains and contusions are the most frequently reported injuries.
- Common reported accidents are falls, cuts and grazes.
- Some 66% of all accidents are preventable.

Temperatures below 20°C experienced in polar cruising increase unsafe behaviour. Cold temperatures cause clumsiness and decrease muscle strength.[12]

Inhalation injuries constitute the main risk with on-board fire. Fast airstreams develop in corridors and air ducts. A lack of oxygen below deck occurs early in the fire, and smoke and fumes contain chemical elements of incomplete burning. Survival and injury depend upon the location of the ship, proximity of other rescue ships and sea state. People have a better chance of survival on a burnt-out ship than in a lifeboat.

Overexposure to ultraviolet light

Many passengers overexpose themselves to strong sunlight on cruises, with adverse solar effects compounded by reflection from the sea. Others, especially older people, fall asleep in the sun and are badly burnt. Solar radiation over Antarctica is four times greater than where earth is protected by atmospheric ozone.[11]

Seasickness

All passengers on one ship were affected in rough conditions in the Southern Ocean.[14] Motion sickness can affect many people, even on ships with stabilisers,[3] although it is perhaps less likely to affect passengers with mid-ship, mid-deck, internal cabins. Severe vomiting results in dehydration and interference with routine medication. Favoured drugs are cinnarizine, scopolamine and promethazine.[20,21] Only a third of passengers who are seasick ask for medical help.[19,43] Anti-seasickness medication has a 30% positive placebo effect.[44]

On-board medical facilities

Cruise lines strive to maintain a healthy, safe environment on board. Most large ships have excellent medical facilities, but cannot equate with on shore hospitals. There are no international standards of care for cruise ships. The American College of Emergency Physicians (ACEP) cruise ship and maritime medicine section was founded to act as a resource for cruise industry physicians and departments, and to develop guidelines.

Many ships have medical staffing and facilities in accordance with ACEP guidelines but they do not provide emergency surgery, blood transfusion, extensive laboratory or radiological services. The ship's physician position is determined by custom, not maritime law, and many are employed as independent contractors. Except for ships registered in Norway and England, there are no mandatory international maritime requirements for cruise lines to carry a licensed physician or to have hospital facilities aboard; ships carrying more than 50 passengers, however, generally have both. Quality of facilities, medical practice and physician varies depending upon itinerary, the ship's complement and construction.

North Americans staff about 10% of cruise-ship medical rooms. Staff manage severe blood loss with fluid replacement using intravenous colloids and crystalloids as they do not carry blood products.[14] Most shipboard physicians are not certified in trauma treatment or medical evacuation. There is no internationally agreed standard relating to certification. Many ship doctors are GPs on short-term contracts. This can lead to poor continuity and variable standards.

The ACEP healthcare guidelines may not be followed by smaller ships, or those run by independent companies, which may have limited medical facilities on board – sometimes located in the doctor's cabin. The ratio of medical staff to passengers varies greatly from ship to ship: one of 88 passengers could have a doctor and a nurse, while large ships of 4,000 passengers might also have only one doctor. As an example, the QE2 with 2,921 passengers had a doctor, surgeon and six nurses while the Sensation, with 3,541 passengers, had one doctor and two nurses.

Shipboard medical centres are not hospitals and should be considered first-aid stations for temporary stabilisation until shoreside facilities are reached – a fact rarely appreciated by passengers. The cruise line is liable for physician's negligence in treatment of crew but not in treatment of passengers, providing it endeavoured to hire a competent doctor.

Guidelines for handling emergencies vary from ship to ship, with many having elaborate well-rehearsed emergency response systems and others ad hoc arrangements. The deep-sea evacuation of 4,000 passengers and the crew from a ship in distress in rough weather and high seas, by day or night, remains to be tested in reality. The assumption that passengers are safer on board a crippled ship rather than in lifeboats, is in question after the Concordia disaster. Emergency drills, although realistic, can be counterproductive, with passenger deck assembly for the practice launching of lifeboats on compulsory passenger drills causing bodily harm.

Ship pharmacy and medications

Medications stocked on board vary markedly from ship to ship and record systems for availability and expiry can be poor due to the ever-changing professional resource. ACEP guidelines encourage standardised equipment, supplies and medications but cruise lines do not have to comply. Ships often have no oxygen-saturation monitor to determine blood–oxygen levels, although these are available as standard in most land-based emergency departments.

Passengers with disabilities

A cruise ship is not a safe environment for some travellers but there are few embarkation restrictions. Unqualified or poorly trained medical staff and inadequate medical equipment are serious risk factors for ill or injured passengers.[14] Newer ships are more accessible for people with disabilities. At present only four cruise ships give direct ramp access to lifeboats. Crew members have to be specially trained to assist wheelchair passengers – two per eight-hour shift are required according to latest safety and evacuation regulations (*see Chapter 10*).

Fly cruising

Many passengers now undertake long- and medium-haul air travel en route to the ship and so are exposed to health risks associated with long air journeys. The precautions for long-haul flights to avoid deep vein thrombosis apply (*see Chapter 4*).

Pre-travel risk assessment

It is essential that pre-travel risk assessment is undertaken and pre-travel advice given to older people and those who are chronically ill undertaking lengthy sea cruises. Risks may be reduced by ensuring passengers understand potential hazards, especially during rough seas.

If a person is very unfit, has serious medical problems and is easily confused, a cruising holiday may not be in their best interest.[45] People in poor health or with a history of recurrent serious and chronic illness should pick voyages with short distances between ports with good facilities.

Effective emergency plans, aggressive treatment of serious medical conditions and a proactive evacuation policy will keep the number of deaths at sea low.[46] Targeted safety promotion regarding potential injury is required for older people, especially females.[43] High-risk passengers should seek cruises leaving from and returning to UK ports with inclusive home to port land connections.

Travellers on board cruise ships should be prepared for the possibility of illness and injury, and realise that even minor injury may require evacuation to shore facilities. They should appreciate the limitation of medical facilities and providers on board ship and that continuing care will depend on the nearest port with variable shore.[34]

Checklist for passengers
Passengers should:
- buy adequate and comprehensive travel health insurance
- enquire about the size of ship, distance between ports, quality of medical staff and facilities
- choose a cruise with close proximity of scheduled ports and good evacuation possibilities, if they are likely to require emergency care
- be aware that ship medical rooms should be considered first-aid stations for temporary stabilisation until shoreside facilities are reached
- remember quality of continuing medical care is dependent upon that available at the first port of call
- carry antiemetic medication, a list of medications and medical history, adequate routine medications, anti-diarrhoeal and antiemetic preparations and high-factor sun block
- have pre-travel influenza and pneumococcal vaccine prophylaxis
- be aware of infection risk if they are immunity-compromised passengers e.g. splenectomised, IV infected, or taking steroids or immuno suppressive therapy

- acquire a note from their family doctor recording their medical history and medications
- carry adequate supplies of medications on their person en route and on excursions
- seek mid-ship, mid-deck inner cabins and adopt a supine position parallel to the ship's axis of major motion to minimise effects of motion on vestibular apparatus in rough seas, if they are subject to motion sickness
- be aware of risk of enteritis infection from salads and shellfood on board
- take advantage of alcohol-based aerosol antibacterial hand washes that are provided for embarking passengers and those arriving for meals
- be wary of on-shore water and food
- remember that the precautions for safe air travel also apply on fly-cruises.

Recommended medications and prophylaxis

Favoured drugs for motion sickness are cinnarizine, scopolamine and promethazine.[43,44] Influenzal immunisation and pneumococcal immunisation are also recommended, as are antimalarials, where appropriate.

Land travel

Many ships berth in a different port every day and disgorge passengers for a day of exploration on land. They voyage to many destinations in undeveloped parts of the world where transport and roads can be rudimentary and road traffic accidents common. Many day-trippers take the opportunity to tour the local town and hinterland by coach, on local buses or in hire cars; they often take this transport without thought for the health risk to which they may be exposed.[45] Segway transporters are proving a hazardous transport mode for passengers who perceive them as a mobility aid.

On vacation and relaxed people can forget routine precautions for road safety, which they practise at home. They enter vehicles that are not roadworthy and walk highways without regard for personal safety. They hire beach vehicles, safari cars, motorbikes and scooters, and ride them without helmets or seat belts. They often transit over poorly constructed roads and maintained roads with low safety margins, in mountainous and jungle terrain. They jaywalk and traverse poorly maintained pavements, and many do so having imbibed freely on local alcoholic spirits.

Older passengers compound potential safety risks with systemic failings that interfere with balance, gait, agility and disability, thereby disturbing mobility. Forgetting their advanced years, they may unwisely enter rickshaws and tuk-tuks driven by young drivers inured to accident risk, unaware that road traffic accident is a likely possibility in foreign travel.[46,47]

Statistics show that the chances of being involved in a car accident in mainland Europe doubles, and almost triples in Greece and Portugal and undeveloped countries of Asia and the Caribbean.[48] Accidents cause 20% of all deaths among overseas travellers – they are the second most common cause of death (68%) after heart disease.[48]

Many holiday accident claims occur before holidaymakers even reach their destinations; the UK national estimate for accidents while travelling and touring was 480,664 in 2008. Older drivers are more likely to have accidents involving themselves than other drivers in Britain and are more likely to have accidents on unfamiliar, poor, congested roads abroad. Accidents in vehicles or on the road are one of the riskiest aspects of travel abroad, yet most people worry far more about disease, which causes just 9% of deaths, or terrorism, which presents a negligible risk.[49]

Falls are a common cause of injury abroad and are often associated with alcohol. They are particularly likely in older adults due to poor vision, imbalance and postural hypotension. Walking barefoot or in sandals increases the risk of falls and foot injuries.

Advice for road users while abroad

Travellers should:
- insist on wearing a seat belt when in a car or coach
- check that coaches, buses, taxis or hire cars are roadworthy and safe
- beware of driving in countries with poor traffic regulations such as Egypt and India
- avoid motorbikes as they are particularly dangerous – even in European countries; if using one, wear a helmet
- be careful at night on poorly lit or poorly maintained roads
- be obsessively careful when crossing roads, as zebra crossings are often ignored
- avoid alcohol if deciding to drive but be aware that locals may not do so and that alcohol may disturb balance and gait, making a fall more likely
- wear a helmet and safety jacket if using a bicycle
- think of road-safety precautions
- avoid the attractions of Segway transporters.

References

1 Ward D. Ocean Cruising 2005 Berlitz Pub. London.
2 McIntosh I Health risks for those going on sea cruises. 2006. North European Travel Health Conference. Edinburgh
3 Wheeler R. Travel Health at Sea. Principles and Practice of Travel Med.2001 274-85 Ed Zuckerman J Wiley Chichester
4 McIntosh I. Elderly travellers. In Trav. Med and Migrant Health. Churchill Livingstone. Edinburgh1992 7.107-114
5 Internat. Passenger Survey 2003 HMSO London6.Polonev K/Characteristics of morbidity among passengers. Proceedings 4th. Internat. Conf. Marine Med. Varna 1972, 298-303
6 McIntosh IB Travel and Health in Older People 2011 Fast Print Pub. Peterborough
7 Ulewitz K.1976.Epidemic on a passenger ship. Bull. Instit.Marit. Trop Med. 27.105-8
8 Baterman W. The ugly duckling, a different kind of ship. Can. Med. Assoc. J. 1990142.365-71
9 Travellers' Health,Chap 7. Centres for Disease contol and Prevention Atlanta 2005
10 Smith A. in Travellers Health Ed Dawood R. 4th. Edn. Oxford Univ. Press 2002.277-89
11 Davies J. Polar cruise ships travelling Antarctica and the Arctic Brit. Trav. Health Assoc J. 2006 7.48
12 Davies J. Antarctic tourism and its risks. Brit. Trav. Health Assoc J. 2006.7.35-8.
13 Prociv P Health aspects of Antarctic tourism J Trav Med. 1998 4 210-21957-1993
14 Dahl E. Anatomy of a world Cruise. J. Trav. Med6.168-71
15 Polonev K.Characteristics of morbidity among passengers. Proceedings 4th. Internat. Conf. Marine Med. Varna 1972,298-303
16 British Travel Health Assoc. J Shipping News.2006 54-55
17 Peake D. Grey C. Ludwig MR Descriptive epidemiology of injury and illness among cruise ship passengers. Ann. Emerg. Med. 1999.33.67-72
18 Baterman W. The ugly duckling, a different kind of ship . Can. Med. Assoc. J. 1990 142.365-71
19 Martinovic N Morbidity of passengers and crew Adriana Trav. Med .Internat.1997 15.194-199
20 Jareman B Problems of medical care on a passenger ship Bull Instit. Marit. Trop. Med.1988. 39 137-48,
21 Carter. Shipboard medicine on package cruises Brit. Med J. 1972 550-53
22 DiGiavanna T Rosa T Shipboard Med. Ann Emerg Med. 1993 10.1639
23 Dahl E.Passenger mortalities aboard cruise ship. Internat. Marit.Health.2001.519-3
24 Hudson Neilson P Dahl E. Factors associated with injuries aboard ships J.Trav. Med.2006 13.67-
25 Oliver . Health problems at Sea Practitioner 1977 21,202-10
26 McIntosh I. Health ,hazard and the higher risk traveller. Quay Books Mark Allan Pub Dinton 1993 23-34
27 Elbert h. 100 years of public health authority in Hamburg. Bull. Instit. Marit. Trop Med. 1992 43.5-11
28 McIntosh I Travel, trauma, risks and health promotion. Quay Books. Marl Allen Pub. Dinton. 1998
29 Minooee A. Rickman L Clin Inf Disease 1999,29,737-44.
30 Beyrer K Lai S Dreesman et al Legionnaires disease outbreak associated with a cruise ,liner Aug.2003. Govt. Instit of Public Health. Hannover Germany. Sept29.2006

31 Jernigan Doffman J. Certon MS. Et al Outbreak of Legionnaires disease among cruise ship passengers . Lancet 1996 347 494-99
32 Kura E.Ammemura J Yagita K. Outbreak of Legionnaires disease 2003 PMID 9876197. Pubmed.
33 Azara A Piana A Sotjui G et al BMC Public Health 2006 18.100
34 Quarantine div. Centres for Disease Control and prevention CDC1998a, 1998b.Mortlality and morbidity report. 47.638
35 Health Canada 1998.Influenza outbreak Canada Communicable disease report. 24.9-11
36 CDC(Quarantine div. Centres for Disease Control and Prevention. Guidelines. jan 28. 1999.
37 Quarantine div. Centres for Disease Control and prevention 1CDC 2000a.b. 2001.Report 50
38 WHO Compendium of food and waterborne disease and Legionnaires disease associated with ships 1970-2000. 2002WHO/WHO/01.
39 Daniels N Neimann J Karpati A Travellers' diarrhoea at sea et al J Inf Dis 2000 181 1495
40 Koo D Maloney K Tauxe R epidemiology of diarrhoeal disease outbreaks on cruise ships 1986 –1993 JAMA 1996 275 545-7
41 Snyder J Wells JG. Ashuk J. outbreak of invasive E.Coli gastroenteritis on cruise ships Am J. Trop
42 Consumers Assoc.UK Cruise ship hygiene. Report 2005 Which.
43 McIntosh I Motion Sickness J.Trav. Med. 1998 5.89-91
44 Pingree B.INM investigation into drugs for sea sickness .J. RN Med. Service. 1994 80.76-80
45 Brennan F. A guide to healthy cruising. Brit. Trav. Health Assoc.J. 2000 1, 17-20
46 McIntosh I.Pitstops and pitfalls – A health guide for older travellers Quay Pub.Mark Allan Pub. Salisbury.1996
47 McIntosh I Health and safety on Cruise ships Brit.Trav. Health Assoc. J. 2007 9.10-17
Iain B. McIntosh
48 Internat. Passenger Survey 2007/8/ Office Nat. Stats. London
49 Mackay I Accidental trauma and the vacationer. 2011 Brit.Global Trav health assoc J 18b 3-5

6

Travel Induced Disorders

Hot, arid, dry and humid environments

The effects of travel-related illness on older people are poorly recorded. One general practice-based study of medical intervention for illness sustained abroad and its impact on over 65 year olds showed that almost half became ill. Much was minor in nature and responded to self-medication but ill health often interfered with holiday plans and, for some, ruined the vacation.[1] Adventurous older people are increasingly exploring distant parts of the globe with hostile climates, which present a challenge to health. The world traveller is exposed to several natural and environmental forces that can have an adverse on health; these are outlined in this chapter.

Disturbance in electrolyte and fluid imbalance

When exposed to high environmental temperatures, poor control of fluid balance can have an adverse effect on the wellbeing of older travellers. Body-fluid regulation is critically affected by age-related changes in function of sweat glands and kidneys, and in the sensation of thirst. Older people are more vulnerable in a very hot, arid or humid environment than the young, due to:
- increased frailty
- load of chronic conditions
- reduced efficiency of adaptive processes
- poorer control of fluid balance.

Increasing age brings decline in body mass – the percentage of water in the body in older people is lower than in young adults – and the decrease in intracellular volume is more marked than in extra cellular volume. Losing a litre of water has a proportionately greater adverse effect in older people.[2]

Under heat stress, the regulation of body fluids depends upon kidney and sweat-gland function as well as thirst sensation. Homeostasis is affected by intrinsic and extra renal control mechanisms. The ageing kidney exhibits detrimental anatomical and functional change over time. Renal mass is lost and there is a decrease in renal blood flow, with an almost linear decline in the glomerular filtration rate.[3]

Attenuation of renal tubular activity results in impaired renal response to arginine vasopressin. Older people are more sensitive to water depletion, are less responsive to the renin-angiotensin-aldosterone axis and have decreased plasma renin and aldosterone activity, which predisposes them to natriuresis and salt depletion. The decline in renal function also ensures they are less able to excrete a salt load or to adjust to salt deficiency. Even without the effects of renal disease older adults are at greater risk of developing hyperkalaemia due to reduced kidney function and reduced ability to correct acid load.[4]

Fluid deprivation, or restriction in a very hot environment, such as the tropics, can have a deleterious effect on the older traveller. In older people, control systems for thirst and satiety are attenuated. There is a reduced sensation of thirst. They have a higher osmotic operating point for thirst awareness and a decreased response to unloading of baroreceptors by hypovolaemia.[5] Due to this lack of awareness, there is a higher risk of dehydration occurring. There is also a marked atrophy of sweat glands with ageing, as well as reduced neurohumoural control. Diminished sweating capacity contributes to thermo-regulatory failure, compounded by impaired vasodilatation. Both water deficiency and salt deficiency heat exhaustion occur in older people who exercise hard in conditions of heat extremes.

Dehydration is the most common fluid and electrolyte imbalance in old adults including three elements:

Isotonic dehydration involves a balanced loss of solutes and water, which occurs with severe vomiting or diarrhoea – common occurrences in world travellers.

Hypotonic dehydration occurs when sodium is lost at a greater rate than water, resulting in serum sodium concentration of <130mmol/litre.

Hypertonic dehydration is when water losses exceed those of sodium, and serum sodium concentration is >145mmpl/litre. This can occur with fever or decreased water intake.

Hypernatraemic dehydration also often occurs in older people in very hot conditions as an end result of heavy sweating, as sweat is a hypotonic salt solution.

Comorbidity and the presence of pre-existing conditions in travellers – common in world wanderers who are older – can increase the likelihood of illness from exposure to enduring heat and humidity extremes.[6] Drug medication can interfere with the excretion of free water and diuretics have a high incidence of adverse effects on fluid balance.[7] Medical conditions that reduce cardiac and renal reserves can affect the capacity to respond adequately to heat stressors. Chronic renal failure – the end point of diabetes mellitus, hypertension, renal sclerosis or obstruction, and the tendency to slip into cardiac failure – are common conditions affecting older people. Those who are affected easily move into critical water and fluid imbalance when exposed to heat stress.

Summary

Older people are vulnerable in very hot, arid or humid environments due to:
- increased frailty and disease load
- reduced efficiency of adaptive processes and control of fluid balance
- increased sensitivity to water depletion
- less ability to excrete salt load or to adjust to salt deficiency
- greater risk of developing hyperkalaemia
- reduced sensibility to sensation of thirst
- higher risk of dehydration
- diminished sweating capacity.[8]

Identifying those at potential risk

Three groups of older people have been identified as at higher risk of developing heat-exposure problems.
1. *Active people* fit enough to indulge in hard exercise – these can incur significant water and electrolyte losses when pursuing strenuous physical activities in hot climates, particularly if these occur at high altitude
2. *Sedentary older people* who are overclothed, drink inadequate fluids, fail to replace loss of salt, rely on an inadequate adaptive sweating capacity and vasodilatation to dissipate heat
3. *People with chronic conditions,* such as renal or cardiac failure.

Symptoms of dehydration
Classic symptoms of water depletion are:
- fatigue
- giddiness
- thirst with nausea
- vomiting
- muscle cramps.

The condition may result in heatstroke and death. In predominant salt depletion, thirst is less marked but fatigue is more prominent, as is giddiness and vomiting, with potential death from oligaemic shock.

There are *no pathognomonic signs or symptoms*. The most useful indicators are dry mouth, tongue and mucous membranes, sunken eyes, body weakness, and confusion, which are common to other conditions in older people. Thirst is the main presentation in water deficiency, but less so with salt shortage. The volume of urine is low and concentrated.

Decline in glomerular function (decrease by 50% between the ages of 45 and 80 years) and impaired tubular function make an older person more susceptible to go into renal failure with dehydration.

Management
- Those at high risk should be identified before travelling to very warm, humid areas.
- People with diabetes in particular, as well as those with thyroid disease, should be targeted.
- Potential older travellers need advice on risk and preventive measures.
- Ensuring appropriate fluid intake and reducing insensible heat loss by behavioural precautions are important to maintain adequate fluid balance.
- Lightweight, loose-fitting clothing of light colours should be worn.
- Adjustments in medications such as diuretics may be necessary.
- Adequate fluid and salt intake is vital with a recommended daily intake of fluid of 1,600ml/70kg of weight in 24 hours, enhanced in hot, dry temperatures overseas.[8]
- Salt supplementation will be appropriate for physically hyperactive older people, especially those on high treks or desert and jungle safaris.[9] Attention should be drawn to the health hazards of physical overactivity in heat extremes.
- The need to carry water and check for indicators of possible fluid imbalance must be emphasised in pre-travel consultation.

Conclusion
- Fluid and electrolyte imbalance can affect older travellers going to hot climatic regions.
- A reduction in efficiency of renal water and electrolyte regulation, sweating function and thirst sensation makes older travellers a higher risk group.
- Water and salt deficiency heat exhaustion can lead to oligaemia and heatstroke in old travellers.
- Intense physical activity in hot, arid and humid conditions is likely to promote water deficiency in older people.
- Pre-existing cardiac and renal disorders increase the risk of fluid imbalance.
- At-risk world travellers should be identified in pre-travel health consultations and advised of the risk and appropriate precautions to minimise them.

- Adequate water and salt intake, wearing appropriate clothing, avoiding direct sun exposure and being aware of adverse effects and symptoms can ensure travellers maintain good health in very hot, dry environs.

Water and food-borne illness

Gastrointestinal illness is often an unwanted travel companion resulting from eating contaminated food, drinking contaminated or untreated water, or drinking water containing glacial sediment or that with different physical characteristics from the water supply in their home country. Acute gastroenteritis accounts for half of all reported illness in travellers. Of those who are ill, 18% seek local medical consultation while abroad. Some 8% are hospitalised because of travel-induced illness and 11% are ill enough to seek consultation with a doctor on their return home.[10] Some of this infective illness is preventable and may be avoided by good pre-travel advice and precautions.

Acute gastroenteritis
Approximately 10% of subjects with enteric disease during international travel present with vomiting as the primary feature of the disease. Diarrhoea may complicate the illness but vomiting predominates. The two major causes of this illness are viral gastroenteritis (often caused by a norovirus) and ingestion of a preformed toxin of *Staphylococcus aureus* or *Bacillus cereus* from contaminated food. In viral gastroenteritis, the incubation period exceeds 14 hours while, for the intoxications, it is 2–7 hours.[11]

Surveillance of 14,227 air travellers of all ages returning to Scotland from abroad revealed 37% were affected by illness.[10] Alimentary symptoms accounted for 76% of symptoms reported. Older travellers may be more adversely affected by acute gastroenteritis if they become dehydrated and lose electrolyte balance.[12]

Travel-related diarrhoea
Travellers' diarrhoea – the passage of at least three unformed stools over 24 hours, plus symptoms of enteric infection such as abdominal cramps or pain confirms the diagnosis.[13] Prevalence rates vary from 8% to 55% depending on the country visited.[13-16] World travellers are 6.5 times more likely to experience infection than those residing in Britain.[10] Three levels of risk are recognised:
- *High:* 20–55%, in developing parts of the world such as Latin America, Africa and India[17]
- *Intermediate:* in destinations in the Caribbean, southern Europe, Israel, Japan and South Africa

- *Low:* <4%, in travellers visiting low-risk regions, including North America, Western Europe, Japan, Australia and New Zealand.

Risk is associated with destination, length of stay and season. Some 30–50% of travellers will develop travellers' diarrhoea during a two-week stay in high-risk areas.[19] Many older travellers return home with the infection and seek treatment from family doctors.[20] Eighty per cent of infection is caused by *E.coli* with *Campylobacteria* and noroviruses also responsible.

Ageing changes make it more likely that older travellers are vulnerable to travellers' diarrhoea and its complications.[18] The increased incidence of achlorhydria associated with ageing, caused by chronic atrophic gastritis, may permit ingested bacteria to survive transit through the gut. Shortening and broadening of the villi in the small bowel and atrophy of mucosae cause toxins to take longer to transit the intestine. In people who are very old, associated dehydration and loss of body salts may endanger life.

Symptoms

Diarrhoea frequently starts 2–3 days after exposure to infection or a new environment; a second episode often follows a week later. Untreated, the condition lasts about four days, with 1% of the affected experiencing symptoms for a month. Some cases develop into dysentery – diarrhoea containing blood – usually caused by *Shigella dysenteriae*, or *Entamoeba hystolytica* – an important management distinction.

Inappropriate or delayed treatment, and failure to prescribe appropriate anti-diarrhoeal agents, can mean the illness is unnecessarily prolonged. Mortality due to travellers' diarrhoea is uncommon but 1% of people are ill enough to require hospital admission.[21,22] Affected people who consult a doctor are likely to be older, in poor health and taking regular medication.[23,24]

Infection risk

Causation, prophylaxis and treatment (see Chapter 7)

Conclusion

Pre-travel health advice regarding avoidance, prophylaxis and treatment of travellers' diarrhoea should be given to any older travellers who are vulnerable. Self-medication for travellers' diarrhoea can help to reduce the duration of the illness.

Patients should be encouraged to carry over-the-counter medications such as loperamide and self-treat simple acute episodes of travellers' diarrhoea. Use of an antimotility agent and an antibacterial will bring fastest relief.

High-altitude illness

Many older people are adventurous and participate in holiday packages that can expose them to high-altitude environments. Several of the world's airports, such as La Paz and Cusco, are 3,000m above sea level and arriving passengers can succumb to altitude illness on arrival. Standard tours across the altiplano of Chile, Bolivia, Peru, the Andes, Rockies and Himalayas can expose travellers to high altitude.

In a case report, an older woman developed acute mountain sickness (AMS) in a taxi, crossing the high mountain pass between Marrakesh and the Sahara. Himalayan tours with no age exclusions are popular and travellers frequently get altitude sickness on walking treks in Nepal and Bhutan. Many tourists are unaware of the health risk they run by exposing themselves to high altitude; this can induce illness from AMS.

The partial pressure of oxygen in the atmosphere diminishes with increasing altitude. Older people with diminished lung capacity and function (*see Chapter 1*), when exposed to lack of oxygen, are more disadvantaged compared with those who are young. They are also vulnerable to complications of exposure to increasing altitude. Travellers living at high altitude can experience headaches, breathlessness, poor sleep and loss of appetite. These symptoms of AMS are uncomfortable but not life threatening. If symptoms become severe and an increase in altitude continues, an increase of fluid in the brain (high-altitude cerebral oedema – HACE) or fluid in the lungs (high-altitude pulmonary oedema – HAPE) can happen. These conditions can kill quickly.

Older people are also at greater risk of stroke and retinal artery occlusion due to the increase in viscosity in the blood, which occurs with altitude. Altitude starts to have an effect at 1,500–2,000m. The body tries to make up for the change in oxygen levels over a few days of exposure.[25,26]

Given enough time to adapt, most people can adjust to altitudes of up to about 5,000m (such as Everest base camp in Tibet). The body slowly adapts to lower oxygen levels – acclimatisation. People acclimatise at different speeds Ascending too fast to above 2,500m and maintained, or increased altitude thereafter exposes the individual to altitude illnesses that are common. There are no indicators to indicate those at high risk with first exposure to a high-altitude environment; however, if an individual has experienced symptoms on previous exposure, they are more likely to experience them on further exposure (*see Chapter 11*).

Symptoms
- headache
- nausea
- vomiting
- fatigue
- poor appetite
- dizziness
- sleep disturbance.

Dehydration with fluid and electrolyte imbalance in older adults can also add to the risk from AMS. High-altitude environments are often very dry, with limited water sources. Strenuous activity, overheating and inadequate fluid intake makes dehydration a significant risk for those who travel at high altitudes.

Management guidelines
Pre-travel precautionary advice is important, and includes the following:
- Travel slowly at altitudes of >3,000m.
- At the end of each day, sleep no more than 300m higher than on the previous night. Going higher is possible if there is decent to lower level to sleep each night – 'walk high, sleep low'. If this is impractical and descent is not possible, an organised rest day before further ascent allows the body time to catch up.
- Consider using a carbonic anhydrase inhibitor prior to entering this environment. Acetazolamide (Diamox) can be used to reduce the effects of AMS and is useful if large height gains are unavoidable. It does have side-effects of sudden paraesthesia in limbs and increases the risk of dehydration.[27,28]
- Use a simple scorecard to measure disturbances to normal breathing and sleeping, and question whether symptoms are getting better or worse.
- If symptoms worsen, descent is obligatory – to a level that is at least 500 – 1000m lower for sleeping).
- Give the body extra time to acclimatise.
- Maintain a high fluid input to avoid dehydration.

Kinetosis

Kinetosis (motion sickness) occurs where there is disagreement between visually perceived movement and the vestibular system's sense of movement.

This can occur on any form of transport; most people are affected on ships and small boats, in cars and coaches. Dizziness, fatigue and nausea are the most common symptoms of motion sickness. About 33% of people are susceptible to motion sickness even in mild circumstances, such as being on a boat in calm water, although nearly 66% of people are susceptible in more severe conditions. Older people are no more susceptible than the young; however, prolonged vomiting can bring electrolyte disturbance and dehydration, which has more serious consequences in this group.

It should also be noted that antiemetic medication can also interact or interfere with routine medication.

Seasickness
All ship passengers can suffer in rough conditions, particularly in the Southern Ocean and Drake Passage. Most cruise ships however have stabilisers that diminish roll and reduce the number of affected passengers. Cabins at the centre of the ship display least vertical acceleration (*see Chapter 5*).

Vehicle sickness
The effect is worst when looking down and is significantly lessened by looking forward and outside a land vehicle. The front seat of a car, forward coaches of a train, upper or wing seats in a plane may give you a smoother ride. Looking out of the car or coach into the distance can reduce effects; reading aboard is best avoided.

Medication
Prophylactic medicaments should be taken an hour or two prior to exposure to the unstable environment. Favoured drugs are cinnarizine, scopolamine and promethazine. Scopolamine was more effective than cinnarizine but, in mild motion conditions, cinnarizine is better tolerated. A placebo effect of 33% is shown by any preparation used.

Psycholgical effects of travel

Psychological illness
Britons face travel over, under or across the sea when going abroad. Air, land and sea transit can create anxiety in older travellers. The slowing of mental responses to stimuli and central processing information, as well as a slower reaction to cognitive tasks when peopel get older makes them more vulnerable to the stressors now inseparable from global relocation.[29] Passage to and through air terminals, rail terminals and sea ports has become more stressful and anxiety provoking. There are concerns about the mechanical safety of aeroplanes and rational fears of hijack, terrorist attack and the physiological effects of prolonged travel on the venous circulation (*see Chapter 9*).

Many older people find conventional travel modes and translocation moderately or severely stressful, with many fearful and some phobic of travel. Anxiety generated by relocation and transportation is associated with travel fatigue, which can last for a day or two after arrival.[30] The increase in heart rate and blood pressure associated with the anxiety of airport transit may only discomfit a traveller who is fit, but it can be disadvantageous in older people. In those with cardiac problems, this may precipitate arrhythmia, myocardial infarction and stroke.[31]

Terrorist attacks brought a disproportionate public psychological response in that, many potential travellers gave up flying and took alternative transport. Analysis of fatal accidents showed the number of Americans who lost lives driving on roads, to avoid flying, was higher than all those killed on affected flights. Their behavioural response was disproportionate to the actual personal risk of flying. This risk misperception with a change in behaviour provokes unnecessary and inappropriate anxiety.

Worries about developing deep vein thrombosis with prolonged flying are common. The public is relatively well informed about risk, but poor in risk assessment. The disproportionate reaction merits reconditioning of the individual and education in risk assessment.[32-34]

Health professionals working in travel health should be aware of the psychological effects of relocation and transit, as well as the risk to the wellbeing of older and vulnerable people embarking on international travel. They deserve to:
- be risk assessed before departure
- receive information on potential health challenges, as well aseducation regarding misperceptions
- be encouraged to take measures to minimise any threats.

They should also be identified and offered counselling and treatment. Appropriate advice and improved pre-planning could diminish the impact of many travel-induced stressors.

Management
- Provide informative facts on actual risk, dread risk and correc any misconceptions
- Recommend pre-planning travel programmes to decrease stress
- Recommend precautions, e.g. deep vein thrombosis
- Offer advise on available therapy (e.g. panic states and phobias).

References

1 McIntosh I Power K. Travel induced illness in the elderly 1991 Scot. Med.11. 4.14-15
2 Allison S. Lobo D. Fluid and electrolytes in the elderly. Curr. Opin. Clin. Nut.r Metab. Care 2004 .27-33

3 Lye M. Disturbances of homeostasis in Tallis FC (Ed) Geriatric Med. and Geront. 5th Ed. London Churchill Livingstone 1998 925-48
4 Biswas K Mulkerrin E. Potassium homeostasis in the elderly QJ Med 1997 90. 487-92
5 Kenney W Chiu P. Influence of age on thirst and fluid intake Med. Sc. Sports Exercise 2001 33. 1524-32
6 Gurwitz G Field T et al Incidence and preventability of adverse drug events in in older persons in ambulatory sweating.J Amer Med Assoc. 2003 289.`1107-11
7 Schwartz J. Who is sensitive to extremes of temperature? Epidemiol. 2005 16 61-7
8 Collins K Fluid balance of elderly people in hot environments. Geriatric Med. 2009.385-90
9 Department of Health. Heat wave plan for England. Dept of Health 2005
10 Cossar J. Review of travel associated illness 1988 Trav. Med.50-54
11 Dupont H Systematic review: the epidemiology and clinical features of travellers' diarrhoea 2009 Alimentary Pharmacology & Therapeutics30, 187–196, August
12.McIntosh I. Travel in the elderly 1992 .Chap 7. Quay Books. Lancaster
13 DuPont HNL. Guidelines on acute infectious diarrhoea in adults. American Journal of Gastroent. 1997; 92: 1962-75
14 Gorbach SL, Peltolah H. Textbook of Travel Medicine and Health.1997, (Eds. R Steffen and H Dupont). Becker Publications, Hamilton, Ontario.
15 Reed J. McIntosh I. Power K. Travel Illness and the Family Practitioner. J Trav Med 1994, 1.192-7
16 Farthing M. Travellers' Diarrhoea. Gut. 1994, 35: 1-4
17 Fletcher P. Benefit/risk considerations with respect to OTC de-scheduling of loperamide. Arzneim Forsch 1995, 45: 608-13
18 Caroll B. Behrens R. New approaches to management of travellers' diarrhoea.2012 Emporiatrics Spring 7-9
19 Diemert DJ Prevention and Self-Treatment of Travellers' Diarrhoea 2006 .Clin Microbiol Rev. July; 19(3): 583–59419
20 McIntosh I., Reed JM, Power K Travellers' diarrhoea and the effect of pre-travel health advice in general practice. British Journal of General Practice, 1997, 47, 71-75.
21 Dupont HNL. Guidelines on acute infectious diarrhoea in adults. American Journal of Gastroenterology. 1997; 92 : 1962-75
22 Peltola HP. Gorbach LS Travellers' diarrhoea in Textbook of travellers' health .Ed. Dupont. Steffen 1997 Decker. Canada
23 Zeichner LO Ericson CD. Travellers' diarrhoea in Principles and practice of travel medicine. 2001 ed. Zuckerman Wiley Chichester.
24 Diemert DJ Prevention and Self-Treatment of Travellers' Diarrhoea 2006 .Clin Microbiol Rev. July; 19(3): 583–594.
25 How do older persons tolerate moderate altitude?. Roach RC. Houston CS. Hogigman B et al. West J Med. 162: 32-6 1995
26 Ventilatory sensitivity to CO_2 in hyperoxia and hypoxia in older humans. Poulin MJ. Cunningham DA. Paterson DH et al. J Appl Physiol. 75:2209-16, 1993
27 McIntosh I Prescott R Acetazolamide in prevention of acute mountain sickness. 1986 J. Int. Med. Research. 14(5) 285-7

28 Kerr A Prescott R McIntosh I Acetazolamide in prevention of acute mountain sickness –a double blind cross-over study. 1981 Brit. Med. J. 283. 811-13

29 Gurcharan SR Essentials of Ger. Med. 2010 2nd. Ed. Radcliffe Pub. London

30 Waterhouse J Reilly T Health Problems 2004 Sports Sc.(10) 946-

31 DeHard R Halth issues of air travel Ann Review of Pub, Health 2003 24. 133-5

32 Gikenzer G Dread risk, Sept 11 and fatal accidents 2004 Psychol Sc. 15.286-7

33 Gauld J McIntosh I Attitudes to travel after terrorist events of 2001 2002. J. Brit. Trav. Health Assoc3.62-7

34 Swanson V McIntosh I Perceived threats to life and limb 2004 J Brit Trav Health Asoc. 5.48-52

7

Infection and Disease

Immunisation

The ageing of populations in developed countries has greatly increased the number of older world travellers, with estimates of 13% of travellers being at least 65 years old. In tropical areas, 5–8% of travellers are older persons. Immunisations are recommended for older people because age generally aggravates the impact of infectious diseases and these individuals often have chronic medical conditions.

The immune system deteriorates in old age, especially where immune response is dependent upon cellular immunity and humoural response. The number and functions of T-lymphocytes decrease, but B-lymphocytes are not altered. There is reduction in peak antibody response to immunisation and reduction in duration of antibody response to it. The response to vaccinations is therefore slower and lower in efficacy in older people. Reduced ability to seroconvert is attributed to immunosenescence. This has multiple elements and is difficult to measure. It includes T-cell reduction from thymic involution, less effective antigen presentation through monocytes, and reduced killer cell toxicity.[1]

Vaccination requirements for older travellers are broadly similar to those for younger people except that additional factors have to be considered. Loss of immunity, the effect of routine medications and seroconversion after vaccination are relevant in this group. People going on trips involving travel in confined spaces with other travellers, such as bus trips and cruise ships, are at additional risk as are older people with reduced immunity, such as those who have HIV, are taking high-dose long-term steroids or are receiving chemotherapy. Another complicating factor is that older travellers may often have a vague knowledge of past immunisation records and infectious diseases.

Older adults are especially vulnerable to certain diseases, such as influenza and pneumonia. In 2008, adults aged 65 and older comprised 90% of deaths that occurred from complications related to influenza and pneumonia. Pneumonia is a major cause of morbidity and mortality in older people, especially in those with chronic medical conditions such as chronic heart and lung diseases. Influenza is another prime cause of death in old people. Influenza, pneumococcal, herpes zoster, tetanus, poliomyelitis, hepatitis and typhoid fever vaccinations are commonly recommended for senior citizens before world travel. The effects of age-diminished immunity response are observed with vaccinations against tetanus, flu, pneumococcal infections and hepatitis B.[2]

Influenza

Influenza is a perennial rather than a seasonal disease in the tropics, and this vaccination should not be overlooked. Influenza and pneumonia are responsible for about 8% of all deaths in old people, with influenza being the fourth most common cause of death, after cancer, heart disease and stroke.

There is limited evidence of the benefit of the influenza vaccine in the over-65s from randomised controlled trials but cohort studies suggest that those who are vaccinated fare better in terms of reduced hospital admissions and total mortality. Evidence of benefit is sufficiently strong that influenza vaccine is recommended throughout Europe. The success of the vaccine depends upon seroconversion in the individual, and then the extent to which the strain in the vaccine matches the circulating viral strain. Seroconversion after vaccination occurs in 60% of community-dwelling subjects who are around 60 years old, 30% of those aged 70–80, and 12% of those over 80. Annual influenza vaccination is recommended for those aged over 65 and should be offered to all global older travellers if they have not been protected. The seroconversion, after vaccine, is 50% from age 60–70 years, 31% for ages 70–80, and only 11% for those older than 80 years. Vaccination reduces morbidity by 25%, admission to hospital by 20%, pneumonia by 50% and mortality by 70%.[1-8]

Pneumonia

Pneumococcal disease is caused by the bacterium *Streptococcus* resulting in pneumonia, meningitis and septicaemia, which can be life threatening. Vaccination is recommended for older adults over 65 years of age as they are more vulnerable to infection. Pneumococcal vaccine is effective in 60% of older recipients. It is indicated every five years for those over 65 years of age or with chronic diseases and post splenectomy. The 23-valent pneumococcal polysaccharide vaccine is used in most European countries for adults aged over 60 and is particularly indicated for those: with asplenia; who are immuno-compromised; who have chronic cardiac, renal, pulmonary or liver disease; and who have had organ transplants. Meta-analysis has shown a 36% reduction in pneumococcal pneumonia, but no overall effect on pneumonia mortality.[8] The efficacy varies with the age of the population studied and the endpoint used: in adults aged 65–74 years, the vaccine is 70–80% effective; this falls to 53–67% in 75–84 year olds, and even further to 0–22% in the group aged 85 years and above.[1,2]

Tetanus

Tetanus is fatal in 32% of people over 80 years old, so this vaccination is important. Adults are now recommended to have a tetanus booster at age 50 unless they have had a booster in the previous 10 years.

Diphtheria

Diphtheria is caused by the bacterium *Corynebacterium diphtheriae*, which infects the upper respiratory tract. A grey membrane may form in the throat and obstruct breathing. The bacteria also produce a toxin that may affect nerves and the heart. Adults are recommended to have a diphtheria booster vaccination at age 50 unless they have had a booster in the previous 10 years. Diphtheria and tetanus boosters are usually combined in one injection.

Herpes zoster

Herpes zoster (shingles) is caused by the chicken pox virus (varicella zoster). When infected for the first time, it causes chicken pox but the virus stays in the nerve cells, kept in check by the immune system. With age, this control is less effective; the virus may be reactivated and cause shingles. Older people may develop complications of shingles with enduring pain, or the rash may spread to the eye. A vaccine for herpes zoster was licensed in 2006 in Europe for adults aged 60 or over; in 2007, recommendations were amended to include adults aged over 50 years. The use of the herpes zoster vaccine reduced the incidence by 51%, reduced the incidence of post-herpetic neuralgia by 66% and the overall burden of illness due to zoster by 61%.[9] The vaccine has an uncertain duration of benefit and the severity of post-herpetic neuralgia is greater above 70 years.

Vaccination against zoster is recommended for adults aged 60 and over, unless they have already received a dose of zoster vaccine, are allergic to any of its ingredients, or have another disease or are receiving treatment that significantly lowers their immunity. Only one dose of zoster vaccine is needed.[9]

Hepatitis A virus

Hepatitis A virus (HAV) exposure in unprotected adults may cause severe disease and serious symptoms, with risk of both morbidity and mortality increasing with age. With hepatitis A, there has also been shown to be an association between an age of >40 years, severe morbidity and high mortality: the mortality rate is 2.5% for patients who are >40 years of age compared with a rate of <0.1% among younger patients.

As seroprevalence of HAV is low in industrialised countries and an increasing number of older people travel from areas of low HAV endemicity to those of high endemicity, pre-travel vaccination is warranted. Vaccination of older people against HAV may be associated with reduced seroprotection, since the immune response decreases with age. Studies with monovalent hepatitis A vaccine or combined hepatitis A and B vaccine show good efficacy in adults in general. Administering monovalent hepatitis A vaccine in older people showed a reduced seroprotection of approximately 65% after a single primary dose in subjects over the age of 50 years. Seroprotection was 98% in this age group after receiving a booster dose.

Giving a combined hepatitis A and B vaccine in those aged over 40 years showed similar seroprotection (99–100%) against HAV compared with a monovalent vaccine after receiving three doses. Based on available data, travel health professionals should screen older travellers to areas endemic for HAV for the presence of naturally acquired immunity and, if found susceptible, immunise them well in advance of their trip to allow time for post-vaccination antibody testing and/or administration of a second dose of the vaccine.[10]

Poliomyelitis
Naturally acquired anti-poliovirus immunity does not seem to decrease with age, unlike anti-diphtheria and anti-tetanus immunity.

Tuberculosis
The tuberculin skin test is an easy method to check risk in older people. A negative result indicates depressed cell-mediated immunity.

Yellow fever
Older travellers aged over 60 years who have not previously been vaccinated against yellow fever are at a higher risk of side-effects from the yellow fever vaccine. Serious adverse reactions to immunisation increase from one in 250,000 to one in 50,000 in the over-60s who have not been immunised previously.[11-14]

Malaria (see Chapter 3)
Malaria is one of the most prevalent global diseases, with an infected population of 300–500 million and 1.5–3.5 million deaths reported annually. The major killer is *Plasmodium falciparum*, which causes multi-organ involvement and, in the absence of prompt and appropriate treatment, is associated with high mortality rates. Extensive advice on the correct use of exposure and chemoprophylaxis of malaria is especially important for travellers above the age of 60. Old age is a risk factor for complications of malaria in the non-immune traveller with higher risk for a severe course of malaria in older people. There is significant evidence for a correlation between age and the frequency of complications in malaria such as cerebral involvement, respiratory failure, renal failure, anaemia and hyperparasitaemia.

In patients over 15 years of age, 37.1% developed a severe course of malaria, whereas in those 60 years and above this percentage increased to 61.5%. The age distribution in the group with severe malaria was significantly shifted towards older people (P=0.016, Mann-Whitney test).

The duration of hospitalisation also increased with age from an average of five days for the group younger than 45 years, to 21 days for older people aged 60 years and above.[15,16]

In a national Israeli analysis of *P. falciparum* malaria in non-immune patients, there was a significantly higher rate of severe disease and mortality among those patients who were over 40 years of age.[16] In an Indonesian study, mortality from malaria was highest in the youngest (<2 years) and oldest age groups (>40 years) – 2.2% and 2.5% respectively – compared with 0–0.9% for patients who were 2–40 years of age.[17]

In patients who died of imported *P. falciparum* malaria in 1959–1987 in the United States, a breakdown of the study population by age groups showed that there was an increment in mortality by age in the 0–19, 20–39, 40–69 and 70–79 year old age groups; case fatality rates were 0.4%, 2.2%, 5.8% and 30.3% respectively.[18] Other studies show similar results. The number of severe cases increased with age: 3.2% of cases in patients who were <30 years of age; 5.3% for patients aged 30–39 years; 9.8% for patients aged 40–49 years; and 23.5% for patients >50 years of age.[19] There was a 2.3% case fatality rate in patients with malaria due to *P. falciparum*, with increments in mortality by age. The mortality rate was 0.5% in patients aged 21–30 years, 2.3% in patients aged 31–40 years, 1.7% in patients aged 41–50 years and 5.4% in patients >51 years of age.[20]

These studies included a mixed population of non-immune travellers and immigrants, and all examined different end points (either severity or mortality of malaria). Age (over 40 years) is the most important risk factor for predicting severe malaria. In five studies with a total of 4,146 patients who had malaria due to *P. falciparum*, the case fatality rate was 1.1% among the patients who were <40 years of age, compared with 5.3% in patients who were >40 years of age.[19,20]

VULNERABILITY WITH AGE

The reason for increased vulnerability when older than 40 years age is not clear. One explanation may be the underlying medical conditions of the older patients. Baird[16] hypothesised that different immune responses related to age may be responsible for the different outcomes. The susceptibility of the older population to the negative effect of cytokines excreted during the disease may be higher. Older persons may use prophylaxis less than younger patients (79% of the older patients did not take any prophylaxis, compared with 52% of the younger patients in one study). Complete prophylaxis was taken by only 2% of the older patients, whereas 10% of the younger patients took it. These findings may not be generalisable but, if they are, they may explain the higher attack rate in the older population.[17]

Many senior citizens have chronic medical conditions and are on several medications that can interact with antimalarial prophylaxis and complicate preventive interventions. For instance, some antimalarials lower insulin requirements in patients with diabetes and can lead to hypoglycaemia in those treated with insulin or oral hypoglycaemics such as glibenclamide. Both chloroquine and mefloquine also have the potential to increase the risk of arrhythmias if given with other anti-arrythmic agents such as amiodarine. It is best to avoid a range of cardioactive drugs including beta-blockers, anti-arrythmics and calcium antagonists in combination with mefloquine. This is due to the risk of prolonging the QTc interval and inducing other cardiac adverse effects (*see Chapter 7*).

Recommendations

Clinicians should provide aged travellers with specific instructions for prophylaxis of malaria, encourage complete compliance and vigorously treat patients when they show the first clinical signs of malaria. Medical history, current medications and decreased immunity status have to be considered.

Recommendations should be based on individualised, customised analysis of infection risk with a review of travel venue, prevalence of malaria in the area and whether *P.vivax* or *P.falciparum* is locally endemic and exposure is continuous or sporadic.

Concise risk appraisal is mandatory to provide the traveller with accurate information on personal risk while exposed to mosquito bites on a short vacation. Global travel in this group is frequently in cities and urban areas with exposure only during daytime hours. Many older tourists are only exposed to the local environment on daytime coach tours and will spend much of their time in air-conditioned buildings and coaches, with minimal exposure to biting mosquitos. Passengers on cruises visiting endemic areas will often be offshore at dusk and during the night and daytime exposure will be limited.

The health professional should consider whether the risk of serious side-effects from prophylactic medication may be greater than the risk of acquiring the disease. Standby emergency treatment may be an option in those only exposed to a risk for short time in a lower-risk area.

The need for barrier prevention of bites needs to be emphasised with the wearing of trousers and long-sleeved garments, and the repeated application of insect repellent containing DEET.[21]

PROPHYLAXIS

No reduction in antimalarial dosage is required on the basis of advanced age. However, older travellers are more likely to have underlying disorders, for example renal or liver impairment, which may necessitate antimalarial dose reduction. The increased likelihood of older travellers taking additional medication for chronic conditions will influence the choice of chemoprophylactic agent.[22]

Chloroquine, proguanil, chloroquine plus proguanil, mefloquine or doxycycline may be appropriate. All have potential side-effects and their use has to be carefully considered if there is chronic disorder and the traveller is on routine medication.[21-26]

Drug interactions[8]

Proguanil may enhance the anticoagulant effect of warfarin, a medication commonly taken in older patients. Mefloquine antagonises the anticonvulsant effect of antiepileptics and interacts with a number of cardiac drugs. Mefloquine prophylaxis is contraindicated in those with current or previous history of depression, neuropsychiatric disorders or epilepsy, or those who are hypersensitive to quinine. The metabolism of doxycycline is accelerated by carbamazepine and phenytoin.[2,27]

Tetracyclines possibly enhance the anticoagulant effect of coumarins (e.g. warfarin).

Travellers should start taking antimalaria tablets more than one week (ideally 2–3 weeks, in the case of mefloquine) prior to their departure. A baseline INR should be checked prior to starting chemoprophylaxis, and re-checked after one week of taking chemoprophylaxis.

If a traveller is away for a long period of time, the INR should be checked at intervals at the destination. Once chemoprophylaxis has been completed, the INR should be checked again to restabilise anticoagulant therapy.

Liver disease

Most antimalarial drugs are excreted or metabolised by the liver with a risk of drug accumulation in severe liver impairment. In severe liver disease all antimalarial drugs are contraindicated, with the possible exception of atovaquone plus proguanil.

For moderate impairment proguanil, or atovaquone plus proguanil or mefloquine may be used. In mild impairment, chloroquine or proguanil, or chloroquine plus proguanil, or atovaquone plus proguanil or mefloquine, may be used. Doxycycline should be used only with caution.

The choice of chemoprophylaxis should be made after discussion with the hepatic specialist. The Child-Pugh classification is often used for grading liver function (accessible at www.emea.europa.eu/pdfs/human/ewp/233902en.pdf)

Renal impairment

Chloroquine is partially excreted via the kidneys, while proguanil is wholly excreted via the kidneys. For chloroquine, a dose reduction for prophylaxis is required only in severe renal impairment. Proguanil should be avoided, or the dose reduced. Atovaquone/proguanil is not recommended for patients with a creatinine clearance of <30ml/minute.[28] Doxycycline or mefloquine may be used in severe renal failure.

Alternative medications are being explored and vaccination possibilities researched. The therapeutic efficacy of new products such as artemesinin – the active ingredient of the plant artemisia in killing parasites – has been established. Consideration is now focusing on management change, with selected travellers to lower-risk areas being given antimalarial testing kits to be taken if fever intervenes. If blood tests positive for infection, an antimalarial medication would then be taken to treat the infection.

Artemesinin has few side-effects and may prove a useful option for the older traveller, particularly if they have concomitant medical conditions and are on several routine medications. For instance, West African coastal cruise passengers making an occasional visit to a malarial area in daytime might consider this possibility. With compliance being an issue in this group, good mechanical barrier protection and prompt treatment when necessary may avoid prophylactic side-effects, a greater risk to the individual than the chance of a bite from an infected mosquito.[28-30]

This approach would depend upon: appraisal of risk; the provision of adequate information, medication and testing kits to the individual traveller; their compliance; and efficient follow-up on return to the UK.[29,30] If prophylaxis is not recommended, professional advice on adequate bite prevention, recognition of malaria symptoms and prompt treatment with a product like artemesinin, rather than a prophylactic intervention response, is vital. This option may be appropriate for non-adventurous, older seniors on short trips abroad, living in air-conditioned rooms in city centres, who are not going on safari, up-country or who are living on board a ship overnight and are likely to be poorly compliant in taking prophylactic medication. Their actual exposure to mosquitos may be minimal and adverse reactions to antimalarial medication may present a higher risk than malarial infection.

Renal and hepatic impairment concomitant with ageing in the older traveller who has pre-existing illness, the traveller who is on medications or drug interactions may slant the risk assessment towards non-drug malarial prophylactic recommendations.

Dependence upon standby emergency treatment requires the travel health professional to identify and analyse the malarial risk and acquire knowledge of the traveller's:
- current health status
- clinical history
- medications
- travel itinerary
- willingness to accept stand by emergency treatment and comply with instructions
- ability to make an active personal response to malaria symptoms.
- competence to do a blood test
- ability to promptly treat with antimalarial medication if tested positive.

Travel-related diarrhoea

Travellers' diarrhoea is the predominant medical problem associated with international tourism in terms of frequency, and personal and economic impact.[31] It can have deleterious effects on older tourists who suffer from it if there is marked fluid loss with disturbed electrolyte imbalance. This and related dehydration may increase the likelihood of angina and arrythmias, including atrial fibrillation, and myocardial and cerebral infarction. Decreased renal function makes it also more difficult for these individuals to maintain water and electrolyte balance.

Vomiting and diarrhoea with fluid and electrolyte imbalance may also have an impact on chronic disorders such as diabetes mellitus and the absorption of routine medications may be disturbed in the ill.[32] Older travellers are more likely to acquire gastrointestinal infection than younger people due to lower immunity; they will also be less able to combat the infection. If older adventurous travellers do become ill from diarrhoea while overseas, a delay in access to supportive medical and nursing services may compound the health problem.

Travellers' diarrhoea – defined as the passage of at least three unformed stools plus a sign or symptom of enteric infection, such as abdominal cramps or pain[33] – is the most frequent health problem to afflict global tourists. The range in frequency of it is between 10% and 60%, with the highest rates seen in Latin America, Africa and India. The lowest rates (<4%) are seen in travellers in low-risk regions, such as North America, Western Europe, Japan, Australia and New Zealand.

Many older travellers return home with the infection and seek treatment from family doctors.[34] Estimates suggest 50,000 travellers a day suffer from travellers' diarrhoea in high-risk countries.[35] To keep this in perspective, acute non-travel related diarrhoea of presumed infective origin affects 20% of England's population annually, resulting in 3.4 million professional consultations. One in six seek GP treatment. About 6% of adults report an acute occurrence of diarrhoea in the preceding two-week period when living at home.[34]

Professional management of acute episodic diarrhoea varies greatly and doctors often delay therapeutic intervention or limit prescription of appropriate medication. Inappropriate or delayed treatment and failure to prescribe appropriate antidiarrhoeal agents can mean the illness is unnecessarily prolonged.[36] Mortality due to travellers' diarrhoea is uncommon but, 1% of people are ill enough to require hospital admission.[35,37]

Risk is associated with destination and length of stay, and dependent upon the ingestion of contaminated food or water, with the most common cause being bacteria. Countries can be identified as low-, medium- and high-risk with risk altering seasonally in temperate climates. It has been estimated that 30–50% of travellers will develop travellers' diarrhoea during a one or two-week stay in high-risk areas.[38] Affected people who consult a doctor are likely to be older, in poor health and taking regular medication.[39]

Travellers' diarrhoea is largely caused by detectable and undetected bacterial enteropathogens. The most important group are enterotoxic *E. coli* (ETEC),[40] entero-aggregative *E. coli* (EAEC)[41] and probably diffusely adherent *E. coli* (DAEC).[42] While DAEC causes a majority of cases in high-risk regions, invasive enteropathogens, including *Campylobacter jejuni*, *Shigella spp* and *Salmonella spp* more commonly are encountered in southern Asia than in Africa and Latin America.[40-42]

Risk areas for transmission of travellers' diarrhoea

Low risk
North America, Australia, New Zealand, Japan, northwest Europe
Medium risk
Eastern Europe and former eastern bloc countries, South Africa, the Caribbean
High risk
The Middle East, Southeast Asia (not Singapore,) North and Central Africa, South America

Causes

A number of travellers' diarrhoea cases remain without cause after comprehensive microbiological evaluation (20–40%); this is most probably due to undetected bacterial enteropathogens as antibacterial drugs are remarkably successful in treating the undiagnosable proportion of disease. In up to 80% of cases the infection is caused by *E. coli*, with strains of *Campylobacter jejuni* causing many cases occurring in southern Asia. Enteric viral infections such as noroviruses are the most commonly implicated nonbacterial cause of travellers' diarrhoea, responsible for 10% of the disease. Norovirus and rotavirus are responsible for most of this illness, which can be debilitating in older travellers. Parasites can be found in only about 2–10% of acute cases.[43] Micro-organisms responsible for travellers' diarrhoea include:

Bacteria
- ETEC
- EAEC
- *Campylobacter jejuni*
- *Salmonella spp*

Parasites
Fewer than 10% of cases of travellers' diarrhoea are caused by protozoan parasites. The most common include:
- *Giardia lamblia*
- *Cryptosporidium parvum*
- *Cyclospora cayetensis*

- *Entamoeba histolytica*
- viruses
- norovirus
- rotavirus.

Prophylaxis and treatment

Precautions to minimise the risk of developing travellers' diarrhoea emphasise avoidance of potentially contaminated food or drink, and the taking of prophylactic measures, including both non-pharmacological and antimicrobial strategies. Adherence to instructions and compliance is universally poor however, with older travellers no exception. Where food and water are concerned, 'boil, cook, peel or avoid it' is good advice.

The second-generation prebiotic food supplement B-GOS, taken immediately prior to and during travel, may be of value in preventing or diminishing the impact of travel-related diarrhoea.[44] If diarrhoea does develop, a combination of an antibiotic and an antimotility agent is usually effective treatment.[38] Cochrane database review confirms that doxycycline, ciprofloxacin and trimethoprim-sulfamethoxazole are useful prophylactic antibiotics.[45]

Health professionals are reluctant to prescribe antidiarrhoeal medication. The belief that antimotility drugs should not be used in acute diarrhoea, where fever may indicate an invasive pathogen infection, has been widely held. Professional response may be based on personal beliefs that diarrhoea is nature's way of clearing the body of infectious agents and that antimotility drugs may prolong or worsen the infection by reducing stool output.

In one study over half the GPs and nurses questioned agreed with the statements "anti-diarrhoeals keep toxins or pathogens inside the intestine where they do more damage to the gut" and "antidiarrhoeals prolong illness by delaying excretion of the pathogen" – a premise not supported by research-based evidence. Few doctors confirm they would recommend and prescribe antidiarrhoeal medication.

In the management of an adult presenting with diarrhoea, a third of family doctors would take no action for 24 hours, with 12% delaying for 48 hours in the case of travellers' diarrhoea. Half would recommend oral replacement therapy. Many would advise the patient to avoid solid food over this time, although starvation as treatment has no scientific basis and may encourage fluid loss.[46] Two-thirds of sufferers actively treat their diarrhoea, with half self-medicating and the others seek professional prescription. Antimotility agents, available as public pharmacy products, are used widely by many older travellers without adverse effects.[47]

ANTI-MOTILITY AGENTS

Loperamide (Imodium) is the anti-motility agent of choice for travellers' diarrhoea. The drug brings symptom relief. It is a peripherally acting opiate without abuse potential, which does not cross the blood-brain barrier and hardly reaches the systemic circulation due to its mainly liver and faecal excretion. In addition to an anti-peristaltic effect, it increases intestinal absorption of fluid and electrolytes. When used as sole therapy, loperamide provides good relief for mild to moderate diarrhoea compared to placebo or bismuth subsalicylate. A 4mg. dose in a healthy adult does not slow orocaecal transit and in diarrhoea states will normalisetransit times.[47] There was no prolongation of illness or complications when administered with antimicrobials in cases of diarrhoea where invasive organisms were identified 48.49 It reduces the number of unformed stools and shortens duration of symptoms. When compared to antimicrobial medication alone, they do not prolong fever or delay pathogen excretion in stools.

ANTIBIOTICS

Treatment with antibiotics is effective against enteropathogens.[50] Trimethoprim/sulfamethoxazole resistance is however widespread. Ciprofloxacin is often employed empirically with single-dose therapy effective in most cases.[51] Problems with fluoroquinolones have emerged relating to tendinitis and tendon rupture.[52] Both fluoroquinolones and ciprofloxacin may deplete colonic flora[53] and predispose persons treated with these drugs to *Clostridium difficile* colitis.[54] *Campylobacter* strains from diverse regions have shown an increased resistance to the fluoroquinolone class of drugs.[55] Antibiotic therapy is recommended either with or without loperamide for travellers with moderate to severe symptoms (three or more unformed stools during an eight-hour period, particularly if associated with nausea, vomiting, abdominal cramping, fever or bloody stools). Antimicrobials reduce the duration of diarrhoea, as well as reducing related symptoms such as abdominal cramping and time spent incapacitated.[38]

Rifaximin. This drug is a semisynthetic, non-systemic antibiotic, with very little drug passing through the gastrointestinal wall into the circulation as often occurs with other orally administered antibiotics. It has been compared with placebo and ciprofloxacin for treatment of travellers' diarrhoea in randomised, double-blind clinical trials. It is highly effective at treating travellers' diarrhoea, with few side-effects and a low risk of developing antibiotic resistance. It is not effective against *Campylobacter jejuni*, and there is no evidence of efficacy against *Shigella* or *Salmonella* species. Oral rifaximin is a safe and effective treatment of travellers' diarrhoea caused by non-invasive pathogens and can be used with loperamide.[56-62]

Prophylactic antibiotics should be considered for older people who are at high risk of travellers' diarrhoea and who have:
- increased susceptibility to infection or are immunocompromised, e.g. people receiving chemotherapy or immunosuppressive drugs

- a high risk of complications if they were to develop travellers' diarrhoea, e.g. chronic gastrointestinal disease (such as Crohn's disease, ulcerative colitis)
- an ileostomy or colostomy
- type 1 diabetes mellitus, renal disease, congestive heart failure in whom diarrhoeal illness might severely impact on their health
- a critical trip in prospect, which would be seriously disputed by a diarrhoea episode.

People taking acid-suppressive drugs, e.g. proton pump inhibitors, should not be routinely offered antibiotic prophylaxis unless they have a high risk of complications.

Empirical antibiotics may be appropriate for people who are travelling to high-risk locations where access to medical assistance is poor or not available and for whom antibiotic prophylaxis is not the preferred choice.[63,64,65]

Table 1. Medications for travellers' diarrhoea[33]

Ciprofloxacin	potential side-effects: tendonitis and rupture, *Clostridium difficile* colitis, *Campylobacter* strains often resistant
Rifaximin	not effective against invasive forms of travellers' diarrhoea, good safety profile
Azithromycin	short-lasting nausea, effective against bacterial forms and febrile dysenteric travellers' diarrhoea

Acute gastroenteritis
Approximately 10% of subjects with enteric disease during international travel present with vomiting as the primary feature of the disease. Diarrhoea may complicate the illness but vomiting predominates. The two major causes of this illness are viral gastroenteritis (often caused by a norovirus) and ingestion of a preformed toxin of *Staphylococcus aureus* or *Bacillus cereus* from contaminated food. In viral gastroenteritis, the incubation period exceeds 14 hours; for intoxications, it is 2–7 hours.

Salmonella infections and typhoid fever is discussed later in this section.

Summary

All older travellers to high-risk regions should exercise care in disease prevention by careful selection of safe foods and water. Those planning a trip to a high-risk region and senior adventurers visiting places distant from emergency health care should take with them loperamide to treat milder forms of travellers' diarrhoea and antibacterial medication for a severe infection.[11,33] Rifaximin is recommended in UK guidelines for self-treatment of diarrhoea and, in certain situations, for use as chemoprophylaxis;[81] with its low side-effect profile, it may be suited to older travellers. There is debate as to whether patients should self-medicate from a personal travel kit in developing countries or whether they should consult local doctors. A minority of the latter use obsolete antimicrobials polypharmacy and have a high rate of invasive procedures with a theoretical risk of nosocomial infection – concerns that justify pre-travel provision of antimotility agents and antibiotics in order to combat an episode of travellers' diarrhoea.[66, 67,68]

Other infections

Sedentary, non-adventurous, older world travellers living in hotels and participating in coach tours are less likely to acquire infections that often affect the more adventurous young. However the senior citizen, sitting by lake or seaside, having a forest picnic and overnighting in a hotel can be exposed to insect bites, skin trauma and suffer prolonged healing. Ageing brings lowered immunity, impaired peripheral circulation, poorer skin repair and ankle oedema from cardiac conditions, which often result in adverse reactions to minor afflictions. Bites from insects, even when not threatening systemic disease, can be troublesome. These are a serious threat to diabetic and immunocompromised older travellers. Simple bites from ticks, bed bugs, lice, fleas and sand flies may result in more than a short-lasting localised itch, with potential for skin breakdown, ulceration and a lengthy healing process.

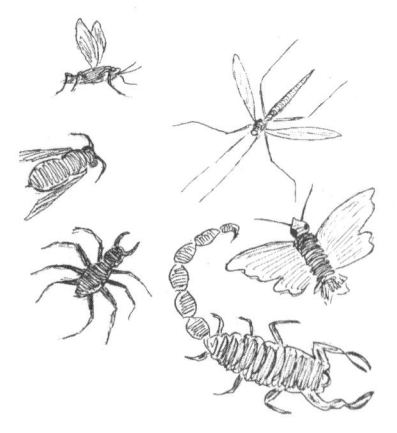

Bed bugs *(Cimicidae)* These have increased in prevalence and show increasing resistance to pesticides. They can inhabit top-quality hotels and bite bed sleepers. They are small parasitic insects feeding on human blood and are mainly active at night, biting mainly on legs and feet. They feed unnoticed on hosts, but bites become intensely itchy and can cause skin rashes and allergic symptoms. The itch encourages scratching and excoriation. If there is ankle swelling, as often occurs in travellers and those with cardiac problems, or the limb is oedematous, sores and ulcers can develop. [69]

Treatment is symptomatic. Clean bites with an antiseptic and elevate the leg if there is oedema. A topical antihistamine cream will diminish any itch, but the bites create lumps in the skin that continue to itch and can take several weeks to resolve. Scratching breaks the skin so secondary infection can result, particularly in oedematous lower limbs common in older people.

Fleas are insects of the order *Siphonaptera*, which are wingless insects with mouthparts adapted for piercing skin and sucking blood. They are external parasites, living by hematophagy off the blood of mammals such as cats, dogs and humans. The wingless insects have tube-like mouth parts, adapted to feeding on the blood of hosts. They move through hairs, feathers or under clothing. The tough flea body is able to withstand great pressure – even hard squeezing between fingers is normally insufficient to kill a flea. They can be eliminated by rolling briskly between the fingers to disable them and crushing between fingernails, or by direct contact with anti-flea pesticides. Their bites are itchy;when scratched they can become infected and be a problem on swollen limbs.

Treatment. Clean bites with antiseptic and apply topical antihistamine cream.

Sandflies are a species of flying, biting, blood-sucking Diptera encountered in sandy areas. Their bites leave large, red itchy bumps that may turn into a rash. These bumps are often more itchy than mosquito bites and tend to last longer. Some sandfly genera of the *Phlebotominae* subfamily are primary vectors of leishmaniasis and pappataci fever, both confusingly referred to as sandfly fever. In the New World, leishmaniasis is spread by sandflies. Belize and Honduras are notorious in the Caribbean for sandfly populations.

Prevention and treatment. Tourists to sandy areas should carry antibug spray containing high concentrations of DEET, and apply antiseptic cream to the bites.

Biting midges. *Ceratopogonidae*, are a family of small flies (1–4mm long) in the order Diptera. They are closely related to *Chironomidae*, *Simuliidae* (or black flies), and are found in almost any aquatic or semiaquatic habitat throughout the world. Many are pests in beach or mountain habitats. The blood-sucking species may be vectors of disease-causing viruses, protozoa and filarial worms. In humans, their bite can cause intensely itchy, red welts that can persist for more than a week. The discomfort arises from a localised allergic reaction to the proteins in their saliva, which can be somewhat alleviated by topical antihistamines. They are notorious for multiplicity of bites and intensity of itch produced and are particularly prevalent in the Scottish Highlands and northern latitudes of Scandinavia.

Prevention and treatment. Use of fine-screen head veils and spray containing high concentrations of DEET and application of antiseptic cream to bites.

Lice Infestation with *Pediculus humanus capitis* (head lice) occurs worldwide, and is hyperendemic in many developing-country populations. Tourists travelling in close contact with indigenous natives in crowded buses, trains and markets in Africa, Asia and South America can become infested. Transmission route is by head-to-head contact. Pruritus – an immune-mediated reaction to components of lice saliva – is the common symptom and may interfere with sleep. Typically, there are reddish, intensely itchy papules, frequently in the retro-auricular area of the scalp. Left untreated this becomes intensely irritating and skin infections may occur if bites are scratched with excoriation.[70]

Treatment. There are no functional head-lice repellents. Hair combing removes most eggs and lice.

Chemical. Pediculicides containing insecticide with neurotoxic action are used but are not effective against eggs younger than four days old. Increasing resistance is occurring. Topical insecticides – commonly pyrethroids and organophosphates – are used but insecticide resistance is a problem worldwide;[71] these are unsuitable on broken, secondarily infected skin. Published results of Cochrane Review, found no evidence that any one pediculicide has greater effect than another.[72]

Pyrethroids have a knock-down effect. Permethrin can kill during application and also has a long-term residual effect. Most adverse reactions are local and mild. Evidence of efficacy only applies to permethrin 1%.[73]

Organophospates. Malathion inhibits acetylcholinesterase causing louse death by hype-excitability and exhaustion. It is safe if pure, but takes 20 minutes to be applied. It can cause skin irritation and asthma attacks.[74]

Physical. Dimeticone (92%) has a physical mode of action and suffocates lice, larvae and eggs. The volatile dimeticone vaporises, thickens and seals the tracheal tubes irreversibly and suffocates all three stages of development of nymphs, larvae and eggs.[75]

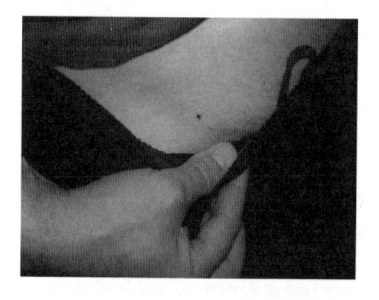

Ticks *(Ixodidae)* are small arachnid external parasites, living on the blood of mammals, birds and, by default, humans. Ticks are vectors of a number of diseases, including Lyme disease (*Lyme borrelosis*) and tick-borne encephalitis (TBE). Tick-borne illnesses are caused by infection with a variety of pathogens, including rickettsia and other types of bacteria, viruses, and protozoas.

The bite is often on the legs and thighs. It is initially painless but, after about 36 hours, the site begins to itch; the arachnid may be seen with its head buried in the skin once it has started feeding. If the tick is removed within the first 48 hours of contact, the risk of infection is low. If a herald patch develops around the bite site some days later, Lyme disease has to be considered and treatment with a tetracycline instituted. Doctors and nurses often miss the diagnosis and fail to appreciate the significance of the bites. Older travellers visiting rural areas and spending time in public spaces such as picnic spots, parks and gardens are at risk from tick bites. There is a high prevalence in northern Europe in the vacation months of July and August.[76]

Treatment. Embedded *Ixodidae* should be removed mechanically with forceps and every effort made to ensure the tick's head and mouthparts are not left attached to the person after removal. The site should then be swabbed with an antiseptic cream.

Dengue fever Dengue fever now occurs in 110 countries and its more severe effects can be life threatening for vulnerable older travellers who are susceptible to haemorrhage and low blood pressure. All travellers are exposed to the risk of infection from daytime biting mosquitos, which can result in dengue haemorrhagic fever and shock syndrome. The mortality incidence from such infections is estimated to about one in 100,000 travellers exposed, dependent on location and climate, which approximates to the incidence of traveller mortality from motor vehicle accidents.

Typhoid fever WHO rates typhoid incidence in most developing countries as high or medium. Caused by the bacterium *Salmonella typhi*, vaccination should be offered to all bound for risk destinations.[77] South Asia followed by the Middle East and Central Africa pose particular risks to travelers.[78] Efficacy is less than for most other travel vaccines and travellers should be aware that infection remains possible. Contemporaneous intake of oral typhoid vaccine and antimalarials with antibacterial activity should be avoided.[79]

Yellow fever Thymus disorders that alter immune-cell function (such as myasthenia gravis) are contraindicated for yellow fever vaccine but indirect radiation therapy is not.

A certificate waiver issuer should complete the Medical Contraindications to Vaccination section of the international certificate (ICVP) and issue a signed, dated exemption letter on letterheaded stationery. This should state the contraindications to vaccination and bear the vaccination centre stamp to validate the ICVP and inform the traveller of increased risk of yellow fever infection associated with non-vaccination .

Rabies is a zoonotic virus infection of mammals transmitted to humans when the skin barrier is breached by bite or scratch, usually by a rabid dog. The cause of 97% of human rabies cases are in Asia, parts of the Americas and large parts of Africa. Dogs remain the principal host. India has been reported as having the highest rate of human rabies in the world, primarily because of stray dogs. In 2007, Vietnam had the second-highest rate, followed by Thailand. In these countries the virus is primarily transmitted through canines.[77]

Rabies is almost invariably fatal if post-exposure prophylaxis is not administered prior to the onset of severe symptoms. The rabies virus infects the central nervous system by following the peripheral nerves to the brain, ultimately causing disease death. The incubation period is usually a few months, depending on the distance the virus must travel to reach the central nervous system. Once the rabies virus reaches the central nervous system and symptoms begin to show, the infection is effectively untreatable and usually fatal within days.

Early-stage symptoms of rabies are malaise, headache and fever, progressing to acute pain, violent movements, uncontrolled excitement, depression and hydrophobia. Periods of mania and lethargy eventually lead to coma, with primary cause of death usually respiratory insufficiency. The older traveller with lowered immune status is vulnerable and should avoid contact with animals in countries where rabies is present. All mammal, bites, scratches and licks on broken skin should be cleaned immediately with treated with an antiseptic; immediate post-exposure prophylaxis should be taken if there is a rabies risk. Pre-travel consideration should be given to tetanus booster and rabies vaccination.[80]

Pre exposure rabies prophylaxis immunisation provides the traveller with time to seek help and also reduces the post-exposure treatment needed. Over the age of 45 years, the uptake of rabies vaccine is reduced and a booster dose 12 months after the primary regime is recommended. The traveller aged 65 years and over should receive this primary course intramuscularly. Anyone bitten by an animal suspected of having rabies or in rabies endemic countries should wash the wound for 15 minutes with soap and water and apply iodine or alcohol to the wound. A reputable health facility should then be sought immediately for the initiation of post-exposure rabies treatment.

Vaccination and malaria prophylaxis resources

- Travax *www.travax.nhs.uk*
- NaTHNac *www.nathnac.nhs.uk*
- Guidelines for Malaria Prevention in UK Travellers, HPA, Jan 2007 *www.hpa.org.uk*
- Immunisation against infectious disease – *The Green Book www.dh.gov.uk*
- Health Information for Overseas Travel – *The Yellow Book* NaTHNac
- International Travel and Health *www.who.int/ith/en/index.html*
- Centers for Disease Control and Prevention *www.cdc.gov*
- The British Society for Rheumatology. *Vaccination in the Immunocompromised Person – Guidelines for the Patient Taking Immune Suppressants, Steroids and the New Biologic Therapies*, 2002: www.rheumatology.org.uk/includes/documents/cm_docs/2009/v/vaccinations_in_the_immunocompromised_person.pdf

References

1 Bourée Immunity and immunization in elderly. P.Pathol Biol (Paris). 2003 Dec;51(10):581-5.

2 Rey M. How to manage vaccinations in the elderly traveller .Bull Soc Pathol Exot. 1997;90(4):245-52.

3 Goodwin K et al Antibody response to influenza vaccination in the elderly: a quantitative review. Vaccine 2006;24:1159-69.

4 Michel J-P et al., Advocating vaccination of adults aged 60 years and older in Western Europe – Rejuvenation Research 2009;12(2):127-136.

5 Dawood R. Vaccinations requirements in Travellers Health 2012 Oxford university Press Oxford

6 Potter JM, O'Donnel B Serological response to influenza vaccination and nutritional and functional status of patients in geriatric long term care. Age Ageing 1999;28:141-5.

7 Mangtani P, Cumberland P, Hodgson CR, et al. A cohort study of the effectiveness of influenza

vaccine in older people, performed using the United Kingdom general practice research database. J Infect Dis 2004;190:1–10.

8 Jefferson T, Rivetti D, Rivetti A et al. Efficacy and effectiveness of influenza vaccines in elderly people: a systematic review. Lancet 2005;366:1165-74.

9 Michel J-P et al., Advocating vaccination of adults aged 60 years and older in Western Europe – Rejuvenation Research 2009;12(2):127-136.

10 Genton B, D'Acremont V, Furrer HJ, Hatz C, Louis Loutan Hepatitis A vaccines and the elderly. Travel Med Infect Dis. 2006 Dec;4(6):303-12. Epub 2005 Nov 28.

11 Immunisation against infectious disease – 'The Green Book', Dept of Health (various dates)

12 WHO: Yellow fever vaccine safety, as in Weekly Epidemiological Record (WER) 7 January 2005

13 Lindsey NP, Schroeder BA, Miller ER, et al; Adverse event reports following yellow fever vaccination. Vaccine. 2008 Nov 11;26(48):6077-82. Epub 2008 Sep 20. [abstract]

14 Roukens AH, Visser LG; Yellow fever vaccine: past, present and future. Expert Opin Biol Ther. 2008 Nov;8(11):1787-95.

15 Stich A, Zwicker M, Steffen T, Köhler B, Fleischer K: [Old age as risk factor for complications of malaria in non-immune travellers]. Dtsch Med Wochenschr; 2003 Feb 14;128(7):309-14

16 Baird JK, Masbar S, Basri H, Tirtokusumo S, et al. Age-dependent susceptibility to severe disease with primary exposure to Plasmodium falciparum. J Infect Dis 1998;178:592-5.

17 Schwartz,E Sadetzki S , et al Age as a Risk Factor for Severe Plasmodium falciparum Malaria in Nonimmune Patients

18 Greenberg AE, Lobel HO. Mortality from Plasmodium falciparum malaria in travelers from the United States, 1959 to 1987. Ann Intern Med 1990;113:326-7.

19 Calleri G, Lipani F, Macor A, Belloro S, Riva G, Caramello P. Severe and complicated falciparum malaria in Italian travelers. J Travel Med 1998;5:39-41.

20 Sabatinelli G, Majori G, D'Ancona F, Romi R. Malaria epidemiological trends in Italy. Eur J Epidemiol 1994;10:399-403.

21 World Health Organization International travel and health. World Health Organization, G Geneva, 2005.

22 Chiodini P, Hill D, Lalloo D, Lea et al .Guidelines for malaria prevention in travellers from the United Kingdom. London, Health Protection Agency, January 2007.

23 Meier CR, Wilcock K, Jick SS. The risk of severe depression, psychosis organic attacks with prophylactic antimalarials. Drug Safety.2004; 27:203-13.

24 Wells TS, Smith TC, Smith B et al.Mefloquine use and hospitalizations among US service members, 2002-2004. American Journal of Tropica lMedicine & Hygiene. 2006;74:744-9.

25 Taylor WR, White NJ. Antimalari l drug toxicity: a review. Drug Safety.2004;27, 25-61.

26 Ohrt, C, Richie TL, Widjaja H et al .Mefloquine compared with doxycycline for the prophylaxis of malaria in Indonesian soldiers .A randomized, double-blind ,placebo-controlled trial. Annals of Internal Medicine. 1997;126:963-72.

27 Bryant SG, Fisher S, Kluge RM.Increased frequency of doxycycline side effects. Pharmacotherapy.1987;7:125-9.

28 Blackwood T Malaria old and new .2011 J.Brit. Trav health Assoc xvi 2011 34-5

29 Jelinek T, Grobusch MP, Nothdurft HD.Use of dipstick tests for the rapid diagnosis of malaria

in non-immune travelers. Journal of Travel Medicine.2000;7:175-9.
30 Valecha N Phyio P. Mayxay M Randomised study of dihydroartemisinin v. srtensusnate-mefloquine for falciparum malaria in Asia PLoS ONE 2010 5..
References
31 Leroy H. Arvieux C et al A retrospective study of 230 consecutive patients hospitalised for travel related illness. Eur.J. Clin. Microbiol.Infect. Disease. 2008 (11) 1137-40
32 Bracewell C.Gray R. In Essential facts in geriatric medicine 2nd. Ed.Radcliffe pub. Abingdon
33 DuPont HNL. Guidelines on acute infectious diarrhoea in adults. American Journal of Gastroenterology. 1997; 92 : 1962-75
34 McIntosh I., Reed JM, Power K Travellers' diarrhoea and the effect of pre-travel health advice in general practice. British Journal of General Practice, 1997, 47, 71-75.
35 Peltola HP. Gorbach LS Travellers' diarrhoea in Textbook of travellers' health .ed. Dupont. Steffen 1997 Decker. Canada
36 McIntosh I Power K Reed J World traveller, family doctor and the need for pretravel health education 1994 Scot. Med J.39-40-44
37 Zeichner LO Ericson CD Travellers' diarrhoea in Principles and practice of travel medicine. 2001 ed. Zuckerman Wiley Chichester.
38 Diemert DJ Prevention and Self-Treatment of Travellers' Diarrhoea 2006 .Clin Microbiol Rev. July; 19(3): 583–594.
39 Prevention of diarrhoea The Centres for Disease Control and Prevention (CDC) 2007 report. Atlanta
40 Jiang ZD, Lowe B, Verenkar MP, et al. Prevalence of enteric pathogens among international travellers with diarrhoea J Infect Dis 2002; 185: 497–502.
41 Adachi JA, Jiang ZD, Mathewson JJ, et al. Enteroaggregative Escherichia coli as a major etiologic agent in travellers' diarrhoea in 3 regions of the world. Clin Infect Dis 2001; 32: 1706–9
42 Meraz IM, Jiang ZD, Ericsson CD, et al. Enterotoxigenic Escherichia coli and diffusely adherent E. coli as likely causes of a proportion of pathogen-negative travelers' diarrhea – a PCR-based study. J Travel Med 2008; 15: 412–8.
43 Dupont H Systematic review: the epidemiology and clinical features of travellers' diarrhoea 2009 Alimentary Pharmacology & Therapeutics30, 187–196, August
44 Drakoularakou A, Tzortzis G, Rastall RA et al. A double-blind, placebo-controlled, randomized human study assessing the capacity of a novel galacto-oligosaccharide mixture in reducing travellers' diarrhoea. Eur J Clin Nutr 2009; 1-7.
45 The Cochrane Database of Systematic Reviews-travellers' diarrhoea The Cochrane Library 2003 London
46 Swanson V. McIntosh I.Howell K.A study of gps attitudes to acute diarrhoea management. Scot. Med. 1999.18.6-7
47 Wingate D. Phillips S. Lewis S et al Guidelines for adults on self medication for the treatment of acute diarrhoea. 2001 Aliment. Pharmacol.Ther. 15.773-82
48 Van Loon FPL. Double blind trial of loperamide for treating acute watery diarrhoea in expatriates in Bangladesh. Gut. 1989, 30: 492-5
49 Murphy GS. Ciprofloxacin and loperamide in the treatment of bacillary dysentery. Annals of

Internal Medicine. 1993, 118: 582-6
50 Gomi H, Jiang ZD, Adachi JA, et al. In vitro antimicrobial susceptibility testing of bacterial enteropathogens causing traveler's diarrhea in four geographic regions. Antimicrob Agents Chemother 2001; 45: 212-6.
51 Salam I, Katelaris P, Leigh-Smith S, Farthing MJ. Randomised trial of single-dose ciprofloxacin for travellers' diarrhoea. Lancet 1994; 344: 1537-9.
52 Gomi H, Jiang ZD, Adachi JA, et al. In vitro antimicrobial susceptibility testing of bacterial enteropathogens causing traveler's diarrhea in four geographic regions. Antimicrob Agents Chemother 2001; 45: 212-6
53 Johnson PC, Ericsson CD, Morgan DR, DuPont HL, Cabada FJ. Lack of emergence of resistant fecal flora during successful prophylaxis of traveler's diarrhea with norfloxacin. Antimicrob Agents Chemother 1986; 30: 671-4.
54 Norman F, Perez-Molina J, De Ayala P, Jimenez B, Navarro M, Lopez-Velez R. Clostridium difficile. difficile-associated diarrhea after antibiotic treatment for traveler's diarrhea. Clin Infect Dis 2008; 46: 1060-3.
55 Vlieghe ER, Jacobs JA, Van Esbroeck M Trends of Norfloxacin and Erythromycin Resistance of Campylobacter jejuni/Campylobacter coli Isolates Recovered From International Travellers, 1994 to 2006
56 Taylor DN, Bourgeois AL, Ericsson CD et al A randomized, double-blind, multicentre study of rifaximin compared with placebo and with ciprofloxacin in the treatment of travellers' diarrhoea. J Trop Med Hyg. 2006 Jun;74(6):1060-6.
57 DuPont HL. Systematic review: prevention of travellers' diarrhoea. Aliment Pharmacol Ther 2008; 24 Lowe B, Verenkar MP, et al. Prevalence of enteric pathogens among international travelers with diarrhoea J Infect Dis 2002; 185: 497
58 Steffen R, Sack DA, Riopel L, Jiang ZD, Sturchler M, Ericsson CD, et al. Therapy of travelers' diarrhea with rifaximin on various continents. Am J Gastroenterol. 2003 May;98(5):1073-1078.
59 DuPont HL, Jiang ZD, Belkind-Gerson J, Okhuysen PC, Ericsson CD, Ke S, et al. Treatment of travelers' diarrhea: randomized trial comparing rifaximin, rifaximin plus loperamide, and loperamide alone. Clin Gastroenterol Hepatol. 2007 Apr;5(4):451-456.
60 DuPont HL, Jiang ZD, Ericsson CD, Adachi JA, Mathewson JJ, DuPont MW, et al. Rifaximin versus ciprofloxacin for the treatment of traveler's diarrhea: a randomized, double-blind clinical trial. Clin Infect Dis. 2001 Dec 1;33(11):1807-1815.
61 Layer P, Andresen V. Review article: Rifaximin, a minimally absorbed oral antibacterial, for the treatment of travellers' diarrhoea. Aliment Pharmacol Ther. 2010 Jun;31(11):1155-1164.
62 Infante RM, Ericsson CD, Jiang ZD, Ke S, Steffen R, Riopel L, et al. Enteroaggregative Escherichia coli diarrhoea in travellers: response to rifaximin therapy. Clin Gastroenterol Hepatol. 2004 Feb;2(2):135-138.63.
63 DuPont HL, Haake R, Taylor DN, Ericsson CD, Jiang ZD, Okhuysen PC, et al. Rifaximin treatment of pathogen-negative travelers' diarrhea. J Travel Med. 2007 Jan-Feb;14(1):16-19.
64 Huang DB, DuPont HL. Rifaximin – a novel antimicrobial for enteric infections. J Infect. 2005 Feb; 50(2): 97-106.
65 Ericsson CD. Safety and Tolerability of the Antibacterial Rifaximin in the Treatment of Travellers

Diarrhoea. Drug Safety. 2006;29(3):201-207.
66 summarieshttp://www.cks.nhs.uk/diarrhoea_prevention_and_advice_for_travellers#
67 DuPont HL, Ericsson CD, Farthing MJ,. expert review of the evidence base for self-therapy of travellers' diarrhoea. J Travel Med. 2009 May-Jun;16(3):161-71.
68 Wyss MN, Steffen R, Dhupdale NY,.Management of travellers' diarrhoea by local physicians in tropical and subtropical countries--a questionnaire survey. J Travel Med. 2009 May-Jun;16(3):186-90.
69 Melrose A. Bedbugs and bites. 2010 Brit.Trav. Health Assoc. J 15. 24-5
70 McIntosh I Louse infestation in Travellers 2011. Brit.trav. health Assoc. J. 16.45-7
71 Heukelbach J Management and control of head lice infestations 2010Unined Verlag AD Bremen
72 Cochrane Database Syst Rev. 2001 and Cochrane Database Syst Rev. 2000 (2)CD001165
73 Picollo MI.Vassenna Cv et al. Resistance to insecticides and and effect of synergistson permethrin activity in pediculosis capitis.J.Med. E6tomol.2000.37.721-25
74 Gao GR.Yoon KS et al Esterase mediated malathion in the human head louse. Pestic. Biocham. Physiol.200685.28-37
75 Ricchling I Bocleler W. 2008 Lehtal effects of a treatment with dimeticone on insects –Insights in to physical mechanisms. Arzneimitelforshung 58. (5) 248-54
76 McIntosh I Lyme disease and facial palsy. 2012 J. Prevent. Med. In press
77 Steinberg EB, Bishop R, 28Haber P, et al. Typhoid fever in travelers: who should be targeted for prevention? Clin Infect Dis 2004; 39:186–191.
78 Ekdahl K, De JB, Andersson Y. Risk of travel-associated typhoid and paratyphoid fevers in various regions. J Travel Med 2005
79 Shirakawa T, Acharya B, Kinoshita S, et al. Decreased susceptibility to fluoroquinolones and gyrA gene mutation in the Salmonella enterica serovar Typhi and Paratyphi A isolated in Katmandu, Nepal, in 2003. Diagn Microbiol Infect Dis 2006; 54:299–303.77
80 Denduangboripant J, Wacharapluesadee S, Lumlertdacha B, et al "Transmission dynamics of rabies virus in Thailand: Implications for disease control". 2005 BMC Infect Dis 5: 52. doi:10.1186/1471-2334-5-52
81 www.travax.nhs.uk

8

Psychological Problems

Travel anxiety

Global travel is an indulgence for many older people. Some however, are fearful of travelling by air, under and over water and in enclosed spaces – prerequisites for those departing from Britain. Those with phobias may exhibit avoidance behaviour and refuse to contemplate leaving the UK, to the disadvantage of a partner. Recent climatic, terrorist and financial events have made all forms of transportation a more worrying experience, adding to common fears of travel in a ship, aircraft or through a long tunnel.

Transportation concerns
Concerns about aeroplane mechanical failure no longer predominate, but air travel is still regarded as the most dangerous and anxiety-provoking travel option by the general public.[1] Media reports of travellers marooned for days in airports in Britain and Europe have altered the public perception of risk relating to air transportation and have increased focus on airport problems. While mild flight anxiety is common and causes little disruption, severe anxiety can cause in-flight emergency and even prevent travel by air altogether, disadvantaging the individual as well as those accompanying them. This chapter focuses on anxiety problems related to older people and air travel but the same principles apply to anxiety surrounding other modes of transport.

Loss of luggage, cancelled flights, rerouting and being stranded have brought anxieties about this travel mode more in line with the proportionate risk of an unwanted event occurring to the traveller. Paradoxically, as the risk of mechanical aeroplane failure and physical danger has waned, the likelihood of major psychological trauma in air travel has increased. Major delays, prolonged waits in packed airline lounges, vast queues in airports and the uncertainty of arrival and departure have impacted on the public psyche. Land and sea transport have also been affected by weather, as well as terrorist and traumatic events, with passengers marooned on motorways, rail lines and in terminals, and evacuating capsized ships. Older people may have some experience of such adverse events, which can generate legitimate fears and anxieties that do not affect the young who may be less aware of potential travel problems.

Behavioural change

These occurrences are bringing behavioural change, particularly in seniors. Older people are more vulnerable to uncontrolled situations. Common features of old age, such as indecisiveness, slower problem solving, inflexibility, poor memory, cognitive decline and tardy adaptation,[2] aggravate personal reaction to the often frenzied environment in airports and rail stations, where all onward movement can abruptly cease. Pre-flight worries and anxieties are added to the concerns older travellers have of actually flying. Their cumulative effect can promote tension and angst, with psychological effects resulting in adverse physiological responses, cardiac stress, possible heart attack and stroke.[3]

Terrorist and environmental factors brought a fall in air travel in 2010 that was disproportionate to effects relating to the financial recession. Travel operators specialising in travel for older people reported a coincident increase in passengers seeking to avoid the fly part of the cruise experience by use of UK ports for arrival and departure. The Passenger Shipping Association noted that 10% more passengers set sail from a UK port that year than in the previous year. Older people free from time constraints are avoiding potentially stress-provoking airports. Other behavioural responses are also evident, with 42% of travellers admitting to repeatedly checking travel documents prior to an international journey. These compulsive tendencies are greater in womenl a third admit they check passports at least five times from arrival at the departure point to boarding, although they do not normally exhibit obsessive behaviour.[4]

Flight anxiety may predispose passengers to stress-related illnesses and cardiological problems, which can result in-flight emergencies.[3] Apart from potential health-damaging effects, this may also have an adverse effect on social interaction.[4] Stress of air travel has been found to disrupt passengers' behaviour.[5] Stressed and anxious passengers may become more demanding, dissatisfied and easily agitated in communication with the crew or other passengers. Fatigued and overwrought, they can exhibit disruptive behaviour ranging from verbal to severe physical aggression.

Air transport-related anxieties may be enhanced in anxiety-prone personalities; those who are very old and vulnerable can be affected by different cultural values and external environmental influences. All shape the subjectively affected cognitive and emotional impact of the overall flying experience. Airport environments and flights often pose novel situations where limited personal control, bureaucracy, as well as overt and covert regulations add to frustrations. Attribution of blame and satisfactory redress from frontline staff, which might diffuse build-up of stress, rarely occurs, as they too have scant control over the predicament. Air travellers are reacting to these psychological pressures by changes in behaviour, which are belatedly being recognised by the transport industry.

Travel-related stress in older travellers often starts before airport departure, with the change from being at home with established routines. The land journey can be affected by adverse road/rail conditions and the traveller is stressed by the time they arrive at the departure terminal. Stress mounts incrementally with progression through airport security, now a major source of psychological disturbance for passengers. The passenger has been reduced to a mere seat number in an uncaring bureaucratic process.

Communication failures are tension-causing when systems collapse under overload. The procedural process is annoying, diminishing and demeaning and, added to inevitable flight delays and failures, continued frustration brings increasing stress, tension and aberrant behaviour in the airport or in the air. Physiological change may endanger health.[6]

Flight anxiety

Prevalence

Flight anxiety can be a debilitating experience for air travellers. It is a common phenomenon observed in 10–40% of air travellers of all ages, dependent on pre-flight and in-flight situations.[1] One study found that fear of flying increases with age in women but not men. However, the cohort only included the 'young' old and had a 70 year old cut-off.[6] In a random sample of 7,074 patients in general practice based on a structured questionnaire listing 13 common fear-provoking objects or situations, 16% admitted to having a phobia and 13% of this sub-group reported fear of flying, with a female to male preponderance of 2:1.[5] This proportion is likely to have increased with recent deleterious change in the pre-flight experience and the terrorist threat to aircraft.

Development

A specific flying phobia occurs when anxiety is triggered only by the flying situation. However, flight anxiety can be part of a more generalised problem, where multiple situations set off the anxiety. It is not always obvious how anxiety problems develop.[7] Some people have more anxious personalities or pre-existing mental health problems that make them more vulnerable to developing anxiety problems.[8-10] Sometimes there is a clear-cut initial trigger, such as a major stressor occurring on a flight or in an airport before or after travel; alternatively there may have been an accumulation of minor stresses prior to flying.

Minor stressors, e.g. loss of luggage, cancelled flights, rerouting, delays and beign stranded, cause uncertainty and a reduced sense of control. Increased security precautions add to delays. There is invasion of individual privacy and potential personal embarrassment if luggage is searched. Enforced removal of shoes, belts and body frisking are an unwelcome reminder of the risk of terrorism. These, with increasingly bureaucratic check-ins, baggage weight restrictions and reduced customer care from budget airlines, add incrementally to stress levels.[11,12]

In a study at Heathrow Airport, passengers had heart and finger monitors fitted to record their blood pressure and pulse rate while in the airport en route to flight departure. Skin conductance – a reliable measure of stress – was also measured. Readings were correlated with the amount of psychological stress experienced.[13] Passengers passing through the airport, who were healthy and not exercising, showed monitored stress levels equivalent to on-duty riot police.

During the test, there were marked physiological changes. ECG and blood pressure monitors showed immediate and sustained changes. Within minutes of entering the terminal, heart rates had increased from 55 beats per minute to over 70 per minute in the non-exercising state. In the average four hours it took to board the aircraft, rates continued to rise to more than 200 beats per minute in transit, with a rise in blood pressure also occurring.

Queues at check-in and security increased blood pressure levels from average of 123/81mmHg to 170/99mmHg. There was a marked increase in skin conductance with a 100-fold rise of that in a relaxed state. Associated stress levels peaked four times but were sustained at a high level overall. Causes of peaking were: queues; unfriendly, unhelpful staff; and lack of information or misinformation. Monitoring on the return journey revealed that return transit through the airport was almost as stressful as departure, primarily because of queues at immigration, security channels and lost luggage.[13] A study of 1,009 passengers transiting an airport reported that 69% said rude staff were a contributory problem to stress; 52% considered this a major cause of travel-related stress.[14]

Older passengers may find stressors at airports, especially protracted delays, even more difficult to cope with as there is a slight decline with age, reaction speed, new learning ability and flexibility.[15] For those who have to contend with additional mobility, sensory or cognitive impairment, their stress levels will be further confounded.[16] The cumulative effect can promote tension and angst, with psychological effects resulting in adverse physiological responses, cardiac stress and possible heart attack and stroke.[17]

Other travel modes

Passengers travelling by road and train confirm the stress felt by delays. The pulse rate of train passengers increased with the queue for departure, delays and while the train was in the Channel tunnel. Car drivers were stressed on boarding ferries and adapting to foreign driving. Only coach passengers remained relaxed during travel.

Behavioural responses

Catastrophic thinking
When a person feels anxious, they interpret their situation as dangerous and think the worst will occur. This can be helpful if the dangers are real, e.g. in the early days of air travel where mechanical failure was common. However, problems occur when the likelihood of danger is over estimated (e.g. people think the plane will definitely crash/be subjected to a terrorist attack) or the ability to cope with the situation is underestimated (e.g. the person thinks the confined conditions or their anxiety symptoms in the plane or airport will cause them to become physically or mentally ill). Catastrophising and rumination about travel can start many weeks and months before the person is due to travel and keeps anticipatory anxiety going, until it can feel unmanageable by the day of travel.

Increased physiological arousal
If a situation, e.g. flying, or even the thought of flying is interpreted as threatening, the 'fight and flight' response is triggered in the body. This is a series of automatic changes in the body to prepare it for defensive action, which can include increased heart and breathing rates, increased muscle tension, nausea and dizziness etc. The degree of arousal can vary from mild stress to a full-blown panic attack.

Safety behaviour
Anxiety is designed to protect the individual from danger. This includes trying to escape from the anxiety-provoking situation. This can cause people to leave airports before boarding or their trying to persuade cabin staff to land early. It also makes the person hypervigilant towards future danger; avoid it if possible, and stay away from anything associated with flight. Anxiety can increase irritability and defensiveness when dealing with others. People try to ameliorate the symptoms of anxiety by recourse to sedatives and alcohol, which can have unwelcome side-effects. Avoidance maintains anxiety since the person never finds out if their fears were justified, nor do they learn to cope with their anxiety. A vicious cycle is set up and anxiety becomes a problem.[18]

Impact of untreated flight anxiety
Many older people decide they will never fly again. Since many have more free time than their younger working counterparts, it may not be that disruptive to their lives to take other forms of transport. They consider the costs outweigh the benefits. However, for others, their flying anxiety becomes a problem they cannot ignore. It may generalise into other areas of life or may disrupt too many meaningful

activities, e.g. visiting family abroad, easily and quickly.

For those able to board, flight anxiety may make the person more irritable and less social during the flight. It can lead to them becoming more demanding, dissatisfied and agitated in communication with crew or other passengers, and may predispose passengers to stress-related illnesses and cardiological problems, which may result in-flight emergencies.[19]

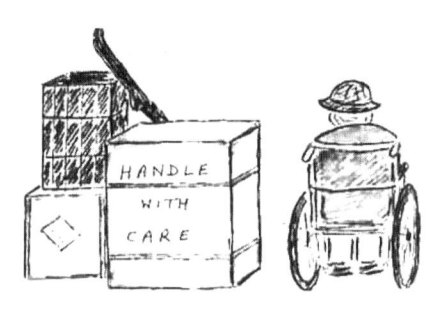

Management of flight anxiety problems

Travel health professionals should have an understanding of passengers' subjective experiences and anxieties regarding flying and coping strategies. Knowledge of psychological aspects of air travel, the specifics of worry experience and anxiety-provoking situations should inform management and direct pre-travel advice to minimise psychological and physiological stress.

Coping strategies
Half of all worried travellers do nothing to minimise their anxieties.[16] Several coping strategies are adopted by passengers for air-travel worries; one study showed that:
- 9% avoid flying if possible
- 16% use relaxation and distraction techniques
- 13% use alcohol to relax in flight
- 6% resort to sedatives.[5]

Many travellers resort to cognitive strategies to diminish and deal with the travel experience, while affluent older passengers, in particular, can reduce the effect of adverse circumstances by travelling in first class.[17]

Coping strategies are thinking patterns and cognitive frameworks that individuals use when stressed and aroused, in order to regulate their emotional state and alleviate anxieties. Passengers distract themselves by reading, writing, utilising relaxation techniques or other activities that direct attention from the flight or pre-flight experience. Listening to music can induce calmness; alcohol, smoking and tranquillisers are also used to handle stress.

Some travellers minimise the seriousness of their flight experience, reflect on personal fears and anxieties over flying, and remind themselves of pleasant experiences – be they relevant or irrelevant to the flight situation – as a strategy to cope with current distress. However many older people have admitted to brooding over worst-case scenarios as the day of departure approached.[17,18]

New coping strategies are being developed in passengers exposed to airport environmental challenges, but they are limited in potential adaptation manoeuvres. Weight restrictions to limit food, drink and pastimes to be taken airside to ameliorate prolonged waiting make it almost impossible to prepare for prolonged delay or a night or two spent on a departure lounge floor. Maladaptation results in aggressive behaviour and has brought a resultant increase in reported police interventions at major airports.[19]

Passengers are now adopting the classical response to potential stressful situations – avoidance.[16] They are seeking alternative means of reaching destinations. Long-distance train companies report increased business with more, well-used trains. Ferry companies to the continent are attracting more travellers. Cruise lines diligently survey regular and potential passengers and report an increasing demand for UK port-to-port cruises.

The travel health professional should have an understanding of passengers' subjective experiences, anxieties about flying and the use of coping strategies. Adequate knowledge on psychological aspects of air travel and specifics of worry experience, along with anxiety-provoking situations, should inform management and direct pre-travel advice to minimise psychological and physiological stress.

Therapeutic approach

Medication

Intending passengers approach health professionals for anxiolytics and sleeping pills to reduce travel anxieties but prescriptions should be resisted. The latter may result in deep vein thrombosis on long flights due to limb immobility, and older people may already be on other medication and risk adverse drug interaction.[20] While medication may seem like a quick fix, it does not allow the person to learn how to manage their anxiety and break the vicious cycle. When drugs are used they ought to be prescribed for the very short term. Benzodiazepines are given for general anxiety, and the is patient advised to refrain from taking alcohol or a hypnotic on the flight. Beta-blockers are used to control peripheral sympathetic responses such as palpitations.

Cognitive behavioural therapy (CBT)

CBT has been shown to be the most effective therapy treatment for flying anxiety problem.[14] Although no work has been done on older people with this problem per se, CBT has been found to be effective for older people with other types of anxiety as long as it is adapted to take into account age-related changes.[21,22] Based on a thorough assessment, CBT works by modifying catatrophising thinking, avoidance and safety behaviour, through psycho-education, graded exposure and the teaching of various skills to deal with anticipatory anxiety, such as relaxation techniques and coping statements. Some airlines may provide CBT-based day courses at airports. However, a qualified therapist can provide imaginal exposure to the feared situation, which can be just as effective. Learning new skills means that it is not a quick fix and therefore has to be carried out a number of weeks or months in advance of a planned flight.

Behaviour modification
Given time before the need to travel, behaviour modification is widely used in clinics to treat phobics. The principal is to expose the patient to the situation that causes distress until he or she gets used to it; attempts are then made to extinguish the fear by relating it to a pattern of response that provokes no anxiety. The problem behaviour needs detailed study in order to arrive at a hypothesis about its genesis and identify appropriate intervention.

Desensitisation consists of two features: muscle relaxation and reduction of anxiety, and the construction of a graded hierarchy of aversive stimuli from information provided by the patient. Such a hierarchy for a flying phobia would consist of arrival at the airport, proceeding to the departure lounge, walking on to the plane, experiencing take-off and landing. The hierarchy can be presented to the patient either in imagery or in reality, and film and tape recordings can be used effectively in desensitisation. Treatment can be assisted by vicarious or participant modelling. Here the therapist approaches the feared object or situation and demonstrates a confident response to it before asking the patient to do likewise.

This procedure has three functions: the model encourages new patterns of behaviour to be adopted; unnecessary responses are inhibited or disinhibited; and the expression of already established responses can be facilitated. Desensitisation works well with social and specific phobias; the disadvantage is that the process is time-consuming and often requires many sessions.

Hypnotherapy
Hypnosis treatment for anxieties concentrates on relaxation techniques and borrows from behavioural approaches, but therapy is facilitated by the induction of a trance state and suggestion.[23,24] Teaching the individual autohypnosis, whereby at a coded signal he/she can recreate the relaxed state acquired at earlier sessions, decreases the risk of dependence and diminishes the time required for therapy.[23-25]

Flying phobias

Flying phobias and fear of tunnels and sea travel are common, affecting old and young. They can inhibit sufferers from undertaking global travel. With good management, disabling fear, disturbed conditioned responses and frantic avoidance behaviour can be replaced by rational activity. In most cases it is not known how a phobia has developed. Sometimes there is a clear-cut trigger such as an unhappy incident occurring on a flight, or someting happening to an aircraft before or after travel. Some are simply conditioned fear reactions. It is likely that we are more genetically predisposed to make fearful links with some situations and objects than with others.

Typically, the older person with a phobia presents to the family doctor a few days before a long planned flight to a popular holiday resort. Months previously the family have convinced a grandparent they can overcome a reluctance to fly and the vacation is arranged. As time for departure draws ever closer, apprehension increases and, shortly before departure day, it becomes apparent to the patient that he or she cannot face the perceived ordeals of an air passage. An acute anxiety state results, which reaches crisis proportions as the family becomes teed up for the vacation. This presents as a specific phobia, which may be associated with panic reaction.[26]

The majority of people with phobias appear to be women, although women may be more likely to report their fears that men. Travel phobias represented 2.81% of phobias reported by women in surveys.[27,28] In a random sample of 7,074 patients in general practice, based on a structured questionnaire listing 13 common fear-provoking objects or situations, 16% admitted to having a phobia and 13% of this sub-group reported fear of flying with a female to male preponderance of 2:1.[29]

The *phobia* is a disproportionate reaction. Fear is a normal and essential condition for everyday living. It is a response to a real or imagined threat with a behavioural element that is often pronounced. Minor fears are within the cultural norm and there is a continuum between mild and intense fears, with the latter usually described as phobia. This is considered a morbid response disproportionate to the causative stimulus. Sufferers often structure their lives to avoid fear-provoking situations. With a phobia, the degree of anxiety and fear is:
- out of all proportion to the evoking situation
- irrational
- cannot be explained or reasoned away
- beyond voluntary control
- leads to avoidance.

It is likely that there are many more people with flying phobias than statistics suggest, as most simply avoid any likelihood of exposure to air travel. There are cognitive, physiological and behavioural components involved:
- The psychic element appears as overt anxiety and an exaggerated arousal response when exposed to the feared situation or even consideration of exposure, e.g. as the day of the dreaded flight draws closer.
- The physiological response results in a sweating, tremulousness, palpitations, dyspnoea and assorted pains from muscle tension. The primeval 'fight or flight' reflexes poorly prepare people for today's flight demands.
- Avoidance behaviour by a travelling executive or relative's refusal to

contemplate air travel introduces a social element that often finally forces the patient to seek professional help.

The phobic cycle is open to curative intervention at three levels: relaxation can be taught to control physical symptoms; cognitive therapy helps to control and change fear-provoking thoughts; and exposure treatment can help to overcome restrictions in lifestyle.[30]

Treatment

Given time, therapy can usually bring alleviation of symptoms and cure and, even at the eleventh hour, patients can be helped towards and along the frightening path from airport to aircraft and on with the flight. A phobia specific to flying can be dealt with most easily but air travel involves more than boarding the aeroplane. Crowded departure lounges will disturb the agoraphobic, the closed inescapable environment of the jet-liner frightens those with a fear of closed spaces, climbing the steps to the doorway of a jumbo jet towering above will upset those with a fear of heights, and the necessity to eat in public will give anxiety to those with a social phobia. All these possibilities must be kept in mind when preparing to treat the patient who wants to make the feared flight and the return.

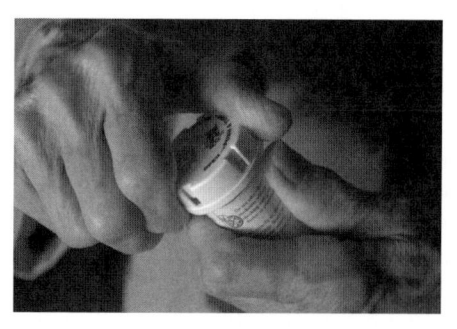

Medication

When drugs are used they ought to be prescribed for the very short term. Benzodiazepines are given for general anxiety, with higher dosage in anticipation of the phobic event.[31] The patient should be advised to refrain from taking alcohol or a hypnotic on the flight. In entrenched agoraphobia with travel phobic manifestations there is some evidence that clomipramine has an antiphobic effect but it has to be given in high dosages. Any antidepressant may well lift a specific phobia that has been a symptom of an underlying depression.

Hypnotherapy

Hypnosis treatment for anxieties concentrates on relaxation techniques and borrows from behavioural approaches, but therapy is facilitated by inducing a trance state and by suggestion.[23,24] The teaching of self-hypnosis, whereby at a coded signal the person can recreate the relaxed state acquired at earlier sessions, decreases the risk of dependence and diminishes the time required for therapy. Graded desensitisation and flooding are both practicable within the trance states, and visual imagery and vicarious modelling can also be used. A modified flooding technique can be used and is very effective for specific phobias such as flying.[25]

Case history
One of my patients, who had patiently built up his business, had a unique opportunity presented to his firm for advancement and profit in the Far East. He had long had a phobia for air travel but unable to resist the opportunity for expansion he made his plans, bought his tickets and, the day before departure, succumbed to panic and terror at the thought of many hours incarcerated in an aircraft. In the surgery he was in a state of agitation but refused to consider a drug prescription as he wished to be mentally fit for tough business negotiations upon arrival in Hong Kong.

He accepted the offer of hypnotherapy with alacrity and, proving to be a good subject, was quickly in a trance and relaxed. Soon he was able to create a visual image of himself boarding and sitting in the aeroplane and, with the continued suggestion of calmness, muscle and mind relaxation, and freedom from tension, he was able to fantasise himself through a prolonged exposure to the feared situation. Given post-hypnotic suggestions that he would remain calm throughout the flight, and that the standard pre-take off and recorded music would relax him, he went off to make a successful return flight and business deal. Even when the jet-liner was buffeted badly by turbulence and suddenly dropped 500 feet, with the dramatic appearance of personal passenger oxygen masks from their overhead stowage, he was able to keep calm. Now, after a decade and many air trips, he remains undisturbed by his once disabling phobia.

Desensitisation can be carried out with little therapist contact, using tape recordings to carry out relaxation and desensitisation procedures; these are a useful adjuvant in desensitisation and hypnotherapy. Book and computer instruction courses offering graded and detailed programmes of relaxation and exposure are available, and have proved of value to many. Several airlines now offer in-flight audio meditation programmes with tips on relaxation from a psychotherapist to help diminish passenger stress.

"Gentle words, quiet words are, after all, most powerful words. They are more convincing, more compelling, more prevailing and successful," an older lady wrote to me on return from her first successful air trip after years of phobic avoidance. However, removal of psychosomatic symptoms before the patient is ready or has built up more socially satisfactory defences, can precipitate more serious difficulties; therapists have to be aware of this possibility.

Severe behavioural disturbance
Older people are not immune to the behavioural disturbance referred to as air rage. A build-up of fatigue, frustration and anger can result in verbal and physically aggressive behaviour to fellow travellers and staff. Over-indulgence in alcohol and medication interaction can result in behavioural misconduct so they should

be aware of this risk. Alcohol intake on long flights is best avoided by those on routine medication and affected by a measure of kidney failure – a consideration for many older travellers as a third of those over 80 will be affected by grade 3A chronic kidney disease.

Early Alzheimer's disease can be seen in the aberrant behaviour displayed by some older vacationers.[32] Sometimes solo travellers, they can be seen wandering round cruise ships and getting lost from tour groups. Their fellows are usually tolerant and supportive but they put their health at risk on ships and in road traffic. Unaccustomed surroundings and travel-related stressors add to their confusional states.

They are particularly likely to become disorientated in airports. In 40% of these early cases some measure of agitation, sleep disturbance, wandering, increased irritability and aggression are apparent. Locational change tends to increase their mental instability and they should be discouraged from participating in holidays with an ever-changing environment, such as a cruise, coach or train tour. If they do travel, antipsychotic medication should be reviewed before departure. They should travel with a companion and provisional plans should be in place for unwanted illness in the accompanying person.

Case history
A 75 year old man had travelled alone to Australia despite a diagnosis of senile dementia. His visit to family was successful but, on the return, tired, dehydrated and confused, he became disturbed and wandered around Heathrow for many hours while transferring aeroplanes. Totally disorientated he missed his onward flight and was only identified as ill and lost by a patrolling policeman after the last flight of the day had departed. He never fully recovered his former cognitive state and was institutionalised when he finally arrived in his home town.

Advice for travellers to reduce pre-flight and in-flight stress and anticipatory anxiety

- Use alternatives to air transport when possible.
- Use direct, daytime flights.
- Book into airline courtesy lounges.
- Travel in best affordable class.
- Book into local hotel accommodation, the night prior to departure.
- Prepare for delays and take reading material, games, emergency food and water.
- Avoid air travel in winter, the strike season at Christmas and Easter and around public holidays.
- Use relaxation techniques or distraction, such as reading or listening to music.

- Take advantage of in-flight audio meditation programmes.
- Avoid smoking. Lighting up can reduce withdrawal symptoms and bring a relaxed, feeling but the nicotine input actually increases arousal.

Conclusion

Although anxieties about air travel and flying-related phobias are increasingly common, coping strategies can ameliorate their impact. Relaxation techniques can be beneficial. Anxiolytic medication should be avoided for air travel. Travellers with a phobia need not despair; fear can be disabled and avoidance behaviour identified so older people can fly if they so choose. Health professionals should:
- be aware of the psychological manifestations that can affect the global older traveller
- identify the problems in pre-travel consultation and
- direct individuals to the appropriate therapist.

References

1 McIntosh, Swanson, Power, F, 2006 Prevalence, intensity, and sex differences in travel related stressors, Journal of Trav Med, 3 (2), 96-102.).
2 Clarke DM Perry L Psychoger, Ed Bayne J 1987 chap.1 Kingsley Pub. London
3 Cohen G Manual of Geriatrics Ed Abrahams W Berkow R 1090 chap 85 Merck New Jersey
4 Blackwood T Behavioural change in tourist air travellers 2011 Brit Global Trav Health Assoc 18.19-20
5 McIntosh, Swanson, Power, et al , 1998. Anxiety and health problems related to air travel, Journal of Travel Medicine, 5 (4), 198-204.
6 Fredrikson M, Annas, P., Fischer, H, 1996 Gender differences in the prevalence of specific fears and phobias, Behaviour Research & Therapy 34:33-39
7 France R.Robson M., 1986. Behaviour therapy in primary care 66.Croom Helm Publishers.
8 Bor, 2007. Psychological factors in airline passenger and crew behaviour: A clinical overview. Travel Medicine and Infectious
Disease, 5 (4), 207–216.
9 Hayes S. Feinleib. M 1980 Women, work and coronary heart disease: prospective findings from the Framingham Heart Study, Am J Public Health 70: 133-141.
10 Abubakar and Mavondo, 2002. The determinants of anxiety in air travel: an exploratory study. ANZMAC Conference Proceeding
2741-2747
11 Cox ID, Blight A, Lyons JP Air-terminal stress and the older traveller Age Ageing. 1999 Mar;28(2):236-7.
12 McIntosh IB 2003 Flying-related stress. In Bor, R. (Ed.),Passenger behaviour (pp. 17-31). Ashgate Publishing:Hampshire.
13 Lewis D. Heathrow stress equal to facing riots.2007.Neuroco International . Travel Telegraph. Aug. 8

14 Kraaij,Garnefski, & van Gerwen, 2003 Cognitive coping and anxiety among people with fear flying. In Bor, R. & vanGerwen, L. (Eds.), Psychological Perspectives on Fear of Flying .Ashgate Publishing
15 Christensen, H 2001, What cognitive change can be expected with normal ageing, Aus NZ J Psychiatry 35: 768-775
16 10Bor, R. (2003). In Bor, R. (Ed.), Passenger Behaviour Ashgate Publishing
17 McIntosh, I. B. 2003. In Rostrum Brit. Soc. Med Dental Hypnosis
18 Oakes, M and Bor, R 2010, Psychology of the fear of flying part 2: Critical evaluation of current perspectives on the approach to treatment 8: 339-363
19 McIntosh I Psychological and behavioural Change in Vacation Air travellers. Travelwise. 2011
20 Goodyer L Travel Medications ants Older Travellers 2011 Brit Global Trav Health J 18.12-14
21 Hendricks GJ, Oude V, Oshaar, RC, Keijers, GP 2008, CBT for late life anxiety disorders: A systematic review and meta-analysis, Acta Psychiatr Scand 117: 403-11.
22 Laidlaw, K, Thompson, L; Gallagher-Thompson D, Dick-Siskin, L Cognitive Behaviour Therapy with Older People, Wiley: Chichester.
23 McIntosh I.1981. Hypnotherapy: The case for the GP. Psychiatry in Practice, November 1981.
24 McIntosh I Compendium of hypnotherapy 2000 Brit Socy Med Dental Hypnosis Chap y Monument Press Stirling
25 McIntosh I Brief selective hypnotherapy in treatment of flying phobias Brit Trav Health Assoc J 2007 39-40
26 Agras S., Sylvester., and Oliveau D., 1969. The epidemiology of common fears and phobias. Comprehensive Psychiatry, 10: 2, 151
27 Wilson G., 1967.Social desirability and sex differences in expressed fear. Behaviour research and therapy, 5: 136.
28 Burns L., Thorpe G., 1977.Fears and phobias. Journal of international Medical Research, 5: Suppl. 1: 132-139.
29 McIntosh I., 1980.Incidence, management and treatment of phobias in a group medical practice. Pharm. Medicine 1, 2: 77-82
30 Van Gerwen, Spinhoven, D 1997;People who seek help for fear of flying: Typology of flying phobics, behaviour therapy, 28 (2), 237-25107 9,595,923
31 Tyrer P., 1989.Treating Panic. British Medical Journal, 298: 201.
32 Connolly P Dementia management, 2011 Ger Med 41 Supp. 5 34-40

9

Heart and Diabetes Problems

Older global travellers experience higher morbidity and mortality rates than if they had stayed at home, due to travel-related infection, trauma and environmental factors. Pre-existing conditions such as chronic respiratory cardiovascular diseases and diabetes mellitus also affect morbidity and mortality statistics, especially with older seniors.

Cardiovascular problems

Several factors increase risk of a cardiac event during travel and at foreign locations. Psychological pressures on travellers have increased in recent years, due to terrorist threat and heightened security precautions resulting at airports, rail terminals and ferry ports. Traffic congestion and new environmental and climatic features have adverse impacts, creating delays, stress and uncertainty affecting the traveller's physiological and psychological stability, which can push vulnerable individuals into systems failure. Increased cardiac, respiratory and metabolic demands of relocation may become life threatening, at a time when immediate emergency medical care may be absent or inadequate. Travel health insurance protection can also be limited, as required by medical need. Insurers can only provide the best medical evacuation resources available locally. Optimal care is unrealistic in transit locations, such as an aircraft, and in many global tourist destinations. Cardiovascular events cause nearly half of deaths during air travel followed by traumatic incidents; they are the second most frequent reason for evacuation.

Fatalities in world travellers[1]

Condition	%	Condition	%
Cardiovascular disease	49.0	Cancer	5.9
Trauma	22.0	Other conditions	2.9
Medical, non-cancerous conditions	13.7	Infectious disease	1.0

Travel to departure point

Anxieties about leaving home, airport travel, transportation and destination develop and heighten as departure day nears. Time constraints and deadlines create stressors and psychological arousal. Physical demands from luggage hauling, long walkways and the transfers from rail station to air or sea port add to in-transit stressors. Fit, healthy older people may cope but the increased physiological and psychological burden may push those with a pre-existing medical condition into cardiac or respiratory failure, or precipitate myocardial and cerebrovascular accident. Prolongation of travel due to transport delay – a common feature of modern travel – increases the risk of a dangerous medical event.

Air transportation

This travel mode, with commercial jet liners flying at an altitude of 10,000m can expose the traveller to arterial oxygen desaturation with a change in cabin pressurisation, enforced immobility and potential dehydration. These effects can induce:

- dyspnoea and pulmonary oedema
- chest pain and angina
- cardiac arrhythmia
- venous constriction and deep vein thrombosis.

Cardiac contraindications and restrictions to commercial flying[1,2]

- unstable angina
- uncontrolled cardiac arrhythmias
- uncontrolled hypertension
- myocardial infarction – seven days (if complicated MI ≥4–6 weeks)
- severe or non-stabilised heart failure
- coronary artery bypass graft procedure, open heart surgery ≥10–14 days
- angioplasty, stent ≥3–5 days
- severe symptomatic valvular heart disease
- implantable cardioverter defibrillator (ICD): prohibition on flying, until condition considered stable, when ICD has delivered a shock.[1]
- pacemaker or ICD insertion: flying acceptable after two days. If pneumothorax at insertion, flight only possible after two weeks.[1]
- post-ablation intervention: flight acceptable after two days but increased risk of venous thromboembolism.[1]

Other contraindications to flying

- acute deep vein thrombosis – no flying until patient is stabilised on anticoagulants
- cerebrovascular accident – if uncomplicated, individual may fly within

three days (airline clearance required if travelling within 10 days)
- brain surgery – no flying for 10 days after event
- epileptic seizure –one day delay before flight
- subarachnoid haemorrhage –10 days' delay
- stent, mechanical valve in place – these will not trigger an alarm on security machines
- pacemaker/ICD: metal casings may trigger alarm. Hand-held metal detector should be requested and the operator advised not to place it directly over the pacemaker or repeatedly sweep it over the device

Over-loaded

Effects of pre-existing cardiac disease

Older travellers with existing cardiac ischaemia and rhythm irregularities may find symptoms exacerbated in the cabin environment. Those with pacemakers and cardio converters may experience problems with security scanners, which can affect electronic devices. They should anticipate medical problems and carefully plan their journey.

Travellers with heart disease should
- Pre-plan the journey by land and air, with the same care taken over accommodation.
- Purchase comprehensive travel insurance and understand provisions and exclusions.
- Acquire pneumococcal immunisation and influenza immunisation.
- Choose antimalarial and antiemetic drugs, and be aware of contraindications and drug interactions.
- Consider use of executive airport transfer lounges to diminish airport stress.
- Consider cabin upgrading for less stressful flying.
- Advise airline of travel (via passenger medical clearance unit).
- Complete medical information form (MEDIF) and travellers' medical card (FREMEC for frequent travellers). For stable, non-progressive, chronic conditions, the airline will wish to confirm that the potential traveller can walk 100m on the flat, at a normal pace without severe breathlessness.[3]
- Notify airline in advance of need for porter, electric buggy, wheelchair and airport oxygen.
- Not all airlines supply oxygen at take-off and landing. Oxygen must be booked in advance (portable cylinder, fixed rate of 2–4L/min by Hudson mask/nasal cannula). Oxygen concentrators are available (concentrate

oxygen in ambient air by removing nitrogen). Some airlines charge £50–100, others the price of another seat.
- For upper-class passengers there may be no facility for oxygen for take-off and landing, as the oxygen cylinder cannot be stowed safely.[4]

In flight
- Support stockings should be worn – ideally applied recumbent before leaving home.
- Warfarin should be continued as normal.
- Diuretic medication should be taken as usual.
- Adequate and spare drug medication must be carried in hand luggage.
- Exercise limbs and walk about the aircraft and in transit when possible.
- Adequate non-alcoholic, non-carbonated fluids should be taken in flight.[5]

Air, coach, car travellers and peripheral vascular disease

Air travel brings increased risk in older people from VTE. Risk increases[1] when the flight is less than four hours and peaks at more than eight hours' flight duration.[6] Length of coach and car travel with prolonged immobility may increase the risk.

Risk factors for VTE:
- immobilisation (75% of cases, with higher risk in non-aisle seating)
- dehydration, from haemoconcentration and hyperviscosity of blood
- hypobaric hypoxia
- recent surgery (operative surgery lasting more than 30 minutes in the previous four weeks increases risk)
- gross obesity
- malignancy
- thrombophilia, Factor V Leiden, antithrombin deficiency,
- past VTE
- plaster of Paris splints on lower limbs.

VTE precautions
- *Support stockings* (but not if existing peripheral arterial disease). Below-knee hosiery should be fitted to the individual; the hosiery should be rolled on and applied with the leg elevated, or at least horizontal, prior to home departure.
- *Aspirin* is not recommended as side-effects may outweigh benefits of use. Aspirin has only been shown to be efficacious in arterial blood research.
- In high-risk patients, a recommended precaution is the prescription of LWMH, e.g. dalteparin 2,500–5,000u to be administered subcutaneously before outward and return flights.[2,6]
- *Warfarin* medication may need alteration in routine administration with

long flights and trans-meridian travel. For instance, with a traveller on warfarin flying direct on an 11-hour flight to Kyoto from the UK, the first regular dose of warfarin on that day needs to be changed.[4] The passenger will be affected by dietary change and a possible increase in alcohol input, leading to a change in gut flora and possible vitamin K balance. This can increase the INR. With altitudinal change having a hypoxic effect on coagulation and drug metabolism, at altitudes >2,400m aircraft cabin pressure, there is a 2.7-fold increased risk of INR values being abnormal.[7]

The first regular dose of warfarin for the day needs adjusting if crossing more than six time zones from the UK, e.g. Britain to mid-United States or East India.

In travel: **WEST** – increase dose by quarter, as the traveller is facing a longer day. **EAST** – decrease dose by a third. The INR should be repeated after two weeks at the destination.

Heart disease and illness while abroad

There is an increased likelihood of trauma and infection overseas, which can increase cardiac load and precursor for cardiac ischaemia and failure. Travellers' diarrhoea with dehydration, electrolyte and metabolic disturbance can bring system failure in older people. Prescribed diuretics and ACE inhibitors should be reviewed and specialist advice sought if there is severe vomiting, diarrhoea, dehydration, hypotension, oliguria, 3kg weight loss, pulmonary or peripheral oedema.

- *Photosensitivity* can be caused by drugs such as thiazides, doxycycline, amiodarone.
- Travel-generated *anxiety* may merit use of a beta-blocker.
- *Paroxysmal supraventricular tachycardia* can be precipitated by physiological or psychological stress. This can be terminated with reflex vagal stimulation, Valsalva manoeuvre, carotid sinus massage, by plunging the face into ice cold water or taking large sips of ice cold water. If recurrent, medication such as a beta-blocker plus verapamil may be required.

Diabetes-related problems

Diet and medication are challenges for the globtrotters with diabetes. Cultural changes in eating and diet habits resulting from relocation may require a change in caloric intake and an adjustment in medication. Crossing time zones and altered meal content and times can upset metabolic balance. Adverse temperatures, hypothermia and hyperthermia can cause morbidity, while failure to protect insulin and maintain adequate personal stores of drugs for diabetes can be dangerous.

Conventional medication for diabetes may be unavailable at the destination or not equivalent in efficacy; in parts of Asia and Africa, it may even be fake.[8] Vulnerable patients with diabetes are more exposed to trauma and infection, especially in developing countries. Global travellers with diabetes must pre-plan the journey well in advance and seek professional travel-clinic advice before embarking on international trips to developing and remote countries.

Diabetes is not a contraindication to travel but problems may arise during travel, including loss of diabetic control, travel-related infections, traumatic emergencies, repatriation and practical problems of carrying and storing insulin and associated equipment.

Travel clinic considerations[9,10]

The travel health professional should discuss
- adequate and correct medication – (glucagon to be administered by a travelling companion; Glucogel; Hypostop Gel); written professional declaration may be needed to explain the medical need for needles, syringes, pens, vials, monitoring devices and an NHS repeat prescription form
- all recommended vaccinations – these may give a temporary rise of blood sugar
- glucose-testing equipment, glucose tablets, syringes/needles, needle disposal container
- malaria chemoprophylaxis and insect repellents
- travel insurance (full declaration of clinical status required) – exclusions should be avoided (diabetictravel.co.uk specialises in travel insurance for people with diabetes)
- European Health Insurance Card
- MedicAlert® identificaton.

Traveller considerations during journeys
- Anticipate delays, the freezing of insulin supplies in hold and lost luggage and the need to carry emergency snacks as well as insulin/food and travel sickness medication.
- All medication, testing equipment, lancets (capped) and glucometer should be carried in hand luggage.
- Exercise limbs and walk about travel vessel.
- Support stockings should be applied to limbs before departure from home.
- Comfortable shoes or slippers should be worn on aeroplanes, trains or long-distance coaches.
- Avoid alcohol in transit.
- Tight glycaemic control during air travel is not necessary, but avoid hypoglycaemia.
- Avoid walking barefoot on the beach or at poolside to avoid laceration and infection.

Insulin and airport security advice
- Carry a prescription matching the patient's name and the product (insulin, glucogel) in the box and on the label.
- Carry insulin, glucagen and glucogelin in cabin luggage. Baggage stored in cargo is subject to powerful X-rays and severe changes in pressure and temperature.
- Request hand-inspection of insulin, which can safely pass through X-rays. (Note that stability is affected by repeated exposures.)

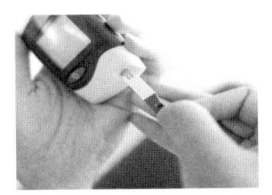

Change in insulin medication[11]
In those with type 1 diabetes on insulin travelling to San Francisco (13-hour flight, eight-hour time difference, nine time zones), the total dose of insulin needs to change by 2–4% per time zone crossed.

Increase or decrease in total dose required?
- Travel up to eight hours – stay on 'home time' for meals and injections.
- North to south travel requires no change.
- Travel over eight hours (more than six time zones) – adjust dose of insulin by 2–4% per time zone crossed (approximately a third of the daily dose).[5]

In Travel From East And North To South And West With more than once daily insulin dosage, monitor blood glucose frequently in-flight and accept there will be a relative hyperglycaemia. In *westbound* travel with a longer day, increase time between injections twice, by 2 to 3 hours each time. Increase insulin daily dose by 2–4% for each hour of time shift. In *eastbound* travel (shorter day), shorten time between injections. Decrease daily dose of insulin by 2–4% for each hour of time shift (approximately a third of the daily dose).[6]

Westbound travel (longer day) If on a single dose, take usual dose on day of departure. On twice-daily dose regimen take usual dose on day of departure then another 18 hours after morning dose; if blood glucose is greater than 13mmol/l, take one-third of usual morning dose followed by a snack or meal, then usual morning dose at destination.

Eastbound travel (shorter day) For single dose or twice daily (10–12-hourly dose) take usual dose on day of departure. In morning at destination: two-thirds of usual dose 10 hours after morning dose. If blood glucose is >13mmol/l, take remaining third of usual dose followed by a snack or meal (if on twice-daily dose regimen add this third to afternoon dose). On second day take usual dose.

Oral hypoglycaemic medication
- Stay on 'home time' for meals and medication.
- Adjust on arrival; sulphonylurea dosages may need to be altered to avoid hypoglycaemia.
- Carry glucose tablets.

Insulin at destination
- Some countries only have insulin U-40 or U-80 strengths, therefore take an adequate supply. Beware of fake products in Asia and Africa (*see Chapter 12*).
- Adjust the dose of insulin if undertaking increased activity, overeating or less active than normal.
- Hot climates lead to increased absorption of insulin, bringing risk of relative hypoglycaemia (dose may need to be reduced).
- Travel to areas of high altitude can cause insulin to expand and contract, causing air pockets within the cartridge or pen.
- Practice a few 'air shots' to ensure absence of air bubbles before injecting. Alternatively, revert to using a syringe and needle – it is usually possible to draw insulin out of a cartridge.
- If travellers' diarrhoea occurs, do not stop insulin or tablets but monitor glucose frequently and adjust insulin dose accordingly. Hydrate and correct caloric input with carbohydrate-containing salt/sugar solution (eight level teaspoonfuls of sugar in one litre of safe water).

Conclusion

People with diabetes can travel the world in good health with careful pre-planning and preparation. Visitors to more adventurous and exotic destinations should seek professional travel health clinic advice well in advance of departure. Insulin and diet may have to be altered en route and at destination, and special arrangements may need to be made to protect the insulin from environmental effects. Travel health insurance should be comprehensive and availability of good health and repatriation facilities confirmed before leaving the UK.

References

1 Causes of Mortality in Travellers Hargarten et al. Ann Emergency Med 20:622-626, 1991
2 Cardiac devices1. Smith D et al. Fitness to fly for passengers with cardiovascular disease. Heart 2010;96:ii1-i6. doi:10.1136/hrt.2010.2030911.
3 McCarthy A. Chapter 24 in Keystone et al. Travel Medicine. 2nd edition, Mosby Elsevier 1.
4 http://www.britishairways.com/health/docs/before/airtravel_guide.pdf
5 Cannegieter SC et al. Travel-related venous thrombosis: results from a large population-based case

control study (MEGA). PLoS Med 2006;3:e307
6 Schwarz T et al. Venous thrombosis after long-hall flights. Arch Intern Med 2003;163:2759-64
7 The Traveller on Warfarin1Ringwald J, et al. Travel and oral anticoagulation. J Travel Med 2009;volume 16, issue 4:276-283
8 Bygbjerg IC. Fake malaria drugs.Ugeskr Laeger. 2009 Mar 2;171(10):815-7.
9 Sane T et al. Travel related morbidity in travellers with diabetes Br Med J 1990;301:421
10 The Diabetic Traveller. Adapted from Benson E, Metz R. Management of diabetes during intercontinental travel. Bull Mason Clinic 1984-85;38:145-151 Practice Nursing 13(6): 259 – 262 (Jun 2002
11 Kassianos G Travel and Health in older people. 1012 in Chap 7. Fast print Pub. Peterborough

Handout leaflet

Travel tips for people with diabetes
Plan well ahead of departure and consider destination and trip activities.

Visit GP or diabetic advisor early to organise immunisations, supplies and equipment.

Acquire a letter from your GP confirming your diabetic status, and need for needles.

Get a prescription for medication to last longer than the trip schedule.

Acquire EHIC card, diabetic identity bracelet and list of medications for emergency situations.

Carry on your person: copies of prescriptions; pharmacy and GP contacts; testing strips; glucometers.

Be aware that exact replacements of drugs and equipment may not be available and fake medications are commonly on sale in Arica and Asia.

Organise health insurance and advise that diabetes is a pre-existing condition. (Diabetes UK can assist with appropriate policies).

Acquire and check the validity of an EHIC when travelling within Europe.

Airport security or immigration may request medication information.

Be familiar with an insulin pump and know how to adjust it with changes in time zones.

Carry a spare blood-test machine, spare sensors, spare insulin and spare insulin pens.

If travelling by air, 'diabetic meals' may not be most appropriate. Check carbohydrate intake regularly and, if required, top up with snacks en route.

Insulin care Keep insulin on your person or carried in hand luggage at all times and keep it out of direct sunlight or freezing conditions, such as an aeroplane hold. In hot/cold regions, store in wide-necked vacuum flask or insulated storage bag. Special insulin wallets can be used on the aircraft with no need for refrigeration; these should be carried in hand luggage.

If on an insulin pump, take spare reservoirs, infusion sets, an inserter and a bottle of insulin as well as some spare pump batteries.

If travelling by car, coach or train, assume travel will extend over one additional day. If traveling by air, assume three additional days.

Carry a readily accessible medical history in case of hospitalisation. Include the name and contact information of your home physician as well as family emergency contact numbers, medical ID cards and current prescriptions.

If travelling alone, the glucagon emergency should include written, concise and easily understood instructions for its utilisation.

At destination
Adjust insulin times on reaching destination.

When travelling west lengthen the gap between insulin doses or add extra food with an extra dose until adjusted; when travelling east, shorten the gap and reduce dosages. Check blood sugar regularly when crossing time zones, to determine any need to adjust dosages. Perfect control might not be possible initially. Anticipate travellers' diarrhoea. Careful attention should be given to food and water ingestion. Monitor blood–sugar levels carefully if vomiting and diarrhoea occur. Maintain a good level of carbohydrate content in your diet. Seek medical advice if the problem continues beyond a few days.

Heat affects the rate at which insulin is absorbed. In a high-heat environment, insulin is absorbed quicker. It is important to monitor blood levels in hot weather and adjust your diet as required. (In very hot/cold climate monitoring strips may over/under read.)

In a cold climate, insulin is absorbed slower. Monitor blood–sugar levels in extreme conditions and never allow insulin to freeze.

If insulin comes in a U-100 pack, check the conversion rate in countries where it comes in U-40 or U-80 preparations.

Carry an extra set of batteries for the glucose meter (or insulin pump if a portable unit is used and requires them).

Set a travel alarm to ring every four hours to help you stick to regular eating habits when abroad; keep it by the pre-packaged emergency snack.

Information sources

Diabetes UK (formerly The British Diabetic Association) www.diabetes.org.uk

Packing a Carry On for a Cruise www.ehow.co.uk/how_6521103_prepare-diabetes-travel-pack.html#ixzz0vqcZIkEj

10

Frail and Disabled Travellers

The physically frail, disabled and handicapped traveller

The majority of older travellers are relatively fit and aged between 65 and 80 years. Cruise ships often have a preponderance of senior passengers. The percentage of the population aged 65 and over increased from 15% in 1983 to 16% in 2008, an increase of 1.5 million people in this age group. By 2033, 23% of the population will be aged 65 and over.[1] Population trends indicate an increasing number of people living to beyond 80 years. Many will have enjoyed previous global travel or visits to relatives far afield, and will desire to venture abroad again.

A considerable number of older travellers have some measure of physical incapacity. A minority will be physically disabled and dependent on walking aids and wheelchairs. Five million disabled people in UK are over state-pension age.[2] Individual disabled travellers have successfully undertaken journeys to some of the world's most remote places.

Determined, goal-orientated, physically challenged people can – and do – make remarkable global voyages. In Western society, holiday-making and travelling have become civic rights. Handicapped people, however, frequently find this right to travel difficult to implement. Mobility barriers, poor communications and unpleasant social contacts with non-disabled people, and uncaring discrimination act as disincentives.[1] If health and transportation hazards can be overcome, international travel can widen restricted horizons and bring rich individual reward. Travel health professionals can facilitate the ease and comfort of the journey for the intending disabled traveller.

Some older people intent on world travel suffer from loss of essential faculties and physical impairment due to stroke and chronic arthritis, or major joint surgery. Poor balance adds to mobility difficulties. Despite frailties, most can travel where they will, with adequate preplanning and preparation. Some even find that transfer to a drier, sunny environment improves symptoms and enhances motility.

Physical handicap is not an insurmountable barrier to international journeying but the need for cautious, anticipatory travel planning and medical assessment is a vital prerequisite if these travellers are to relocate in safety.

Pre-travel consultation
Most will benefit from a pre-travel health consultation. Proposed route, transportation mode and destination are major considerations in determining the additional hazards of travel presenting to people who are handicapped. The health professional should be aware of the difficulties that can present to the disabled traveller, especially if they are wheelchair bound.

Gradually, access improvements are being made for travellers with disabilities who wish to holiday abroad. Ease of travel for these people revolves around foreign location, local transport and accommodation facilities, and the nature of the disability. The travel industry is slowly endeavouring to accommodate the needs of those who are disabled and their incapacity should not preclude desired international travel. However, increasing age is accompanied by increased incidence of stroke, Parkinson's disease, disabling arthritis, loss of function and faculties such as deafness and sight.

Inadequate or non-existent facilities for those who are physically disadvantaged are the norm in developing and impoverished countries, and in much of Eastern Europe and Asia. Some societies are psychologically unprepared to recognise the special needs of those who are functionally disabled and may even positively discriminate against those who are physically incapacitated. Sometimes, individuals suffering severe physical frailty, functional disability and handicap should be advised to restrict foreign travel to countries best equipped to accommodate their needs. Countries with the best facilities for the disabled are:

- UK and Ireland
- Scandinavia
- northern Europe

- Republic of South Africa
- New Zealand
- Australia
- Hong Kong and Singapore
- United States and Canada[2]

This does not mean that these countries present no problems for travellers, but there is state provision for those with functional incapacity. Psychologically too, the populations of these countries are likely to react positively in support of individuals with physical limitations. At a local level in all countries, however, there may be failure to provide the support necessary to maintain the smooth progress of the physically challenged en route or in transit. In some countries, such as the United States, antidiscrimination laws may inadvertently act to this group's disadvantage, e.g. early flight boarding restrictions in some states.

Disabilities
Handicap and disability can be divided into categories such as visible and non-visible conditions, and ambulatory and non-ambulatory states – drop-foot resulting from stroke is a visible, ambulatory condition, while deafness is a non-visible one. Public support is more likely to be offered for visible handicap as the disability is obvious.

Pre-travel documentation
The majority of travellers leave the UK by air. People with acute and chronic conditions should, in advance of the trip, complete and submit to the chosen airline the MEDIF form as an indication that they are a passenger with special needs. The international air transport association has produced MEDIF and FREMEC cards for completion by disabled, potential passengers. Part 1 of the MEDIF, the INCAD is a record of current incapacity to be completed by the passenger. Part 2 requires completion by the passenger's doctor.

For most permanently disabled people, a medical report on their current state is needed to permit airline transportation. The completion of a FREMEC form does not eliminate the need for prior notification of the disability for requirements of flight, but can be used to ease transit for frequent airline passengers.

This data transfer is wholly dependent on the accurate completion of questions by the patient and on patient willingness to complete the form in the first place. Many older patients and those who are physically incapacitated still present to airlines without having completed the forms; airline agents can refuse onward transportation. Prior notification of physical incapacity before a flight is essential to ensure appropriate support is available on the day of travel. Blind persons and people dependent upon walking aids and wheelchair transport will also have to advise transportation staff at train and bus stations and at ports of their special needs in transit, boarding and disembarking.

Deafness

Deafness is non-visible, strongly age-related and probably the most prevalent physical impairment in older people. About a third of those over 75 years of age are affected to some degree and 20% aged over 80 years require hearing aids.[3] The older, deaf traveller runs the risk of missing important travel announcements at airports, rail and bus stations, which may mean missed connections, but can be serious in the event of an emergency. Older travellers often switch off hearing aids when inundated by the cacophony of noise inseparable from busy transport transit points. Many people, whether they are hearing, deaf or have tinnitus, find that flying can cause pain or discomfort in ears and temporary hearing loss.

If travelling alone, older people who are very deaf person should inform the transport carrier and agencies of the need for special consideration. Couriers and travel stewards need to be briefed to keep a watchful eye on them and ensure that there is adequate visual display information available. Many international airports now have special phone links for the hard of hearing, which use microcomputer technology. Deaf people can type in queries on a special telephone link and receive a typed reply in response.

Train travel for deaf and hearing-impaired passengers has improved considerably with the introduction of new rolling stock and disability training for many frontline staff. When buying a ticket from the booking office at most major UK and European train stations, it is usually possible to amplify sound via an induction loop system, with the switch set to the 'T' setting on the hearing aid. Most public-address systems in airports should have induction loop facilities; text phones, public telephones with amplification and induction loops should also be available. Staff at airport information desks should be able to tell people where to find these.

Vision support services for blind or visually impaired people at airports on request include someone to:
- meet and guide through check-in, baggage check and customs controls
- advise personally when the plane is boarding if in a 'silent airport'
- help with boarding the plane and stowing any luggage

At a security search, impairment should be explained to airport security staff and bags should be repacked in a specific order, so essential items can be located.

Guide dogs should be allowed to travel free of charge, in the passenger cabin.

Visual impairment

A quarter of a million of the UK population is registered as blind or partially sighted and 2 million have some sight loss, with three-quarters of the group being over 65 years of age.[3] Nearly 90% of older people wear spectacles and studies suggest 20% of 80 year olds are unable to read newsprint even with prescribed spectacles. Cataract and age-related macular deterioration occur in 20–40% of persons between 65–74 years; glaucoma affects 20% of others.[4]

- *Hypertropia* (far sightedness), when the point of focus lies behind the retina, is the most common refractive defect.
- *Myopia* (near sightedness) occurs where the point of focus is in front of the retina.
- *Presbyopia,* an error in the refractive abilities of the eye, is a hypertropia for near vision. It develops with advancing age and results from a physiological change in the accommodative mechanisms by which the focus of the eye is adjusted for objects seen at different distances. The lens gradually becomes less pliable and eventually cannot accommodate in response to the action of the lens muscles with a resultant failure to focus well for near vision. Remedial action is possible by wear of corrective spectacles.
- *Cataract* may be caused by senile degeneration, with gradual, painless loss of vision. If the opacity is in the centre of the lens short-sightedness develops early and a presbyopic person may discover they can read without glasses. The condition is treatable with corrective spectacles and surgery; cataract surgery is the most frequently performed surgical operation in Western society.
- *Senile macular degeneration* is a leading cause of visual impairment in older people and there is no known predisposing factor.

Many older people now spend long vacations in countries with nearly constant high-intensity daytime sunlight. These two factors may see a rise in cataract formation and macular degeneration. One cause of cataract is oxidation, which can be due to light damage, and there are reports of increased cataract incidence in parts of the world exposed to strong sunlight for long periods.[5]

Light radiation reaching the eye passes to the retina – and the macular part of it in particular – where it is absorbed by photoreceptors, usually protected from the harmful effects of light wavelengths in the ultraviolet range of visible light. With age, the efficacy of the protection declines. Wearing good-quality sunglasses is recommended for older people who venture into strong sunlight, particularly when abroad. Wrap-around glasses offer best protection.

Logistically blindness accounts for fewer travel problems than might be expected. Blind people are not welcome on sea voyages because of inherent shipboard dangers, but cannot be excluded from shipping. In many countries guide dogs cannot accompany blind passengers on external flights across borders, without the dog undergoing lengthy quarantine. In countries such as the UK and United States 'seeing eye' dogs are permitted to ride in the cabin of the aircraft with the owner.

Air transport restrictions

Blind passengers using canes are usually allowed to retain them by their seat on aircraft, but stringent application of security regulations sometimes means that canes are taken away by over-zealous authorities. Swiss airports regard walking poles as offensive weapons and will not permit them into the cabin of the aircraft.[6] Stewardesses will normally provide information regarding seat-row position and guide a blind passenger to appropriate seating and toilet facilities. Airlines exclude blind persons from sitting in exit row seats to ensure the safety of aircraft and passengers.

Some airlines allegedly refuse to allow blind persons to sit at emergency exits, requiring them to sit in rear of the plane. They may also require persons with guide dogs to sit in bulkhead seats or for blind persons to pre-board, be sequestered in a special holding area prior to boarding, or be subjected to special safety briefings and emergency instructions meaning they have to wait until other passengers have deplaned before attempting exit. Although discriminatory, many of these seem sensible safeguards to benefit all passengers.

Ensuring safe travel in older, blind and partially sighted people may require travel with a sighted companion. For educational and other purposes, blind passengers can travel with an escort at reduced rates on British internal flights. Sound health in the travel companion is important.

Case history
The companion to a blind person fell on the first day of a rough weather cruise, breaking the left arm and right clavicle. She found it impracticable to guide the blind person around and he was confined to the cabin for the remainder of the cruise.

Train travel
The introduction of modern rolling stock, better station facilities and staff training has improved the experience of travel by train for disabled passengers but it is important to notify the railway company before the journey to allow support to be put in place. Modern rolling stock often has automated announcements advising station approach. A member of staff should assist train ascent and descent. On many trains, there are Braille buttons for opening doors as well as toilet doors.[7] The train will also have external doors that contrast with the body and interior hand rails to help visually impaired passengers.

Major stations, such as those in cities, will have audio announcements as well as visual screens, informing passengers of arrivals, departures, platform numbers and any delays that may occur. Most platforms now have a tactile edge near the running line to let blind and visually impaired passengers know they are close to the railway line. Unfortunately these refinements that ease travel for those with visual disabilities will not be available when travelling by train across many other parts of the world.

Physical and locomotor disability

There are approximately 10 million adults in Britain who have some form of disability; Leonard Cheshire, a charity that supports disabled people, warns that airports still fail to meet their needs, despite EU laws being introduced in 2008 that make it the responsibility of the airports to provide special assistance. Travel companies are also failing in this respect. Tourism for All, another charity, found that 80% of disabled respondents believed travel agents failed to appreciate their needs and 35% would not consider booking with a mainstream agent for this reason. Expedia, the online travel firm, has launched new search tools to aid disabled travellers find accessible accommodation.

Arthritis and hip replacement may restrict access to trains, aeroplanes and coaches, and the confined space of long-haul flights may create severe cramps and spasm in fixed limbs.[8] Loss of joint mobility may result in difficulty in accommodating limbs to the narrow confines of the aircraft cabin. Cramped legs may increase the risk of development of deep vein thrombosis. Poor balance and postural instability, a feature of ageing, adds to the risk of falls, which are a common occurrence in older passengers in the unstable environment on cruise ships.[9]

Passengers should be advised to avoid seating next to the body of an aircraft, which face bulkheads and where it is impossible to recline seats. The obvious seat positions where there is extra space, at emergency exits, are denied to older people and the incapacitated as airline regulations stipulate that only the fit can occupy this seating; it is only allocated 24 hours before travel. However, an aisle seat has much to commend it for older travellers, as this allows extension of at least one limb into the passageway and eases exit from seating for exercise and toilet purposes. Assistance for passengers with special needs is now the responsibility of a passenger with reduced mobility (PRM) team, employed by the airport and paid for by airlines. A PRM agent is responsible for boarding and seating disabled passengers.

Advice for physically impaired travellers

- Pre-book aircraft, coach and train seating to take advantage of seat positions with additional leg space.
- Purchase executive or club class tickets to have extra leg room.
- Buy entry to executive lounges where feet can be elevated and exercise taken before and between flights, and until a late call to emplane.
- Exercise limbs and avoid venous stasis and possible pulmonary embolism in restricted seating on a protracted airline or coach journey.
- Use constrictive pressure stockings on protracted trips.
- Use a walking pole for additional support.

Between-deck passage on cruise ships without lifts can prove an insurmountable hazard for those with fixed knees and hip deformities. Stairs and companionways can be narrow and steep on board ship, and seven to ten-deck levels are commonplace. Transit of these areas in a swaying vessel is likely to cause falls in older people. On many ships, locomotion difficulties from imbalance and disabled limbs create difficulties on stairs, in long walkways, lurching companionways and decks, with a real risk of falls and fracture in older passengers. Passengers should consider the facilities, lift availability and the suitability of a cruise ship for their particular needs as carefully as their choice of cabin. Older ships have fewer lifts, limited disabled occupancy cabins and steep stairs; newer ships, however, have wide passages and stairways and many open spaces with a dearth of handrails.

Access to lifeboats and emergency disembarkation should also be considered as lifts are rendered inoperative in the event of fire or flooding.[10] Those with spastic limbs from stroke may also find similar restrictions to those experienced by people with arthritis when travelling by sea or air.

Incontinence problems

Toilet access and continence are topics rarely considered by travel agents but exercise the mind of many intending older travellers. The question of toilet access en route and on holiday is a prominent travel-related anxiety.[11] UK or foreign travel brings inevitable restrictions on toilet access and variable toilet facilities. Abroad these are often coupled with limited water supply, inadequate sanitation and poor hygiene. This prospect can be daunting for those with good bladder control; it can inhibit the will to travel in those with urinary problems, who are fearful of possible loss of bladder control and urinary embarrassment, while in the public domain.

Senescence per se does not cause incontinence, although ageing can affect the lower urinary tract and predispose a person to it. Some degree of occasional or regular incontinence is common among older people with up to 71% of those living in the community being affected. Estimates suggest there are 1 million people with incontinence within the UK, the majority being over the age of 65 and female.[11] Many are too embarrassed to discuss their functional disturbance and surveys have shown that only one in five is prepared to discuss this problem with a health professional. The affliction causes many to avoid travel far from home.

The mildly affected, sometimes pressurised into travel by a spouse or offspring, may allow their fears to surface at pre-travel interview. The cause, in absence of a surgical disturbance, is usually due to bladder instability resulting from: an uninhibited neurogenic bladder, which gives rise to urge incontinence; or sphincter weakness giving stress incontinence. Several management procedures can relieve symptoms, bring control or make the condition sufficiently manageable for the individual to travel without undue concern.[12] These should be instituted in the months prior to travel.

Those with normal bladder function, but with other physical disabilities may also meet with functional toilet difficulties while travelling in foreign countries. Poor locomotion or transport abilities, imbalance, lower joint stiffness or rigidity are likely to create problems in toilets commonly met in transcontinental travel. Toilets traditional to the host country may cater only for those who can squat unaided over a plumbing fixture no more than a tiled hole in the ground. In continental Europe and the UK, where sanitary units may be more conventional, toilet seats may also be absent. The ability to hover over a toilet bowl, or perch upon porcelain, in the absence of toilet rails and wall supports is a skill often beyond the ability of older people with arthritic joints and poor spinal function.

Even if older women can manage this functional procedure, there is a 21% reduction in normal urine flow rate and a 19% increase in residual urine volume in the crouching position, forcing further toileting.[13] This, associated with poor renal clearance and the possibility of dehydration and infection on a visit to a tropical country, may lead to urinary tract problems that are sufficient to ruin the vacation. At best, the women with urinary anxieties on a coach tour will be inhibited by the queue to reach the toilet and the line of women waiting impatiently for entry while she micturates.

In aircraft, trains, ships and coaches, accessing toilet accommodation in a lurching, swaying conveyance can risk loss of balance and a fall. Grab handles may be at a premium in the toilet, seating may be too low for the less agile and floors can be awash, making bladder relief a dreaded experience. Aircraft cabin staff can assist passengers to the toilet, but having food-handler status prevents them from providing assistance in the toilet – a consideration some disabled passengers fail to appreciate. The peripheral siting of rest rooms in stations and airports can also defeat older people faced with a long walk to find relief. Inadequately signposted loos are another traveller's hazard and communication difficulties can add to the trauma of the search. The difference between *senora* and *senore* is none too obvious to the linguistically challenged.

Public toilets are rare in developing countries and, when available, are frequently poorly maintained and unhygienic. Toilet paper and hand-washing facilities are luxuries denied to much of the world's populace. Free toilet access is rare and toilet guardians will deny access no matter how great the need for entry, in the absence of appropriate coinage of the country. Coaches in Eastern Europe and developing countries are likely to be without facilities and cramped for space. Onerous demands placed on the bowel by gastroenteritis – the scourge of travellers – with diarrhoea and frequent defecation needs, can further add to individual discomfiture when voiding facilities are inadequate.

Advised of the paucity and variation in toilet facilities common to foreign travel, the older traveller can usually, with sensible preparation, overcome many of these sanitary deficiencies. The informed doctor advising older patients on healthy travel can also help minimise problems relating to feared or actual incontinence. The disorder is frequently neglected, poorly evaluated and ineffectively treated by family doctors. Improved bladder control can enhance the quality of life and can encourage travel. Fundamentally, the condition is due to over or under-activity of detrusor function, or sphincter dysfunction, involving internal or external sphincter, or a combination of both. Infections, medications, loss of muscle tone and diabetes are other relevant features in older women.

Males suffer less from incontinence but they too can have urinary problems that can spoil a foreign holiday. Urgency from prostatism demands immediate access to a toilet, often denied by the waiting queue in long-haul aircraft. Difficulties are likely to relate to prostatic hypertrophy and acute retention. Exposure to cheap wines and spirits often found abroad and on aircraft can lead to excessive alcohol ingestion and acute retention, if the prostate is enlarged. Prolonged intervals between bladder voiding due to transit delays and lack of toilet access can precipitate an inability to urinate. If the journey involves a UK coach tour, this may only result in painful embarrassment and the inconvenience of a trip to a casualty unit, but abroad it may have more serious consequences.

Case history
A fit, retired 67 year old school teacher on a coach tour to Devon from Scotland suffered an acute retention when his much-delayed coach, devoid of a toilet, was held up in a traffic jam on the motorway. He was admitted to an emergency unit, was catheterised and advised to have a transurethral resection. This was done shortly after admission. The operation was successful and he was fit enough to catch his coach on its return journey north.

Another 72 year old was less fortunate. He had always wanted to view the Himalayas and on this holiday of a lifetime he finally reached Kathmandu. Unable to resist the call of the mountains, he arranged a few days' trekking in the Himalayan foothills. The second night out from base, he suffered an acute retention. A passing medic in another trekking group was asked to help. In the absence of a catheter, the retention was relieved by the passage of a stethoscope tube. Although this brought immediate relief, he developed a urinary infection, became pyrexial, then dehydrated. He had to be evacuated back to the capital and, in the absence of wheeled transport, was carried out of the high valleys on the back of a Sherpa porter. Even in hospital his convalescence was protracted and he was very relieved to ultimately return to NHS care and subsequent operation.

Causes of urinary incontinence
1. Detrusor instability – when the bladder muscle or detrusor contracts uninhibitedly, giving rise to urge incontinence, frequency, enuresis and stress incontinence.
2. Urethral sphincter incompetence – when urethral resistance is decreased and stress incontinence occurs.
3. Both conditions can coexist. Both frequently respond to treatment that needs to be instituted at least three months before departure on holiday.

Treatment
If detrusor instability is not due to a neuropathy, bladder retraining is recommended. Retraining instruction involves emphasis on voiding at certain times and holding on for as long as possible. Stress incontinence can respond to pelvic floor exercises, which young older individuals can tackle and practise with success.

The traveller who suffers episodic symptoms of instability with stressful events, e.g. airport transit or aircraft take-off, can be given a musculotrophic drug such as oxybutynin as it has a short half-life. Drug treatment of overflow incontinence is not very successful.

If there is little benefit from drugs, exercises and retraining, the provision of adequate incontinence aids such as Kanga pants and incontinence pads may make short- and medium-distance travel a practicality for those determined on global travel. Urisheaths, catheters and leg bags can be managed successfully en route by older patients, as long as intellectual impairment does not impair good control.

Management
The pre-travel consultation allows nurse or doctor to tactfully explore with the patient any apprehensions regarding continence. If none are admitted, the opportunity should be taken to advise on the variability of access and the quality of toilet facilities likely to be met in international airports and different countries, stressing the inadequacy of those in developing countries.

An information handout can reinforce instructions. Acquisition of passenger leaflets from British Airport Authority airports detailing toilet access should be advised.

Older American ladies on the 'blue rinse' route through the United States travel with a clutch of paper toilet-seat covers, a precaution more appropriate to antiquated washroom fittings in Europe than in the United States and a safeguard that could be appropriate for other older travellers abroad. One older female patient – an intrepid traveller to far-flung places and very familiar with the uncrowned toilet bowls of foreign parts – actually carries her own lightweight, plastic toilet-seat cover with her on her travels!

Ensconced within the tight confines of an aircraft or coach toilet, older people are likely to come to little harm, but traversing aisles and passages in ships on choppy seas or in lurching planes, trains or buses, they run the risk of falls and fractures. Use of a folding walking pole should be suggested, for accessing toilet accommodation on moving transport.

Given enough time before travel, those with occasional incontinence or regular disturbance can often be helped to overcome the problem or make it manageable during travel. Patients may have to be coaxed into giving details of frequency, urgency, nocturia, dribbling and involuntary voiding with coughing and sneezing. These features help identify urgency and dribbling incontinence and provide pointers to management.[14,15] The nurse can obtain the history with the use of simple questionnaires on bladder control. The doctor should make a physical examination of pelvis, rectum and vagina to identify any specific causative factor and referred to the appropriate specialist consultant.

Most patients will be female and urinary tract infections, atrophic vaginitis, cystocoele and rectal overloading have to be considered and treated if found. Prostatism requires a rectal check and prostate specific antigen (PSA) investigation. Review of diuretics, hypnotics and sedatives is required. A midstream specimen of urine (MSU) should be checked for infection and glycosuria. Patients should be encouraged to keep diary records of toilet demands and frequency, urinary volumes and number of incontinence pads used.

All too often no specific correctable cause will be found but bladder retraining exercises and drug therapy can still help many of these potential travellers.

Pre-travel health consultation

History-taking by nurse or doctor should include:

Questions on:
- destination and transportation
- worries about toilet access on the journey
- whether there is a need to get up at night
- making it to the toilet in time, or not
- leaking urine when exercising, sneezing, running, coughing
- problems experienced with emptying the bladder.

Investigations
- MSU (organisms, sugar albumen)
- PSA test
- examination by doctor (if incontinence admitted)
- vaginal and rectal examination to exclude infection, atrophy.

Advice
- possibility of limited facilities (no hand basins, toilet paper, toilet seats,

toilet bowls, wall supports, grab handles, privacy)
- lack of facilities after customs and immigration, during protracted holding manoeuvres before aircraft landing/take-off and in developing countries
- be prepared: carry toilet paper, toilet seat covers, incontinence aids, appropriate continence-inducing drugs in hand luggage
- cystocoele, rectal over-loading and prostatism
- pelvic-floor exercises for the person with stress incontinence, practising interrupted micturition every time she goes to the toilet, and performing the exercises eight times per day
- bladder drill and retraining for people with urge incontinence – secondary to bladder instability, encourage patients to only toilet at certain times, which are progressively lengthened every two days.

Prescription
- Prescribe oxybutinin twice daily as a trial, at least three weeks before departure; if the problem is anxiety related, the drug should be taken before the stressful event.

Wheelchair travel

Wheelchair travellers face access problems with most transport and accommodation in overseas travel.[16-18] They must consider aircraft size, ramp access wheelchair carriage and transit stopovers. The last should be a major consideration as transit points on long-haul flights may utilise an airport in the Middle East or the Gulf states with few aids for the disabled traveller. It is vital that at no point in long-haul travel with transfers that a small plane is used on a feeder service.

Most large international airports now have adequate rampage and wheelchair access and this is true of the majority of cruise ships. Coaches and trains however, even on conventional tours and routes have variable ease of access. Train stations often mean dependency upon lifts, which may or may not be operative. Between-deck lifts on ships may not be available in rough weather or emergency situations, such as fire.[19] British law makes it an offence for providers of goods and services to provide inferior service to a disabled person because of their disability. Disability Discrimination Act (1999) to transport applies only to new trains from 1999 and coaches from 2000, and does not apply to air and sea travel.

Careful, early pre-planning and organisation will smooth the way to a safe journey. Competition between travel services ensures variability and medical counsellors should be prepared to discuss the benefits of shopping around to ensure that passage is with a caring carrier.[20]

Air travel

Prior to purchase of a flight ticket those in wheelchairs should complete the appropriate forms requested by airline management – the Incapacitated Passengers Handling Advice (INCAD) form and/or a Medical Information Form (MEDIF. In smaller airports, wheelchair access and provision may be inadequate or non-existent. At these locations disabled passengers may have to be manually lifted from the aircraft down steps by airport employees. Large airliners now carry sky-chairs – on-board wheelchairs, which expedite movement to the toilet.

Personal transportation of a lightweight wheelchair is advised even when passengers are accustomed to a battery operated one, as they are easy to store on board. Electric chairs are unwieldy heavy vehicles and carrying batteries is often restricted by airlines. The carrying of electric wheelchairs is allowed. An electric wheelchair will be classed as a dangerous material on account of its battery being considered a hazard. A wheelchair powered by a battery that could spill must have the batteries entirely removed. Batteries that cannot spill do not have to be removed from the chair. Airlines must carry mobility equipment free of charge but many airlines only allow one wheelchair per plane.

People who have physical disabilities may have to consider travelling with a companion to expedite transit changeovers and provide en route support. Some airlines charge a nominal fee only for the carriage of such a travel supporter. To travel alone the passenger should be capable of moving from a passenger seat to an on-board wheelchair, as cabin crew are prohibited from lifting passengers in and out of seats.

For safety reasons, airlines are entitled to require that the disabled person travels with a companion if not self-reliant. To travel by air alone, the traveller must be capable of:
- unfastening his/her seatbelt
- leaving their seat and reaching an emergency exit unaided
- donning an oxygen mask and lifejacket
- understanding the safety briefing and instructions given by the crew in an emergency.

If help is required with feeding, administering medication or getting to a toilet, a travel companion is needed.

Every airport in the UK now offers free assistance for disabled passengers to reach and leave planes. The passenger with reduced mobility (PRM) team is responsible for boarding and seating disabled passengers. This applies to visible and non-visible disabilities.

Recommended airlines

Air Canada This airline provides good support within the airport and assistance on board, with regular checks to ensure all is well. On most flights, extra seating is available at no extra cost if needed due to disability. Service animals are allowed, provided they can sit at the feet without protruding into the aisle.

Continental Airlines The airline offers special seating arrangements and on-board assistance, including help for those with mobility problems whether or not they use wheelchairs. They welcome service animals and have a special on-board kennel to make them more comfortable.

EasyJet EasyJet will arrange assistance to get to aeroplane-side with a lift up any steps in a carry chair if necessary. Some support is available on board but there are no aisle wheelchairs. Safety instructions are provided separately for visually impaired and hearing impaired passengers. Service animals can only travel on domestic flights.

Quantas Quantas provides full support from the moment of arrival at the airport, will lift passengers in and out of their seat if needed, and arranges early boarding. Service animals are welcome and, if a carer is needed, both customer and carer travel at a reduced rate.

Virgin Atlantic This airline provides a good support service for visually impaired and hearing-impaired passengers as well as those with mental disabilities who choose to travel alone. There is limited support for mobility-impaired people, but there are spacious adapted toilets on longer flights. Service animals are welcome to travel in the cabin on most major routes.

Airlines must carry mobility equipment free of charge. Disabled travellers must advise the airline when booking and provide them with details of their wheelchair or scooter, particularly if it is powered. Seating on board an aircraft has to meet air-safety regulations. The wheelchair will be stored in the hold of the plane. It is usually possible for the passenger to stay in their wheelchair until plane-side before transfer to an on-board chair – an easy task if there is an airbridge connection. If the plane is parked away from the terminal, passengers will have to use a flight of stairs or a scissor lift to board. If the wheelchair has to be specially packed – especially if it is a powered wheelchair or scooter – it may be necessary to transfer into an airport chair at check-in.

Under European law, disabled people and other people with reduced mobility have legal rights to assistance when travelling by air. Airlines are not obliged to fly disabled passengers; they are flown at their discretion. There are only two specific reasons why they may deny flying access. The first is if there may be a danger to other passengers. The second consideration is the risk of requirement for urgent medical attention, which could force flight diversion.

Medications and air travel

A chronically ill and infirm person can take all medicines needed onto the flight, even if that means exceeding the usual security allowance for liquids. These should be in their original containers with liquids packed separately in a clear plastic bag. Extra water can be carried if needed for health reasons. Prescription liquid medications and other liquids needed by persons with disabilities and medical conditions include:
- all prescription and over-the-counter medications (liquids, gels and aerosols) including petroleum jelly, eye drops and saline solution for medical purposes
- liquids including water, juice or liquid nutrition or gels
- life-support and life-sustaining liquids such as bone marrow and blood products
- frozen items, as long as they are frozen solid when presented for screening.

If liquid medications are in volumes larger than 100ml each, they may not be placed in the quart-size bag and must be declared to the transportation security officer. A declaration of content can be made verbally, in writing, or by a person's companion, caregiver, interpreter or family member.

Declared liquid medications and other liquids for disabilities and medical conditions must be kept separate from all other property submitted for x-ray screening. Repeat prescription forms for the medication should be carried with a list of medications and preferably a note as to their need signed by the family doctor (*see Chapter 12*).

Coach travel

Pre-enquiry must include questions on: the availability of a mechanical wheelchair lift or employees willing to manually assist the passenger; whether the wheelchair can be secured to the floor; the passage permits transfer from wheelchair to seat; and access to on-board toilets? Novice travellers must be aware that in many parts of the developing world tourist coaches will have no toilet and be cramped. Local buses if available, will be grossly overloaded, with a scramble for seats at each stop.

Train travel

There may not only be a gap between platform and carriage but many continental trains have carriage doors raised high above ground. Porterage is now rare at many stations. On-board toilets can be squalid, unhygienic and with flooded floors. Assistance may be only a bell-press away, but speedy aid is dependent on the cooperation of a conductor often many coaches away (*see Chapter 5*).

Cruise ship travel

Many of the large ships have excellent disabled passenger cabins and adequacy of between-deck lifts but older ships still have passage, toilet-access and stair obstructions. Transfer to shore by ship's tender is still common with ladders to be negotiated on and off the ship. Gangplanks can be steep and, even in benign weather, negotiating broad ship spaces can be challenging. In rough weather wheelchairs can be tilted over.

> *Case history*
> *A lady with severe disabilities accompanied by her spouse was travelling to the Arctic on a cruise ship and accommodated in a disabled person's cabin. She required assistance with feeding, toileting and getting to bed. Halfway to Greenland her husband had a severe heart attack and had to be helicoptered to the distant mainland. The wife was left bereft of care. Medical and nursing staff coping with a norovirus outbreak could not help, nor were cruise staff permitted by regulation to give intimate support. Goodwill and ad hoc temporary arrangements provided basic feeding and toilet assistance until she too was flown out on a casualty evacuation flight to Norway in a very expensive repatriation exercise.*

Charities supporting disabled people report that leading travel companies are failing to serve their needs. In one survey, 85% of disabled respondents did not believe travel agents understood their needs or catered for them.[17] Accommodation and access problems regularly arose with bookings; travellers may need to confirm that these considerations have been addressed before travel.

Elevator and facilities access

A lift measuring 3ft 10in (deep) x 2ft 6in (wide) is necessary for wheelchairs with a maximum of two steps for negotiation. Lavatories must measure 5ft 4in x 3ft 7in to allow internal wheelchair manoeuvre. Entrance doors should be at least 2ft 6in wide and walkways ramped where necessary.[18]

Summary

Despite many advances in access to airports and station, aircraft, trains and coaches in the developed world, travelling with a wheelchair remains a challenge and transport services are not user friendly. In the developing world and many foreign parts the experience can prove daunting with vagaries that the best of planning cannot anticipate. Safe world travel is however feasible for most older disabled people guided to realistic goals, on carefully pre-planned individualised journeys. Travelling with a supporter alleviates many problems in transit but their personal health is also a consideration (*see Chapters 4 and 5*).

- World travel is feasible for older disabled people on customised journeys.
- Counsellors must guide towards realistic goals and anticipate problems.
- The individual should consider travel with a healthy spouse, or independent supporter.
- They should be directed towards support organisations for further advice on travel arrangements.
- Safe travel in frail, older people and those with disabilities demands careful pre-travel planning, competent medical assessment, sound counselling and a user-friendly transport mode and destination.
- Within acceptable parameters, world travel need not be out of reach for those with physical and functional limitations. It can expand restricted horizons and be a worthwhile venture.

DISABLED TRAVELLER INSTRUCTION LEAFLET

10 tips for healthy travel

The ease of travel for a person with a disability depends upon destination, transport and accommodation facilities. Plan and prepare in advance before travel abroad.

Plan ahead

Prepare for the journey How do you plan to get to the airport, access transport, store aids or equipment, obtain assistance, order special diets, or access toilet facilities on the aeroplane, train or boat?

Discuss with travel agent accessibility of transport and accommodation, especially if using a wheelchair. If you require assistance for a flight you will be required to complete an Incapacitated Passengers Handling Advice (INCAD) form. The second part of this form – the Medical Information Form (MEDIF) – needs to be filled in by your doctor if you have a medical condition.

Seek advice early for immunisations, malaria prevention, health education, fitness-to-fly certificate, and medical facilities in destination country.

Be honest in stating the degree of the disability.

Acquire medical insurance cover, making sure emergency repatriation is included and maintenance or replacement costs for physical aids, mobility or medical equipment are included.

Carry personal medication that is required in hand luggage on the journey and once at the destination. Carry prescription repeat forms, a list of medications and a doctor's letter for injections. Wear a medicalert bracelet if appropriate.

Maintain hydration Before departure by plane, boat or train, do not reduce fluid intake to reduce the need to go to the toilet. It is important, particularly for flying, that you maintain fluid intake.

Do leg exercises during journeys when sitting for a long time.

Confirm destination arrangements How will you be met and who will meet you at the airport if you need assistance.

Carry names of contacts and telephone numbers of contacts at destination should plans go awry.

Carry a language phrase book and learn key assistance phrases before departure.

CHECKLIST FOR TRAVELLERS WITH EXISTING HEALTH PROBLEMS[18]
Arrange a full medical check-up several weeks before departure.

Ensure adequate and inclusive medical insurance cover including repatriation.

Consider whether special forms should be completed to advise transport agents of disability before departure by air.

Advise airlines of special medical, dietary and mobility requirements.

Re-assess medication before departure. Drug review should pay special attention to diuretics, insulin, hypnotics, H_2 antagonists, anticholinergics, anti-epileptics and interactions with antimalarials.

Adequate medication should be carried in the hand luggage.

Be aware of special risks of high altitude and climate extremes.

Consider the need for supplemental oxygen, if potential respiratory problems in aircraft.

Consider adjustment of food intake and insulin dosage if have diabetes.

On long-haul flights endeavour to exercise legs as often as possible and avoid staying immobile for long periods.

Be aware that medical, transport and toilet facilities en route and at destination may be of poor standard.

Disabled cruise passengers should check the adequacy of medical and access facilities before booking.

Useful contacts

The Disabled Living Foundation (information on flying and travel advice) 380-384 Harrow Road, London W9 2HU

The Royal Institute for the Blind (information on tape for flying and travelling) 224 Great Portland Street, London W1N 6AA

Royal Association for Disability and Rehabilitation (RADAR – produces information for disability and travel) 12 City Forum, 250 City Road, London EC1V 8AF

Heathrow Airport (free guide to facilities *Traveller's Information Special Needs*)

Extensive Advice on Travel for the Disabled at Disabled Travel www.disabledtraveladvice.co.uk

Resources

Health Advice for Travellers. Department of Health. Available free from post offices. Contains basic travel health advice, recommended immunisations, information about travel insurance and entitlement to medical treatment in the European Community.

LaGrow S, Wiener W, LaDuke R. Independent travel for developmentally disabled persons: a comprehensive model of instruction. *Res Dev Disabil.* 1990; 11(3): 289-301.

Airline access rules

Further reading

Walsh A (1991) *Nothing Ventured: Disabled People Travel the World*. Lonely Planet Series, Harrup Columbus. ISBN 0747 102082.

McIntosh I (1993) *Health Hazard and the High Risk Traveller*. Quay Books, Mark Allen Publishing: London.

Dawood R (ed) (2002) *Travellers Health* Fourth edition. Oxford University Press: Oxford.

McIntosh I. Chapter 7. In: Lockie C Walker E et al (Eds) (2000) *Travel Medicine and Migrant Health*. Churchill Livingstone: Edinburgh.

McIntosh. *Pitstops and Pitfalls: A Health Guide for Older Travellers*. Quay Books, Mark Allen Publishing: London. ISBN 1 85642 1163.

National suppliers of medical goods

Travel Medical Centre Ltd – provide sterile injection kits (with intrafusion drips) Charlotte Keel Health Centre, Seymour Rd Eastern Bristol BS5 0UA

Industrial Pharmaceutical Service Ltd – provides travel sterile packs only. Bridgewater Rd, Broadheath, Altrincham WA14 1NA

Philip Harris Medical Ltd – provides travel aid kit with sterile syringes, dioralyte SafariQuip

References

1 Mid-year population estimates, Office for National Statistics; General Register Office for Scotland; Northern Ireland Statistics and Research Agency; Death registrations, Office for National Statistics - http://www.statistics.gov.uk/cci/nugget.asp?id=949
2 Family Resources Survey (FRS) Disability prevalence estimates 2007/8
3 Keyinformationandstatisticshttp://www.rnib.org.uk/aboutus/Research/statistics/Pages/statistics.aspx
4 http://www.rnib.org.uk/aboutus/Research/statistics/Pages/statistics.aspx
5 Neale RE, Purdie JL, Hirst LW, Green AC Neale RE, Purdie JL, Hirst LW, Green AC Sun exposure as a risk factor for nuclear cataract Epidemiology. 2003 Nov;14(6):707-12..
6 In the News British Trav. Health Assoc. J 2010.2
7 Dessary BL. Robin MR. Pasini W. (1997) The aged infirm or handicapped traveller in Textbook of travel medicine and health. Ed. Steffen R. DuPont HL. Decker Pub. Canada

8 Dargent-Molina P, Favier F, et al (1996). Poorer balance and postural stability make falls more likely. Lancet, 348; 145-9.
9 McIntosh I Power K Reed J Prevalence and intensity of travel related stressors.1996 J Trav. Med.96-102
10 Mandelstam D (1986). Incontinence and its Management 2 edn. Croon Helm, London McIntosh I. Health and safety at sea. 1997 Trav. Med. Inter.15.234-7
11 Brocklehurst JC Urinary incontinence in the community--analysis of a MORI poll. BMJ. 1993 Mar 27;306 (6881):832-4.
12 O'Dowd T, MD, FRCGP, Management of urinary incontinence in women British Journal of General Practice, 1993, 43, 426-429.
13 Moore K, Richmond D et al (1991). Crouching Over the Toilet, Brit J Obs Gyn, 98, 569-72
14 Jolleys J (1988). Diagnosis and Management of Urinary Incontinence in Females in General Practice, BMJ, 296,1300-02
15 Fanti J et al (1991). Efficacy of Bladder Retraining in Older Women with Incontinence, J Amer Med
16 Stewart M Physical impairment and global travel Brit. J. travel health 2010.14
17 McIntosh I Disabled travel. In the news. Brit. J. travel health 2010. 15.58
18 McIntosh I. Advice for disabled travellers. In the news Brit. J. travel health 2008 11.54
19 Mitchell M Have wheelchair will travel. 1995. Travel Medicine Internat. 13(5)174.7
20 McIntosh I 1995 Travel and Health in the Elderly. Quay Books . Mark Allan Pub. Dinton Somerset

11

The Older Adventurer

People in the developed world are living longer and often enjoying many years of life after retirement from work. By 2034, 23% of the UK population is projected to be aged 65 and over.[1] Although health expectancy has not improved at the same rate as life expectancy, older people can currently look forward to better health in old age than did those in previous generations;[2] the majority can expect to live in good health well into their 70s. There is a window of opportunity when they can travel extensively and attain longed-for objectives, which time and money may have previously made impracticable.

Speedy transportation by aeroplane has brought the most remote places and distant parts of the globe within reach. Many of the athletic and not so fit are intent on adventure and they travel far and wide engaging in strenuous sporting and physical activities. Eight of the ten world's highest mountains are a mere 24 hours flight away, as are Angkor Wat in Cambodia, Machu Picchu in Peru and

Ayer's Rock in central Australia. Cruise ships berth in Manaus in the heart of the Brazilian jungle, in Arctic Spitzbergen and on the Antarctic Peninsula. Older passengers disembark from aircraft and ships to venture into hinterlands. They yearn to see and enjoy the world's wonders and are prepared for inconvenience, physical discomfort and challenging health demands to meet their desires.

They participate in trekking expeditions and sailing trips; overnight in Dayak long houses and bivouac tents; travel in jeeps, on quad bikes, horseback, jet ski and in canoes to satisfy a thirst for adventure. These locations and activities can challenge the young and be life threatening for people of senior years. They put themselves into a high-risk group of global travellers but good travel planning, pre-travel health consultation, appropriate prophylaxis and sensible precautions can ensure they travel safely and return in good health.

Physical activity can confer benefits in older people.[2] Fitness can help the individual cope with mental challenges in the transition period between occupation and retirement. Higher levels of fitness are associated with a lower risk of developing diabetes and heart disease.[3] People with higher fitness and aerobic capacity have longer life expectancies compared with inactive people.[4] In the absence of serious medical disability, the travel health professional should not discourage their adventurous expectations considering the benefits of pursuing an active lifestyle as age increases.

The older adventurer can be exposed to environmental extremes faced by any traveller to exotic, very hot, cold and high places, and failing organic systems make them more vulnerable. They are at greater health risk from excess heat and cold, due to age-impaired heat regulating systems and poorer peripheral vascular circulation[4,5] (*see Chapter 1*). Older adventurers forsake the comfort of luxurious hotels with high standards of hygiene and sanitation for less salubrious accommodation, where food and water may be contaminated, and they venture into hostile environs where medical facilities may be scarce and distant.[5] They travel off-road, or on roads little better than tracks, in unroadworthy vehicles, in terrain subject to flood, avalanche landslip and the vagaries of monsoon and snow fall.[6] They also expose themselves to risk from trauma and infection.[7,8]

Travellers' diarrhoea with accompanying fluid loss and electrolyte imbalance is a serious threat to older adventurers, who have also to contend with scarce pure water sources and personal carriage of sufficient water supplies. On fast-moving expeditions, recuperation from infection and minor trauma is problematic as rest days are rare. Road traffic and incidental accident are companions to safaris and land and water expeditions, with travellers at added risk, as emergency aid, as well as medical and evacuation resources will often be limited.[9] Contaminated emergency fluid and blood replacement supplies cause further concern. Pre-travel preparations must anticipate these health hazards and seek to minimise their impact (*see Chapters 3, 6 and 7*).

Safari, walking/trekking and small boat mini-expeditions are popular.

On safari and in very warm regions

Reduced capacity of older people to regulate body temperature may lead to heat exhaustion and hyperpyrexia (heatstroke). Dehydration is a constant threat in regions of intense heat and is more likely to occur in older people where there is high humidity.[10] It results from excessive fluid loss due to sweating, coupled with inadequate fluid intake. It can be avoided by ensuring adequate fluid intake of four litres per day. Loss of salt also occurs but can be avoided by a slight increase in dietary salt. Excessive water intake may lead, however, to hyponatraemia.

Heat exhaustion
The condition results from a decrease in plasma volume and reduced cardiac output that becomes insufficient to meet body demands. It is caused by loss of fluid and salt and the person is still able to sweat. Body temperature is usually normal and below 41°C. Symptoms include fatigue, nausea, weakness, dizziness and sometimes cramps.[11]

Treatment of heat exhaustion consists of removal from heat where possible, giving oral fluids and cooling, aggressive cooling being necessary if the body temperature is above 40°C (see below).

Heatstroke (heat hyperpyrexia)[12]
Heatstroke is a serious medical emergency in which there is a breakdown of temperature regulating mechanisms. The classic triad of features is: cessation of sweating; a body temperature of 41°C or more; and disturbance of central nervous system function. The patient should be treated as having heatstroke if any two features are present. Symptoms may include weakness, lethargy, fatigue, headache, dizziness, nausea, vomiting, diarrhoea, cramps, anxiety, confusion, unsteadiness or ataxia, impaired judgement, hyperventilation, collapse and convulsions.[13]

Treatment of heatstroke
Treating heatstroke involves removal of the patient from heat exposure, divesting clothing and reducing body temperature by rapid cooling. Rehydration and maintenance of airway, breathing and circulation are important. Emergency evacuation to hospital for intensive care may be necessary. Rapid cooling may be carried out by ice-water immersion[13] or evaporative cooling using a hammock-like net, spraying with tepid water.[14]

Advice for travellers
- Wear loose-fitting clothing, preferably of cotton rather than man-made fibres, of light rather than dark colour.
- Avoid direct heat from the sun between 11am and 3pm.
- Maintain adequate fluid intake of four litres per day in extreme conditions.

Water activities

Swimming, kayaking, wind surfing and white-water rafting are common pursuits in older adventurers and small inflatable boats are used in passenger transfer in Arctic and Antarctic waters. Low ambient temperatures, wind chill and contact with cold and icy water are hazards with additional risk from immersion, drowning, near-drowning and immersion hypothermia.[15] Immersion in inland lakes brings health hazard from ingestion of contaminated water, leading to gastrointestinal infection and leptospirosis if the water is contaminated with rats' urine.

Poor balance, arthritic joints, postural hypotension and loss of joint elasticity are further problems for seniors who participate in water activities. Many older travellers find themselves by default on river, lake or sea when an agency excursion includes a small boat, canoe or rigid inflatable boat journey. They will nonchalantly board the craft on vacation when they would never contemplate such a manoeuvre on home soil. Cruise ship-to shore transfer by tender is common and transit from a floating bridge on the ship's side to a small boat can test the fit, healthy and young. It can be a death-threatening exercise in the less able and those disadvantaged by age. People often indulge in these water activities without even donning a life jacket, and they rarely consider the sea worthiness of the craft or the consequences of capsize.

Cold-water immersion

Deaths in young people associated with immersion in cold seas and lakes, occur in water with a temperature <17.12°C, 95% of them in water <15°C. As the thermoregulatory ability of older people is impaired, death probably occurs in older people subjected to immersion in water at higher temperature. Older people have a reduced capacity to regulate body temperature when exposed to cold and wet conditions.[16,17.]

Cold conditions are encountered on Arctic or Antarctic cruises, winter sports holidays, at high altitude and at night in desert regions. In these situations older people are at risk of hypothermia. Impairment of peripheral circulation may also expose them to the risk of peripheral circulatory problems. Inadequate food intake and wet or inadequate clothing and sleeping bags predispose to cold-related illness. Those who are ill or injured are also more prone to both hypothermia and cold injury; some medications and the ingestion of alcohol may potentiate the effects of cold.

Hypothermia

Hypothermia occurs when the body core temperature falls below 35°C[18]. Decision making may be impaired at this temperature, and excessive shivering occurs.

Early signs may resemble those of altitude sickness or dehydration. Below this temperature, behaviour becomes inappropriate with clumsiness and confusion. As body temperature falls lower, there is impairment or loss of consciousness and shivering stops. At 30°C, it is difficult to detect vital signs of pulse or respiration. Below 28°C, death will occur unless warming is begun immediately.

Treatment of hypothermia
The person should be insulated from further heat loss both above and below the body, and sheltered from the cold environment. Immediate removal to a warm environment is the ideal but the sharing another person's body heat in a sleeping bag is sometimes the only practicable method of rewarming.

Advice for travellers
In conditions where air temperature may fluctuate suddenly from warm to cold, carry additional insulating clothing, hats and gloves, and layer them on as soon as the temperature begins to fall. Be aware of the wind-chill factor, which can increase cold effects on the body. In extreme cold it is important to operate a 'buddy system' in which travellers look out for signs of illness in each other.

Cold injury to skin
Frostbite occurs when peripheral circulation is reduced in response to cold conditions; ice crystals form within cells causing tissue damage and, in severe cases, gangrene of the extremities. Affected tissue has a pale appearance and a cold and dead feeling to the touch. Frostnip is a less severe form of cold injury in which tissues do not undergo necrosis.

Treatment of frostbite
Affected areas may be rewarmed by immersion in water at, or just above, body temperature. If a foot is affected and the victim needs to be evacuated, it is better to allow walking on the frozen tissue before warming, as less damage will be sustained. Refreezing and thawing must be avoided as this causes further damage, and the use of vasodilator drugs and alcohol is contraindicated. As rewarming occurs, the tissues become red, swollen and very painful with blistering. Apparently dead tissue should not be treated radically in the field by debridement or amputation, as recovery may be greater than first appearances suggest.

Pre-travel consultation
- Advise adequate thermal and loose clothing be worn, as well as insulated footwear.
- Check for medical conditions, such as hypothyroidism, which may impair temperature regulation in cold conditions.
- Check medication, as drugs may impair temperature control.

High-altitude travel

Altitude sickness, often known as acute mountain sickness (AMS), can affect people travelling above 4,000m. Age per se is not a determining factor in the causation of AMS. A study of trekkers in Nepal showed no association between age or gender and the incidence of AMS. The presence of pre-existing heart or lung disease does not appear to increase the risk, nor does the decreased sensitivity of the hypoxic ventilatory response found in older people.[19]

On initial ascent to high altitude there is an increase in pulmonary ventilation, leading to hypocapnia and respiratory alkalosis, which is compensated for by increased renal excretion of bicarbonate and a bicarbonate diuresis. A rise in heart rate also occurs. The body can acclimatise to lower atmospheric pressure and the heart rate gradually reduces again as acclimatisation occurs at moderate altitude. Over a longer period, erythropoietin secretion increases, leading to increased red blood-cell production and a consequent raised haemoglobin concentration and haematocrit. This, in turn, leads to increased blood viscosity and an increased tendency towards thrombosis.[20]

Symptoms
The main symptoms and signs of AMS are:
- headache
- nausea
- vomiting
- fatigue
- loss of appetite
- dizziness
- sleep disturbance.

Acclimatisation can be assisted by the following:

Gradual slow ascent The net height gain in height from one sleeping place to the next sleeping place should be no more than 300m (1,000ft) per day. A few individuals may encounter problems even at this rate of ascent. The appropriate rate of ascent for most members of a group may produce symptoms in a minority of equally fit and healthy people in a group. When flying into a high-altitude airport, symptoms may also occur because, in these circumstances, there is no time for acclimatisation to occur, although it will begin after arrival.

Avoiding over-exertion Over-exertion is known to increase the chance of developing altitude problems. A slow and steady pace is best.

Adequate fluid intake Dehydration may increase the chance of developing altitude problems, although supportive evidence is weak. Fluid loss increases at higher altitudes, partly because of sweating due to exertion and because of evaporation from the mouth, throat and lungs due to the drier air; it is important to avoid dehydration by drinking plenty of water. Tea, coffee and alcohol are diuretics and make the body lose more water than it gains from them.

Acetazolamide (Diamox) The use of acetazolamide (Diamox) has been shown in research studies to improve the body's uptake of oxygen by adjusting the body chemistry and to help either prevent or treat altitude symptoms. It treats the cause of the problem and does not simply mask its symptoms.

Acetazolamide is a carbonic anhydrase inhibitor, which causes the kidney to increase excretion of bicarbonate ions, causing metabolic acidosis. To compensate for this, pulmonary ventilation is increased, increasing excretion of carbonic acid (H_2CO_3, i.e. H_2O+CO_2) via the lungs. Oxygen uptake in the lungs is increased, thereby reducing hypoxia. For prevention, a dose of 125–250mg twice a day, starting 1–2 days before reaching 3,000m is recommended. A higher dose is used for treatment of established symptoms.[21,22]

Acetazolamide is prescribed off-licence for AMS. It often causes tingling in the hands, is also a mild diuretic, and care should be taken to ensure an adequate fluid intake. People with a drug sensitivity to sulfa drugs should not take acetazolamide.[23]

Advice for travellers to high altitude
- Ensure ascent is gradual and slow.
- Avoid overexertion.
- Maintain adequate fluid intake.
- Take acetazolamide 125–250mg twice a day.
- If trekking and climbing at high altitude, endeavour to sleep at low altitude.

Treatment of AMS
- Advise the tour/expedition leader or doctor of the suspected problem.
- Rest at the same altitude, avoiding any unnecessary exertion, and do not ascend further until symptoms have improved.
- Go down to a lower altitude, preferably at least 300m, if symptoms do not improve or if become worse.
- Take acetazolamide, 250mg two or three times a day.

Other medical problems
Mountain and trekking activities involve increased levels of exertion, which may exacerbate pre-existing cardiac or respiratory problems. Many older people have musculoskeletal problems such as osteoarthritis of the knees or hips, or foot problems such as bunions, which may be exacerbated by trekking. Foot care is especially important for people with diabetes. Travel sickness will afflict the

predisposed for many treks or climbs. Safaris may involve long arduous access routes along winding, twisting and steep roads for many hours and days, which will result in travel sickness even in those normally immune to this.

Pre-travel health consultation

- Ensure traveller has a reasonable level of physical fitness, e.g. the ability to walk for several hours per day carrying a rucksack.
- Ensure that clothing, footwear and other equipment are comfortable and suitable for the activity involved.
- Advise of suitable rate of ascent to avoid developing AMS.
- Check that pre-existing medical conditions are stable and controlled, and that all necessary medication is carried, with additional spares in case of loss or damage.
- Ensure traveller carries an emergency medical kit to cover exacerbations of pre-existing medical conditions and to cater for conditions likely to arise during the trip, such as foot and musculoskeletal problems, diarrhoea and minor injuries.
- Ensure that adequate travel and medical insurance has been taken out.

Advice for trekkers and expeditioners

- Organise a pre-travel health consultation.
- Use appropriate prophylactics for altitude and travel sickness.
- Wear comfortable, trekking shoes or boots that have a good tread on the soles; ensure they have been broken in.
- Use two trekking poles to help reduce stress on lower-limb joints. Adjust their length so on level ground the elbow is flexed to 90° when the hand grip is held with the poles vertical. Backpacks should have a padded waist strap, with the shoulder straps adjusted so weight is distributed between them and the waist strap, with an additional strap linking the two shoulder straps adjusted to reduce tension and dragging on the shoulders.
- Wear layered clothing that can be removed or added to, according to the conditions. The inner layer should be of a material that draws sweat away from the skin and the outermost layer should be of a breathable, waterproof and windproof material.
- A good four-season sleeping bag is essential, as nights can be very cold, whether camping or staying in lodges.
- Apply an effective sunscreen and wear UV light-absorbing sunglasses with side panels in the presence of snow.
- Maintain a high fluid intake of purified or bottled water. A useful guide to a good state of hydration is the passage of pale-coloured urine.

- Buy adequate health insurance covering evacuation and repatriation. In Nepal the cost of a helicopter evacuation can be £1,700 per hour;[24] the alternative evacuation mode is on the back of porter, mule or yak, which may result in exacerbation of the medical condition or injury.
- Carry a first aid kit (see *Appendix*).
- Be aware of potential hazards of drowning and hypothermia.
- Use reputable providers of water activities with adequate safety standards.
- Use suitable protective clothing such as wet or dry suits and thermal underwear.

Conclusion

Trauma, infection and health incident are potential hazards for the older adventurer, and emergency healthcare, casualty evacuation and repatriation need to be considered. Pre-travel preparations must anticipate these health hazards and seek to minimise their impact with advice and prophylaxis. Older people can adventure to high and inaccessible places, and indulge in active sporting activities formerly considered the domain of the young, and return in good health. They should, however, be aware of the health risks involved and the potential emergency aid, evacuation and repatriation problems likely to arise if they become ill or have an accident while indulging in these projects. The travel health professional has a major pre-travel management role to play to ensure a healthy outcome.

References

1 http://www.statistics.gov.uk. Accessed 16.4.12
2 Strobl H. Brehm W. Tittlbach S, 2010 Physical activity during the transition period between occupation and retirement.. Zeitschrift fur Gerontologie und Geriatrie. 43(5):297-302,
3 Sieverdes JC. Sui X. Lee DC et al Physical activity,cardiorespiratory fitness and the incidence of type 2 diabetes in a prospective study of men. 2010. British Journal of Sports Medicine. 44(4):238-44,
4 Apor P. Radi A. Orvosi Hetilap. Master sportsmen. Health status and life expectancies of physically active elderly. 2010 151(3):110-3,
5 McIntosh I Maintaining health in the older traveller. 2003 Ger. Med. 33 9 51-7
6 Melrose Accidental trauma and the vacationer 2011 Brit Global Trav Health Assoc J.18 3-5
7 McIntosh I Winter travel hazards for the elderly.2001 Ger Med. 31 18.25
8 McIntosh I Travel and Trauma 1997 Travel Med. Internat. 15.48-51
9 Melrose A Emergency aid, evacuation and repatriation 2011.Brit Trav Health Assoc J 1726-8
10 Schols JM. De Groot CP. van der Cammen TJ.Preventing and treating dehydration in the elderly during periods of illness and warm weather. 2009Journal of Nutrition, Health & Aging. 13(2):150-7
11 Nelson NG. Collins CL. Comstock RD. Exertional heat-related injuries treated in emergency departments in the U.S., 1997-2006. 201. Amer J Prev Med. 40(1):54-60, 2011
12 McLafferty E Prevention and management of hyperthermia during a heatwave.2010. Nursing

Older People. 22(7):23-7,
13 McDermott BP. Casa DJ. Ganio MS Acute whole-body cooling for exercise-induced hyperthermia: a systematic review.. Lopez RM. Yeargin SW. Armstrong LE. Maresh CM. Journal of Athletic Training. 44(1):84-93, 2009 Jan-Feb.
14 Green H. Gilbert J. James R. Byard RW An analyisis of factors contributing to a series of deaths caused by exposure to high environmental temperatures. 2001 Am J Forensic Med & Path. 22(2):196-9,
15 Management of water incidents: drowning and hypothermia. Dean R. Mulligan J. Nursing Standard. 24(7):35-9, 2009 Oct 21-27
16 McLafferty E. Farley A. Hendry C. , 2009 Prevention of hypothermia. Nursing older people. 21(4):34-8
17 DeGroot DW. Havenith G. Kenney WL Responses to mild cold stress are predicted by different individual characteristics in young and older subjects. 2006 Dec. J Appl Physiol. 101(6):1607-15,
18 Wenzel V. Management of accidental hypothermia].. 2007 Anaesthesist. 56(8):805-11, 18. Hohlrieder M. Kaufmann M. Moritz M Environmental cold-induced injury. 2007. Surgical Clinics of North America. 87(1):247-67, viii,
19 How do older persons tolerate moderate altitude?. Roach RC. Houston CS. Hogigman B et al. West J Med. 162: 32-6 1995
20 Ventilatory sensitivity to CO_2 in hyperoxia and hypoxia in older humans. Poulin MJ. Cunningham DA. Paterson DH et al. J Appl Physiol. 75:2209-16, 1993
21 McIntosh I Prescott R Acetazolamide in prevention of acute mountain sickness. 1986 J. Int. Med. Research. 14(5) 285-7
22 Kerr A Prescott R McIntosh I Acetazolamide in prevention of acute mountain sickness –a double blind cross-over study. 1981 Brit. Med. J. 283. 811-13
23 Townend M. 2012 Travel and Health in Older people.In chap 14 Fast Print Pub. Peterborough
24 www.visit-nepal.com/helicopter-tour-nepal.htm.

Appendix

TRAVELLER FIRST AID KIT RECOMMENDATIONS

Medical kit
- **Thermometer**
- **First aid dressings** gauze squares, non-adherent dressing, bandage, fabric plasters, adhesive tape
- **scissors, tweezers** and **safety pins**
- **antiseptic wipes, tincture of iodine,** for cuts and grazes
- **calamine lotion, hydrocortisone cream** for sunburn, skin irritation
- **paracetamol, aspirin, ibuprofen** painkillers, anti-inflammatories
- **promethazine, hyoscine** for motion sickness
- **oil of cloves** and **filler paste** for dental emergency
- **dioralyte** or **rehydrate sachets** oral rehydration agents

- **miconazole cream/powder** antifungal preparation
- **laxative tablets** for constipation
- **antihistamine tablets antiallergic agent**
- **iodine-based water sterilisation tablets**
- **insect repellent** e.g. DEET
- **personal medication** list of prescriptions, doses and a doctor's letter confirming ownership

Reminders
- Have a dental check before you go.
- Visit a travel health clinic for advice.
- Wear loose, open-weave clothing in hot countries abroad.
- Wear layered thermal clothing in very cold countries.
- Treat minor scratches, cuts and bites promptly.
- Take food and water precautions, and know how to treat travellers' diarrhoea.
- Take antimalaria pills and precautions.
- Carry a first aid kit.

Reading list

Health Advice for Travellers. (2012) Department of Health.
Available free from post offices. Contains basic travel health advice, recommended immunisations, information about travel insurance and entitlement to medical treatment at reduced cost for nationals of the European Community.

Dawood, R (2012) *Travellers Health.* Oxford: Oxford University Press.
In-depth information about a wide variety of travel health topics

Howarth, J (1995) *Bugs, Bites and Bowels.* London: Cadogan Books Ltd.

McIntosh I. (1996) *Pitstops and Pitfalls – A Health Guide for Older Travellers.* Dinton: Quay Books, Mark Allan Publishing. ISBN 1 85642 1163

12

Medications

Older travellers are likely to have age-related medical conditions, pre-existing disease and be on medications. Many will be taking routine drugs, often taking several pills per day, and others will be self-prescribing with over the counter (OTC) medicines. The addition of prophylactics for malaria, travel sickness, travellers' diarrhoea and altitude sickness may be contraindicated or bring adverse interaction. The ageing process with impairment of hepatic and renal function may interfere with drug uptake and excretion, thereby diminishing drug efficacy and clearance. The impact of the local environment and travel-related infection – with possible dehydration and electrolytic and metabolic disturbance – may also have an impact on drug absorption. Routine and OTC medications should be reviewed at pre-travel consultation and particularly when prophylactics are being recommended.

This chapter considers prescribed and OTC prescriptions, self-treatment, overseas medication purchase, cross-border carriage of drugs, and the travel first aid kit. Malaria chemoprophylaxis and immunisation are covered in Chapter 7.

Differences in drug effects in older travellers

Pharmacokinetic effects Pharmacokinetics involve the way a drug is absorbed and distributed by the body. In older people, there are changes in bodily drug response due to general declining homeostatic mechanisms; absorption, distribution, metabolism and excretion require consideration. Absorption of drugs by the gastrointestinal tract is not particularly impaired in older poeple, but gastric pH tends to be slightly higher in older people, which may make them more prone to travellers' diarrhoea. Lowered immunity to infection also makes them slightly more vulnerable to diarrhoea, with the risk of electrolyte and metabolic disturbance upsetting absorption. Conditions such as heart failure can potentially reduce blood flow to the gastrointestinal system and also affect absorption. Drugs with anticholinergic properties, such as hyoscine, used as an antiemetic in travel sickness, may also potentially reduce drug absorption.

Body distribution of drugs in older people can be affected by the higher proportion of fat and lower proportion of water in body composition. Reduced drug-binding to plasma albumin can markedly alter the pharmacokinetics of certain drugs and can contribute to changes in drug response, for instance; drugs tend to cross the blood barrier more readily. Any drug with potential central nervous system side-effects may be more likely to cause an undesirable outcome.

Ageing can also reduce response in target tissues due to a decline in regional blood flow, resulting from a fall in cardiac output. A reduction in blood flow in older people is the major factor contributing to a lower ability to metabolise certain drugs by the liver, leading to an increased half-life. Some drugs are affected by decline in liver enzyme activity, sometimes apparent as a reduced first-pass effect. A decline in renal function brings impaired drug excretion with advanced years, manifested by an increased half-life of certain drugs, most apparent with extreme renal dysfunction, or failure. Ten per cent of people aged over 70 years will have some measure of renal dysfunction and be in category 3A of chronic renal disease.[1-3]

Pharmacodynamic effects These are biochemical and physiological effects, and older people may respond differently compared with younger people due to a decline in homeostatic mechanisms. They can be more at risk to the adverse effects of drugs – for instance, proneness to postural hypertension, exacerbated by prescribing medications that can lower blood pressure. Another example would be the older person taking an ACE inhibitor and diuretic, who contracts prolonged travellers' diarrhoea; in such a situation there is a greater potential for serious fluid and electrolyte disturbances.[1]

Polypharmacy The daily ingestion of many different pills is common in older people, so the medication history should always be sought at pre-travel consultation (*see Chapter 2*). The taking of many routine drugs makes interaction more likely. If any drug has potential CNS side-effects, further medication should be prescribed with caution. Pre-travel, the question should be whether prophylactic medication is likely to interact with that taken for chronic conditions.

Drug carriage and purchase abroad

The carriage of personal medications across international borders can meet legal obsatcles. This particularly applies to designated narcotic or psychotropic drugs, which encompasses any medicine that has an effect on the central nervous system, especially if it has abuse potential. Carrying a prescription or note from the prescriber, and keeping medication in original packaging, is advocated but some countries, e.g. United Arab Emirates, ban a range of medicines that are widely acceptable elsewhere, such as conventional antihistamines. It is wise for travellers to acquire medications before leaving home rather than relying on a local supply, even if buying abroad would be much cheaper. In some African and Asian countries, up to 60% of medicines are counterfeit and many locally produced ones are of poor quality.[4]

Travel-related prescription drugs

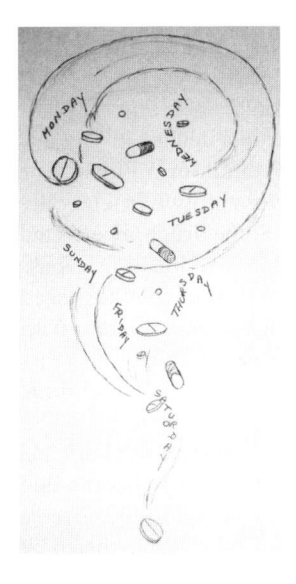

Contraindications Pharmacokinetics and dynamics and should be considered prior to each prescription recommendation by the travel-clinic health professional. Drug–drug interactions, ageing system effects, polypharmacy, the effects of pre-existing conditions such as cardiovascular problems and diabetes and thrombotic tendencies, must be considered.

Acetazolamide Acetazolamide has been associated with a higher risk of metabolic acidosis in older people, those with diabetes and in those with reduced renal function. The clearance of acetazolamide is reduced in the presence of a poor renal function resulting in higher blood levels. There is limited data on the occasional use of low-dose acetazolamide in older people for preventing acute mountain sickness (AMS) but it should be prescribed with caution in such individuals.

Acetazolamide, when used in the treatment of glaucoma, can produce metabolic acidosis of clinical significance, especially in older people and in those with other medical problems. There is also evidence that older people have higher blood concentrations of acetazolamide. The *British National Formulary* recommended dose is 250–1,000mg daily, and many patients take a dosage towards the higher end of that range. There is little evidence on the beneficial effects of low-dose acetazolamide (e.g. 125mg bd) as some authorities recommend for the prophylaxis of AMS. In one study of older glaucoma patients, 75% had blood concentrations increased by a factor of two, which would equate to a dose of 250mg bd. Extrapolating this to the use of the drug for AMS, it seems likely that older people taking it for AMS are indeed at risk of significant metabolic acidosis.[5-8]

Analgesics Painkillers such as codeine, tramadol, non-steroidal anti-inflammatory drugs (NSAIDs) and OTC narcotic analgesics may also cause constipation and are best avoided when carrying medicines across international borders. NSAID-induced peptic ulceration is more likely in older people, as well as the more recently recognised risks of the cardiovascular and renal adverse effects associated with NSAIDs. For occasional use for acute pain, ibuprofen can be carried in the medical kit, with paracetamol.

Antihistamines Hyoscine-containing products for motion sickness are best avoided in older people, due to the anticholinergic side-effects resulting in potential cardiovascular or other problems, such as urine retention. Hyoscine patches in particular seem to be associated with a high incidence of confusion in older people. Hyoscine may also potentially reduce drug absorption of other drugs and routine medications. There is also some evidence of an increased risk of death and mental decline when the over-65s take a combination of drugs with anticholinergic properties, including antihistamines such as chlorpheniramine.

Antimalarials Some antimalarials appear to lower insulin requirements in patients with diabetes and can lead to hypoglycaemia in those treated with insulin or oral hypoglycaemics such as glibenclamide. However, the evidence only relates to treatment doses of such antimalarials rather than prophylaxis. Limited case reports of an interaction between warfarin and proguanil and atovaquone/proguanil resulting in a raised INR have been reported and a similar effect has been observed with doxycycline. The INR of patients taking warfarin after commencing any additional medication, such as antimalarials, should be monitored. The INR should be self-monitored in these people if they will be abroad for longer than 2–3 weeks due to changes in diet and difference in time zones.

Chloroquine has been reported to cause a rise in digoxin levels, but no clinically important interactions have been observed. Chloroquine and mefloquine can potentially increase the risk of arrhythmias if given with other antiarrhythmic agents such as amiodarine. Use of cardioactive drugs, including beta-blockers, antiarrythmics and calcium antagonsists, in combination with mefloquine should be avoided due to the risk of prolonging the corrected QT interval and inducing other cardiac adverse effects. Chloroquine absorption is reduced by antacids based on magnesium, aluminium or carbonate compounds. Caution is recommended when prescribing chloroquine in the presence of renal impairment, but no dosage adjustment is necessary in prophylactic use. As older people are 10 times more likely to die from malaria than young people, special attention is needed to ensure the efficacy of their antimalarial prophylactic.[9]

Anti-motility agents Older people may be more prone to fluid and electrolyte disturbances resulting from a moderate to severe bout of travellers' diarrhoea; the use of oral rehydration therapy and antidiarrhoeal drugs such as loperamide can be justified to control the symptoms. Prolonged therapy may result in constipation however.[1] Travellers often resort to OTC remedies to combat diarrhoea and kaolin products can constipate. Others use probiotics such as bimuno before departure and there is evidence of benefit without adverse effects.

Tetracyclines such as doxyclyine can have their absorption and efficacy greatly reduced by coadministration with antacids based on magnesium, aluminium or carbonate compounds. Quinapril – an ACE inhibitor – contains a magnesium carbonate in its formulation sufficient to cause a significant fall in the absorption of teracyclines. Tetracyclines, such as doxycycline, can cause oesophageal damage if not swallowed when sitting upright and ingesting with plenty of water – a possible problem for those who have difficulty swallowing tablets or are prone to oesophageal reflux.

Increased hypoglycaemia may develop in patients with diabetes who are taking glibenclamide when prescribed ciprofloxacin, particularly in older people.

Quinolones should not be prescribed for them or for older patients on chronic NSAID treatment, as there is a convulsion risk. Tendonitis and tendon rupture have been reported to occur within 48 hours of commencing ciprofloxacin treatment, with risk greater in those over 60 years of age. Usually only a single dose is needed to treat travellers' diarrhoea, but treatment should be discontinued at the first sign of tendon pain. Azthromycin and the macrolides can cause a rise in digoxin levels so the combination is best avoided.[10]

Proton pump inhibitors (PPIs) and H_2 antagonists This group of medicines are commonly used by older people for self-treatment of dyspeptic symptoms as well as being prescribed for peptic ulcer disease. PPIs in particular lower the gastric pH sufficiently to allow a greater burden of potentially pathogenic organisms to reach the gastrointestinal tract and result in a higher incidence of severe forms of travellers' diarrhoea – a particular problem in older people. Those travellers who require continuous PPI therapy might be considered for antibiotic chemoprophylaxis to offer protection against gastrointestinal infections.[10]

Compliance A major problem with older travellers is that they fail to take their diuretics on days of travel because of the fear of limited toilet access en route; alternatively they may pack medications in hold luggage and face drug-access problems when there is travel delay. Air and coach travellers frequently then go into heart failure in the absence of routine medication. The need to continue routine medication and pack medication in hand luggage has to be emphasised. Adherence to medication may be affected due to a change and disruption in routines while away from home and individuals (e.g. people with diabetes) may need advice on time-zone adjustments (*see Chapter 9*).[10,11]

References

1 Goodyer L Travel medications and the older traveller 2011 J Brit Global Trav Health Assoc 18. 12-14

2 Baxter K, Stockley S Drug Interactions 9th Edition Pharmaceutical Press, London 2010Sweatman S

3 Martindale (Ed): The complete drug reference 37th Edition. Pharmaceutical Press. London 2011

4 Bygbjerg IC. Fake malaria drugs.Ugeskr Laeger. 2009 Mar 2;171(10):815-7.

5 Fukuhara Y, Kaneko T, Orita Y. Nippon Rinsho Japanese 1992Metabolic acidosis induced by acetazolamide. J. Clinical Medicine. 50 (9):2231-6,

6 Sporn A, Scothorn DM, Terry JE. 1991Acetazolamide blood concentrations are excessive in the elderly.: Propensity for acidosis and relationship to renal function. J .American Optometric Association. 62(12):934-7,

7 Chapron DJ, Gomolin IH, Sweeney KR metabolic acidosis induced by acetazolamide. Not a rare complication. J. Clinical Pharmacology. 29(4):348-53, 1989Signifiant

8 Heller I, Halevy J, Cohen S, Theodor E1985 Reply Forward. Archives of Int.Med.145 (10):1815-7,

9 Checkley AM, Smith A , Smith V, Risk factors for mortality from imported falciparum malaria in the United Kingdom over 20 years: an observational study. Brit Med J 2012;344:e2116

10 Goodyer L. 2012 Travel and Health in the Elderly Chap 11. Fastprint Pub. Peterborough
11 Kassianos G. 2012 Travel and Health in the Elderly Chap 10. Fastprint Pub. Peterborough

Medication advice for older travellers

- Have routine medication reviewed by a GP if travelling to exotic destinations.
- Remember, routine medicines can sometimes interact with antimalarials.
- Always carry medicines in hand luggage.
- Carry a list of routine medicines.
- Carry a note, and a back-up letter, from your doctor confirming the need for medicines.
- Keep medicines in cool, dry place while abroad.
- Acquire doctor confirmation of the need to carry inhalers, syringes and needles.
- Be wary of taking analgesics across borders and carry authenticated prescriptions for them.
- Carry a yellow fever waiver certificate.

13

Travel Health Insurance and Medical Tourism

Insuring for good healthcare abroad

International translocation without the protection of health insurance protection may threaten the life of the traveller. Many older people in ignorance of risk, or cost saving, choose to globetrot without a travel health insurance package. Older people who are adventurous are at high risk of trauma or ill health while abroad, with cardiac mishap and road traffic accident being the most reported health events affecting senior tourists.

Many fail to acquire adequate health protection and others purchase inadequate cover, do not read exclusive small print in the policy or void it by concealing current infirmity. The number of uninsured or poorly insured older people is likely to increase considerably in future as more insurers refuse to offer policies to older travellers. Many companies have a cut-off age of 65 years, others 70 and few will consider those over 80 years of age. Specialist companies still insure this cohort but the number decreases every year. It is estimated that one in four people go abroad without health insurance. Few people arrange cover for trips of less than five days.[1]

Age Concern believes people over 65 make 5.5 million trips abroad annually, but they are finding it harder to acquire appropriate travel health insurance protection because of upper-age constraints imposed by one in nine insurance providers. Three-quarters will reject applications for those over 75.[1] Four out of five insurance claims relate to medical problems and, although older people do not have more claims, they often cost the insurer more as they are hospitalised more often and for longer.

In the absence of insurance protection, medical and nursing care can be prohibitively expensive:

- A holidaymaker who suffers a heart attack in Greece could face hospital bills of £6,000–7,000.
- Repatriation by air ambulance from Spain could cost £10.000.
- In the United States, treatment for an arm fracture can cost towards £4,000. and a serious accident involving an air ambulance can cost £50,000. Some clinics will only perform operations if they are certain a patient is insured or can meet the bill. Those without insurance could find themselves with medical bills of several thousand pounds, or being refused emergency surgery following injury. Repatriation by air ambulance from Florida to Britain costs about £30,000, with a similar fee for heart surgery there.
- Hospital costs in popular destinations in France, Greece or Spain have ward occupancy rates ranging from £300 daily excluding medical care. Daily ward rates in the United States cost up to £10,000 in intensive care. Some travel health professionals do not perceive it within their role to advise on travel health insurance, but such advice may prove of greater health benefit to the unfortunate ill traveller than recommendations on vaccines and prophylaxis. The adverse impact of a health emergency while the traveller is abroad, especially in developing countries and remote places, may have more dire and immediate consequences than exposure to infection.

Even the best policy will not necessarily provide optimal healthcare. Provision of service by the travel health insurance industry is dependent upon the quality of resources and health professionals, and the evacuation and repatriation possibilities at the venue. Absence or inadequacy of facilities may defeat the service provider, but the insured is usually assured of the best available care, irrespective of cost. The uninsured, at a time of maximal vulnerability, has to cobble together whatever care is attainable, often at prohibitive cost, in a situation where geographic, communication and language difficulties may be intimidating.

Case history

A 62 year old man was recently repatriated from southern Greece. He had developed chest pain 17 days previously, was hospitalised, submitted to angiography, followed by triple bypass surgery and within 10 days was ready to return home by air. A similarly aged patient in the next bed had an almost identical history, but was anxiously worrying about future medical care and home return. He had an ECG result that confirmed myocardial infarction but had only been able to have a cardiogram the previous day, which confirmed the need for cardiac surgery. This was too expensive for him to afford and, denied access to a flight by the airline, he was contemplating a long road and rail transfer back to the UK, where he would join the long waiting list for surgical intervention.

The only difference between the two patients was that the first had bought travel health insurance and the second had not purchased any emergency protection. The latter was dependent upon reciprocal EC arrangements for emergency medical and nursing support and was now facing bills for hospital care. The former had access to the benefits of prompt insurance company attention, immediate medical and surgical intervention and was assured of a speedy repatriation.

The travel health professional – be it nurse, GP or consultant – is uniquely placed to offer unbiased advice about insurance protection and should accept the task as part of every pre-travel consultation. Attention should be drawn to the need for insurance, contingency evacuation, repatriation, financial reimbursement and the requirement to read the small print, check for exclusions and provide information to insurers of pre-existing illness. Many older people travel believing health protection is in place, but are unaware of the exclusions; this can leave them unprotected for the condition(s) most likely to occur while overseas. Others fail to meet contractual obligations to inform the insurer of chronic or existing disorder, which abrogates the policy and, in an emergency, they find cover is not in place or is inadequate.

The travel insurance industry has become more sensitive to higher-risk travellers. Older travellers may now find they cannot acquire cover or can only do so at added cost. Annual travel insurance has been largely withdrawn for older people aged 90 or over. People who have previously travelled extensively, despite past history of cancer and major cardiac problems, now find themselves with hefty extra premium demands, if they can acquire protection at all. Insurance seekers now face a barrage of questions on lifelong health status and current health problems.

The travel health professional should identify the need to advise potential travellers on the hazards of travel without insurance cover. Most travellers are unaware of the inadequacies or expense of healthcare in developing and affluent countries overseas. They need information on health provision facilities and emergency care, evacuation and repatriation possibilities during their travels, to allow them to make an informed choice about the purchase of insurance cover. They should be encouraged to pay additional premiums for peace of mind and health safety, or be made aware that they travel dangerously if they proceed unprotected.

Policy exclusions often remove activities that some tourists will undertake while abroad on vacation. Sailing in small boats, waterway cruising, paragliding, hill climbing, rafting, small aeroplane and helicopter riding, may all be excluded. Older people often appear to cast discretion aside when on vacation and indulge in pursuits they would never contemplate in the home environment. Cover may be absent at the very time when misadventure is most likely to overtake the tourist.

The individual has a contractual requirement to advise the insurance company of actual mishap, medical emergency and potential use of services, although often this is a major task when communications between the traveller's location and the UK may be tenuous.

Case history
A 72 year old man died suddenly in Tibet. Direct communication between the British insurer and the involved family could only be established via a fellow traveller's satellite telephone link with the United States through an associated company. Repatriation of the body was beset with difficulties and was only achieved by land transfer via Nepal. Failure to provide the company promptly with a report may negate the contract and expose the patient to substantial costs they cannot meet. It also deprives the support of their expertise and organisation at a time of greatest need.

Older global travellers are visiting ever more exotic, developing and remote countries where a European Health Insurance Card (EHIC) and healthcare reciprocity with the UK does not apply. This fact and insurer resistance to provide cover, higher premiums, rigid adherence to contractual obligations, will mean that more people will travel without adequate health protection. In an emergency, some will find this seriously affects treatment, rehabilitation and repatriation and they will not receive optimal care in when in urgent need.

All travel health professionals should counsel intending older travellers on the benefits of travel health protection and the adequacies of health facilities at their overseas destination (*see Chapter 14*). Health professionals are uniquely placed to offer unbiased advice about insurance protection and should accept the task as part of every potential or pre-travel consultation. Once clinical fitness for travel has been determined, professional attention should concentrate on insurance cover.

Advice should embrace:
- emergency aid
- evacuation to hospital
- quality of care
- repatriation
- small print in the insurance policy apropos exclusions to cover, terms for pre-existing illness.

Pre-existing conditions and exclusions

Pre-existing conditions can be a catch-all phrase and provide some companies with the opportunity to refuse claims. However, previously declared medical conditions can be accepted with an extra premium. While most ailments will be insurable, illnesses such as heart disease or cancer are likely to be excluded from standard policies. When the insurer contacts the family doctor for personal medical history, the claimant's failure to declare any past illness, or one occurring since inception of the policy, may result in rejection of the claim on the grounds of failure to meet disclosure requirements.

Older holidaymakers are most likely to suffer from disputes about what insurers call "non-disclosure of pre-existing condition" because they are most likely to have suffered relevant illnesses earlier in their lives. The insurer's premise is that they have not had the opportunity to assess risk and might have produced a contract with different terms, if they had known about the existing condition. Few people also realise that inebriation at the time of medical mishap may also negate a later insurance claim.[2]

Case history
An older gentleman had a myocardial infarction on a ship cruising off Greenland and had to be helicoptered to hospital in mainland Europe. The bill was expected to be £30,000 and he left behind a disabled wife who had to be disembarked at the first port of call and flown home at additional cost. Insurance covered his care but not his wife's – an expensive oversight.

All travel health professionals should counsel intending travellers on the benefits and weaknesses of travel health protection and the adequacies of overseas health facilities. The Association of British Insurers urges travellers to carry insurance documents at all times so doctors treating them will know they are insured. The Foreign and

Commonwealth Office (FCO) has warned holidaymakers to be better prepared when taking breaks abroad. They recommend carrying proof of cover on the person, with emergency contact and medical assistance numbers for insurance companies.

Case history
A woman tourist collapsed at the entrance to the Oregon State Legislative building. An onlooker phoned emergency services and a fire engine arrived within minutes. The paramedic crew ascertained she was still living, their second check was to seek and find her insurance document. This was perused. She was promptly placed on a trolley and sped off to a private unit, examined and warded within an hour. In its absence she would have been taken to the local state hospital with a very lengthy wait for attention, with admission being problematic.

Older people should consider travel insurance as a necessity not an option. The travel insurance industry has however toughened its approach to at-risk travellers, particularly older travellers and the very old. This process may now require considerable endeavour and, for some, this is a disincentive to act. Older travellers may now find they cannot find cover or can only do so at considerable added cost. Annual cover has been largely withdrawn for the very old. Patients who have travelled extensively despite a past clinical history now face premium loading, if they can acquire protection at all.

The number of insurers catering for older people has fallen dramatically. An online search a year ago would have provided many sources but few are now displayed and they prove selective. Potential insurance buyers must answer many questions on lifelong health status and current health problems, and may be excluded on initial screening. Any inaccuracy in disclosure at this time or once the cover is in place may void a later claim. Those having difficulties in acquiring cover should insist on bypassing the initial screener and accessing the insurer's clinical appraiser who may have a more realistic stance and be prepared to take on the risk.

Health insurance protection Travel health insurance doesn't cover every eventuality but only closely defined levels of risk. As insurance premiums have fallen in a competitive market, insurers now adhere to policy wording. For example, pre-existing medical conditions of relatives are common exclusions in travel policies. The death of a close relative from a pre-existing medical condition would not be covered under the terms and conditions of many policies, if the condition was known to the customer prior to the commencement of the period of insurance. There is usually no cover in place for cancelling or curtailing a holiday on account of a relative's illness or death if the relative has a terminal condition, or has been to a hospital (including outpatient consultations), or has taken prescribed medication within 90 days of the departure date. Holidaymakers should also remember that if they want to travel for more than 45 days, they must always confirm with their insurer before assuming they are covered.

Case history
A patient returned from a holiday in Morocco having paid a considerable medical care bill, when he developed severe chest pain for which he was hospitalised. He believed his health insurance company would foot the bill but the small print specifically excluded ill health of cardiac cause after he had suffered a previous coronary artery. He had failed to read the insurance document before the premium was paid – an expensive mistake, although not an uncommon one to be made by members of the travelling public.

Insurance provision

The cost of annual, worldwide, multi-trip travel insurance for a couple over the age of 75 can range from £184 to £325 from two insurers. A new service offered to some store credit-card holders provides annual, worldwide, multi-trip travel insurance for couples up to the age of 80 for £120 a year and includes travel to the United States, Canada and the Caribbean. The small print reveals comprehensive levels of cover, including £10m medical expenses and £2m personal liability cover.

A British insurance company has claimed to be the first to offer cover against deep vein thrombosis (DVT). PJ Hayman, an online insurance provider, offers emergency medical assistance cover for travellers contracting DVT, and £10,000 should death occur during the trip or within 72 hours of the policyholder arriving home.

Most cheap policies exclude all claims – even medical claims – made as a result of war, invasion acts of foreign enemies, hostilities or warlike operations (whether war be declared or not), civil war, rebellion, terrorism, revolution, insurrection, civil commotion made in connection with those countries to which the FCO has advised people to avoid "all but essential travel".

Summary

- Older travellers are visiting more exotic, developing and remote countries where EHIC protection does not apply.
- People are booking flights and accommodation separately online (50% of holidays), bypassing the travel agent and making it more likely that many will travel uninsured.
- Insurer resistance to provide cover, higher premiums and rigid adherence to contractual obligations mean more people will travel without adequate health protection. In an emergency this will seriously affect treatment,

rehabilitation and repatriation.
- All travel health professionals should counsel intending travellers on the benefits of travel health protection and the adequacies or deficiencies of health facilities at overseas destinations.

Health insurance and repatriation

Travel insurance, like household insurance, involves underwriters, brokers, claim handlers, customer services and the potential patient. To help process claims, travel insurers have a medical unit. Manned 24 hours a day, 365 days a week by doctors, nurses and support staff, these deal with the first calls, follow up with local doctors and hospitals on a regular basis, confirm a diagnosis and contact a UK GP to ensure the individual had no relevant undeclared previous medical history. If insurance cover is provided, the medical desk assesses the need for medical care. It deals with issues such as the transfer of the client to better hospital care and repatriation to the UK. Repatriation can be non-air (road ambulance from France), scheduled or charter aircraft seats in Europe, or true air ambulance. Costs vary from several thousands to £1 million.

An escort may be required – a non-medical person/doctor/nurse as a team or individual. The accompanying doctor will travel with the patient from overseas to the home bedside. The medical team will be appropriately equipped by the insurer with defibrillators or ventilators as required. Transport is arranged to meet the aeroplane and the patient safely transferred to a pre-arranged hospital. At the point of handover to an NHS or private facility, or to home, the responsibilities of the insurance medical team cease.

Criteria for repatriation include: genuine medical necessity, poor local facilities, difficult access, cost and patient preference (where this is deemed by the insurer to be reasonable). People who rely on the protection afforded by possession of the EHIC are often unaware that it does not cover repatriation, or medical/nursing care for the return to UK.

Exclusions from insurance cover are common. They vary significantly between policies. The following are examples, but often no cover is provided if the policyholder:
- is taking continuing medication
- has had medical treatment or surgery within the last six months
- is suffering from a previously diagnosed psychiatric disorder
- has any AIDS-related complex.

Exclusions are sometimes vague and it is vital to:
- read the insurance small print
- declare past medical history
- get expert travel medical advice.

Consideration Careful thought should be given to travel location and the quality of local facilities for those with pre-existing illness.

Those with breathlessness on the ground should seek expert advice before being exposed to air flight which, despite pressurisation, is equivalent to a height of about 2,500m.

Insurers will pay what they think they need to pay – an air ambulance will not be sent out for a trivial claim and they may insist on land as opposed to air transfer, a nurse rather than a medical escort. Repatriation arrangements often take place when the patient and a supporting relative are in a vulnerable negotiating situation.

EC health protection

The EHIC allows anyone who is insured or covered by a statutory social security scheme of Switzerland and countries in the European Economic Area to receive medical treatment in another member state for free or at a reduced cost, if that treatment becomes necessary during their visit (for example, due to illness or an accident), or if they have a chronic pre-existing condition that requires care, such as kidney dialysis. The intention of the scheme is to allow people to continue their stay in a country without having to return home for medical care; as such, it does not cover people who have visited a country for the purpose of obtaining medical care, nor does it cover care, such as many types of dental treatment, which can be delayed until the visitor returns home. It only covers healthcare that is normally covered by a statutory healthcare system in the visited country, so it does not render travel insurance unnecessary. Many travellers still fail to organise EC reciprocal health protection or are unaware that it requires regular renewal.[3,4]

The EHIC has limitations. Quality of care depends upon national provision, which may be of poorer quality and resources than that provided by the NHS. It does not provide for repatriation. It does not guarantee full financial recompense for medical and hospital bills and does not cover transportation to a hospital. Private health insurance is still advisable in time of need, if only for repatriation cover. A certificate of entitlement by application through a post office, or online is required for cover to be obtained – a minor inconvenience in return for considerable emergency health support in EC countries. This protection should not be spurned and many insurance companies will only provide cover if the insured has utilised EC cover in an emergency.

A change in EC regulations means former certificates are no longer valid. New ones need to be acquired and renewed every three years. Britons still travel without basic EHIC protection. Travellers should be aware that some common tourist destinations such as Turkey and north Cyprus are not within the EC and therefore EHIC does not apply. The card is applicable in all French overseas departments (Martinique, Guadeloupe, La Réunion and French Guiana) however, as they are part of the EEA, but not in non-EEA dependent territories such as Jersey, Isle of

Man, Aruba or French Polynesia. There are agreements to use the EHIC in the Faroe Islands, Greenland, even though it is not in the EEA (www.ehic/ie).

Recommendations
- Health professional should consider it a duty to advise potential travellers on the hazards of travel without insurance cover and recommend acquisition of EHIC protection.
- Older travellers should be made aware of the inadequacies and expense of healthcare in overseas countries to be visited. They should be advised to acquire information on health provision facilities, emergency care and evacuation and repatriation possibilities during travel to permit informed choice. They travel dangerously if proceeding without insurance protection.
- Individuals should be reminded of contractual requirements to advise the insurance company immediately of mishap, medical emergency and potential use of services even when communications between the travellers location and UK may be tenuous. Failure to provide the company promptly with a report may negate the contract and deprive the policyholder of support and expertise in time of need. Failure to utilise EHIC may void the insurance claim.

Summary

- Older travellers should acquire EHIC protection and be aware of its limitations.
- Older travellers may visit more exotic, developing and remote countries where EC reciprocal health protection does not apply.
- DIY holiday arrangements, with many people booking flights and accommodation online and bypassing travel agents, increase the likelihood that people will travel without insurance.
- Insurer resistance to provide cover, higher premiums and rigid adherence to contractual obligations, mean more old people will travel without adequate health protection. In an emergency, this will seriously affect treatment, rehabilitation and repatriation.
- Older people should seek comprehensive travel health insurance cover with protection for pre-existing medical conditions and repatriation from a company offering a medical screening service.

Medical tourism

Medical tourism travel with the prime intent of seeking investigation, treatment and operative intervention abroad is a growing industry in several countries in the developing world. Affluent older people with failing systems and disabilities are attracted to medical tourism as it presents an opportunity to travel and save money. Nearly 450,000 foreigners sought medical treatment in India in 2007, with Singapore not far behind, and Thailand in the lead with over a million medical tourists. In one unrepresentative population sample, one in 20 people interviewed recently have had a medical or dental procedure outside of the UK, or are planning one. [5]

The British Medical Association has stated that thorough research is essential on quality of care and resources before a person should consider going abroad for treatment. Patients should investigate all aspects of the proposed treatment. This must include the health and safety standards of facilities and the potential impact of long-distance travel on the recovery from medication or surgery received while abroad. People with pre-existing illness should therefore satisfy themselves that adequate facilities for treatment will be available if complications arise and that the risk is justified of being out of the NHS umbrella of post-treatment care.

No global regulatory body exists to appraise quality of care provided in overseas institutions engaged in medical tourism. There is a universal body for accreditation, the International Society for Quality in Health Care (ISQua), which has members in 70 countries. MedTral New Zealand also caters for people looking for more affordable treatment abroad. The Joint Commission International (JCI) accredits hospitals, while QHA Trent, a British company, accredits and provides consultancy services for hospitals and clinics globally.

Potential patients should check the surgeon's training, patient testimonials and published adverse events, and whether they are independently verified. Some hospitals refer to overall adverse event rate. If they do thousands of eye operations and endoscopies, their adverse event rate may be very low compared with a unit doing complex major surgery. Checks need also to made on the level of English spoken and aftercare facilities One survey found that 43% of British patients travelled abroad for dental treatment, 29% for cosmetic surgery and the remainder for orthopaedic and infertility surgery.[5,6]

In 2009 more than 50,000 Britons went abroad for surgery and it is anticipated that the number will now be 75,000, according to Treatmentabroad.net, a website for medical tourists. The company provides information on hospitals, clinics and specialists worldwide. Among the more popular treatments are cosmetic surgery and dentistry, which are expensive in the UK and often may not be covered by private insurance. The cost of a cheap flight plus surgery, along with a few days of rest and recuperation, may be much cheaper than having the work done at home. Booking through an agent permits negotiation of an all-inclusive package and patients are likely to get better before, during and aftercare.

Travellers are now having surgery as an extension to a holiday or business trip. It is possible, for instance, to combine cosmetic surgery or dental treatment with a safari in South Africa, and a hip replacement or knee surgery with a trip to Thailand or India. An inclusive check-up provided by BUPA in the UK may cost over

£400; a similar well-person health check at a hospital in Bangalore, including chest x-rays, full torso ultrasound, lung function test, electrocardiogram and a battery of other blood, urine and diagnostic tests, may cost just tens of pounds. Included in the price is a consultation with a doctor to discuss any worrying findings and recommendations on health improvements. The patient is given x-rays, printouts and reports to show their GP at home. Patients should be aware however that consultants overseas will not have access to previous investigations and clinical notes available to the individual when being treated within the NHS at home. This lack of global knowledge of the patient's past clinical exposure may be disadvantageous if the patient has a complex history and chronic illness.

The FCO warns that, although medical and dental treatment abroad may be cheaper, "standards of care in some countries may not be the same as those in the UK, and emergency facilities such as intensive care may not be readily available". In some countries, there may be a risk of transmission of blood viruses such as HIV, hepatitis B and hepatitis C during medical procedures. Tattoos and body piercing should be avoided in overseas situations because of the risk of infection.

People mistakenly believe that travel insurance policies will cover elective surgery abroad, just as they cover an accidental occurrence that leads to requiring medical treatment. Conventional policies and the EHIC will not provide cover for medical costs if the individual has elected to travel abroad for care. Specialist enhanced medical insurance policies are available at an appropriate premium.

Countries involved in medical tourism

Bulgaria Some private clinics are now highly regarded in Bulgaria. Northern Europeans increasingly choose Bulgaria for 'hospital vacations' – receiving treatment at a very reasonable cost compared with Western Europe – followed by recuperation in one of Bulgaria's famous spas. Healing waters at Hissar and Bankya, are thought to bring relief to people with arthritis and rheumatism.

Croatia Medical tourism facilities are well established and often incorporate traditional spa and hydrotherapy.

Thailand The Kasikorn Research Centre reported that 1.28 million expatriates visited Thai hospitals in 2005, generating considerable revenue. Procedures were major surgery, outpatient clinic visits and annual check-ups. Bumrungrad International Hospital treated 400,000 foreign patients in 2005. It has a new 18-storey outpatient centre. Bangkok Hospital, with affiliated hospitals (like BNH Hospital, Samitivej Hospitals and branches in Pattaya and Phuket) is also a popular destination for medical tourists. The standard of treatment and technology can be high, with prices lower than in other countries providing similar quality and technology. Thailand is developing as a medical hub for patients from the United States, Europe, and the Far and Middle East.

India Medical tourism in India has been growing recently and is a popular destination for medical tourists who receive effective medical treatment at lower costs than in developed countries. India's medical tourism sector is expected to experience an annual growth rate of 30%. Estimates of the value of medical tourism to India go as high as $2 billion a year. As medical treatment costs in the developed world surge upwards, westerners consider international travel for medical care increasingly appealing. Roughly 150,000 people travel to India for low-priced healthcare procedures every year. The advantages for medical tourists include reduced costs, availability of the latest medical technologies and a growing compliance on international quality standards. Britons are less likely to face a language barrier in India.

Estimates claim treatment costs in India start at around a tenth of the price of comparable treatment in Britain. Popular Indian treatments are alternative medicine, bone-marrow transplant, cardiac bypass, eye surgery and hip replacement. India is known in particular for heart surgery, hip resurfacing and other areas of advanced medicine. The south Indian city of Chennai nets in 45% of health tourists. Some hospitals in Chennai are equipped with state-of-the-art medical equipment and costs are relatively inexpensive city compared with Mumbai and Delhi. The Indian medical tourist healthcare delivery system is striving to match international standards. Thirteen Indian hospitals have been accredited by the JCI, acknowledging standardised protocols and safety.

South Africa Standards in South African clinics are on a par with UK clinics. Prices and quality of care vary across the country. Patients travelling to South Africa should check their surgeons' qualifications are genuine before treatment. The most popular treatment is cosmetic surgery but the country also provides organ transplants, heart, orthopaedic and obesity surgery, and dentistry.

Surgeons training in South Africa undertake an extensive 12-year training programme before they qualify. Most surgeons study in the United States or the UK before providing care in South Africa.

Patients can expect to save 40–60% on treatment compared with the UK. Hospitals and clinics in South Africa are vying to attract more international medical tourism patients from around the world. Although the cost of medical treatment is not as price-competitive as other popular medical travel destinations, the quality of treatment is very good.

Singapore As a leading healthcare services hub in Asia, Singapore attracts currently 200,000 international patients every year. Many international patients place their confidence in Singapore's world-class healthcare system, which is at the forefront of medical technology and has safety as top priority. The Singapore government aims to attract close to a million overseas patients. Singapore competes with Thailand and Malaysia for a slice of the medical tourism cake.

Malaysia Malaysia is among the world's top five medical tourism destinations for medical tourists selected on quality and affordability of medical care. It ranks third behind Panama and Brazil, and followed by Costa Rica and India. Malaysia's medical tourism industry has seen considerable growth in recent years. From 2001 to 2006, the number of foreigners seeking healthcare services in Malaysia more than tripled from 75,210 patients to 296,687 patients.

Much of Malaysia's attraction lies in the wide array of medical services and procedures available, including dental, cosmetic and cardiac surgeries at significantly lower costs compared with Europe. Thirty-five private hospitals in the country have been identified to promote Malaysia as a health tourist destination. Malaysia's growing reputation on the world healthcare map has also been recognised by a number of international and regional medical associations.

Ukraine The Crimea coast of Ukraine has a long history of spa therapy and is now endeavouring to attract medical tourists from Europe. Standards of care vary with the institution.

Personal health protection advice for the older traveller

Older travellers should acknowledge individual responsibility for personal health maintenance while overseas, and insure themselves against mishap in pre-travel and en-route preparation.[7] They should:
- Acquire appropriate vaccinations and prophylaxis.
- Use mechanical means of protection against malaria, e.g. repellents.
- Take measures to avoid infected food and water.
- Acquaint themselves with health hazards en-route and at destination.
- Be aware of emergency healthcare facilities at destination.
- Carry a list of medications.
- Carry routine medications on their person at all times.
- Recognise the limitations of travel health insurance and EHIC protection.
- Acknowledge that increasing age makes them higher health risk travellers.

References

1 McIntosh I Travel health Insurance, 2007 Brit. Trav. Health Assoc. J.10.58-59
2 McIntosh I Adequate Travel Insurance, 2004 Brit. Trav. Health Assoc. J 5. 41-42
3 McIntosh I EHIC insurance . 2010 In the News Brit. Trav. Health Assoc. J .15.69-60
4 McIntosh I Insurance ,in the news.2011 Brit. Trav. Health Assoc. J .16.37
5 McIntosh I Medical Tourism in the news.2011 Brit. Trav. Health Assoc. J 1637-8
6 Fairhurst R. in Travellers | Health ed. Dawood R. Oxford Univ, Press 2002
7 Turner R in Travellers | Health ed. Dawood R. Oxford Univ, Press 2012

Insurers catering for older travellers

Among the companies that offer full cover are Direct Travel Insurance (0845 605 2700, www.direct-travel.co.uk), and members of the British Insurance Brokers' Association (0870 950 1790, www.biba.org.uk).

People aged over 75 can acquire cover from Saga 0800 015 0757, which quotes on an individual basis depending on health, age and destination. Other providers include: Freedom Insurance (01223 446914, www.freedominsure.co.uk) and All Clear Insurance (0845 250 5350, allcleartravel.co.uk).

Useful websites

www.insuresupermarket.com
www.insureandgo.com
www.flexicover.com.
www.ehic/ie

14

Emergency Healthcare Overseas

Many older people travel the world believing that holiday health insurance will ensure optimal quality emergency evacuation, medical care and repatriation. It may, but much depends upon local facilities at location of injury or illness. The quality and availability of resources varies markedly between regions, countries and localities. Climatic season and transportation infrastructure also affect evacuation and repatriation.

Older people are more likely than the young to become ill while abroad, are likely to be hospitalised for longer and require medical repatriation.[1] Older tourists should be aware of the quality of health resources they may be faced with in time of need. They should investigate and consider the quality of service, speed of response and ease of repatriation when planning their holiday. Travel health professionals should draw attention to these preparations in pre-travel clinic consultations.

Emergency healthcare overseas

The quality of emergency healthcare likely to be encountered by the older traveller, who is more likely than a younger travel companion to need medical aid while abroad, varies markedly from country to country. The quality and availability of emergency evacuation, aid staff, resources and equipment may determine whether the ill or injured will survive an unfortunate medical mishap or accident that occurs abroad. Older people are especially likely to need these services so emergency aid and repatriation should be considered by all older travellers when organising an itinerary – an informed decision can then be made as to whether they should accept the risk of poor medical aid in time of need. This chapter addresses the issue of emergency healthcare in many frequently visited tourist destinations.

Tourist destinations/activities
- North and Western Europe
- Eastern Europe and Danube cruises

- Mediterranean coastlands
- the Baltic and Black Sea cruises
- Caribbean islands
- the Middle East
- North America
- South America
- West Africa and African safaris
- Asia and the Far East
- Australia and New Zealand.

Europe

Many tourists travel within and along the coasts of Europe and ill Britons can now often obtain speedy, high-quality care in countries within the European Union (EU). The European Health Insurance Card (EHIC) covers emergency healthcare in the 27 members of the EU and a few other states. The standard of resources and medical care, however, varies within European boundaries. Britons using this service must present an EHIC card entitling them to free medical treatment within the European Economic Area (EEA). Insurance organisations may not reimburse treatment claims if it has not been produced at the point of treatment.[2] The member countries of the EU (2013) are:

Austria, Belgium, Bulgaria, Cyprus, Czech Republic, Denmark, Estonia, Finland, France, Germany, Greece, Hungary, Ireland, Italy, Latvia, Lithuania, Luxembourg, Malta, Netherlands, Poland, Portugal, Romania, Slovakia, Slovenia, Spain, Sweden and the UK; reciprocation includes the Canary Islands, Azores, Madeira, French Guiana, Guadeloupe and Martinique. The EHIC allows individual access to state-provided healthcare in all EEA countries and Switzerland at a reduced cost or, sometimes, free of charge. Applying for the card is free and it is valid for five years. Presenting the EHIC entitles the bearer to treatment that is necessary during the trip but does not allow travel abroad specifically to receive medical care. However, renal dialysis and management of pre-existing or chronic conditions that arise while abroad are all covered by the EHIC. It allows access to the same state-provided healthcare as a resident of the country visited. However, many of these countries expect the patient to pay towards cost of treatment.

France
Linked closely by rail and sea to the UK, France is the country most visited by Britons. There is no great difference in quality of care between private and public hospitals in France and little difference in price. Treatment, whether private or

public, is not free at the point of delivery. Patients pay the full bill and are then reimbursed later. Being treated in private clinics in France does not mean avoiding waiting lists as they do not exist, but going private does not mean footing the entire bill.[3]

Germany
East German general practice under communism was tightly controlled in large polyclinics. City doctors are now encouraged to run single-handed practices as in West Germany. Visitors pay the GP and claim a refund if they have produced an EHIC card. In Germany, Poland Slovenia, Hungary, Slovakia, Austria, the Czech Republic, Spain, Portugal and Italy, GPs usually work alone and are unlikely to have practice nurses. They also do not practise gynaecology. In Germany, as well as France and Spain, it is now advantageous for travellers who suffer acute cardiac problems to undertake immediate bypass surgery abroad, rather than return to the UK to be waitlisted.[4]

Spain
A network of private and state health institutions and EC reciprocal healthcare ensure Britons can expect as good – and often better – healthcare in an emergency than in the UK. Travel health insurance companies now organise clients requiring cardiac intervention, stent insertion and bypass surgery to receive this in Spain for prompt efficient service. In Spanish hospitals along the tourist-dominated Mediterranean coast, there are dedicated English translators on call to ease linguistic problems. Health centres in Spain and Portugal employ salaried doctors. Home visits are infrequent, with out-of-hours work done by cooperatives working out of hospitals or health centres.

Italy
Italy ranks second on the World Health Organization's list of countries for top-quality healthcare services. However, many public hospitals are overcrowded and underfunded, although medical facilities are adequate for emergencies. Visitors are expected to pay full hospital charges and then claim reimbursement from their insurance provider. In case of emergency, most general and regional hospitals have emergency rooms (*pronto soccorso*), open 24 hours a day.

Greece
Greece's public health system provides free or low-cost healthcare for those who contribute to Greek social security. Although medical training is of a high standard, the health service is one of the worst in Europe, largely because of underfunding. Public hospitals are inundated with patients. Standards of hygiene are high, however, and hospital virus infection almost non-existent. In Greece, GPs are replaced by internists, who are physicians doing primary care work. A large

hospital on Corfu, a favoured tourist island, has recently been completed. In some hospitals patient's eating resources have to be provided by relatives, which present a problem for an ill unaccompanied tourist. Hospital and emergency departments are often manned by private doctors.

Malta and Cyprus
In Malta and Cyprus, favoured holiday spots for Britons of retirement age, most GPs work privately. A large central regional hospital has been completed recently in Malta. In the Maltese state and private sector, diabetes is managed in secondary care and GPs may not even arrange x-rays to check for fractures. In Cypriot and Greek towns, hospital and emergency departments are manned by private doctors.

European river cruises

British tourists visit the European community on land tours and transit many European countries on river cruises. Small ships, without on-board doctors, cruise along the rivers Danube and Rhine and are popular with ageing and often ailing tourists. They are reassured by the thought that reciprocal health arrangements will provide for emergency healthcare. The majority of countries neighbouring the Danube in its long course are members of the EU, with a few exceptions such as Serbia and Croatia. The standard of available emergency medical care and facilities varies greatly with cross-border travel.[5]

In Western Europe, high-quality resources equate with those in the NHS and are immediately available. In eastern European countries, struggling healthcare systems may not provide the urgent care that is required. Immediacy of assistance may also be a problem, as rivers run through many rural areas far from population centres, where ambulance transfer may be unavailable. Private health insurers therefore may not be able, logistically, to provide optimal care for tourists in an emergency. Insurance companies can only provide what is available from local resources and the patient may have to augment financial agreements, with 'informal arrangements' – i.e. bribes.[6]

Romania
This is a poor Balkan country and a relatively new EU member. It is shedding a culture of Communist corruption, when bribery affected every administrative system, including healthcare. Medical care in Romania is generally not up to Western standards, and basic medical supplies are limited, especially outside major cities. The country's healthcare system is so underfinanced it faces imminent

collapse. Even large university hospitals often lack surgical gloves, antibiotics and medication, forcing patients to pay for them. Buildings are in need of repair with rusting surgical instruments, dilapidated examination beds, cracked and damp walls, and dirty toilets being common. Private medical providers meeting Western quality standards are available in Bucharest and other cities but can be difficult to locate.

Doctors are still accustomed to receiving bribes and low average monthly medical wages encourage this. Patients pay more to get good clinical and nursing attention.[6] Transparency International UK ranked Romania as the second most corrupt country in the EU in 2010, behind Bulgaria. A World Bank report concluded that 'informal payments' amounted to £200 million annually. Ethically practising doctors observe that the bribery culture is so established that, when bribes are refused, patients mistakenly believe it a sign that illnesses are incurable; bribes may be expected from tourists who are ill. Costs range from £75 for an appendectomy to £4,000 for more major operative surgery, with prices posted on blogs and websites.

Considerations
Potential health risks within Romania include hepatitis A, polio, typhoid and rabies. Travellers to Romania should ensure they are up to date with all routine and hepatitis immunisations. Dental treatment, tattoos and injections should be avoided when within the country and those neighbouring it.

Travellers seeking medical treatment should choose a provider carefully as quality care is scarce. They should also endeavour to get treatment at a well-equipped centre by travelling to a county or capital city hospital, where staff may speak English. Visitors must tip medical personnel to guarantee sufficient attention is given to their medical conditions.

Hungary
Hungary transformed its healthcare system to a decentralised model and now has EU reciprocity. All citizens are covered, regardless of employment status. Patients make co-payments on certain services, including pharmaceuticals and dental care.[7] GPs contract with the National Health Insurance Fund of Hungary and provide a prescription and referral service.[8] In hospitals, the fee-for-service payment scheme encourages hospitals to treat for financial gain.[9] The system often sees doctors doing nursing duties. Apart from out-of-pocket payments for pharmaceuticals and dental care, 'gratitude' payments – in other words, bribes – by patients, continue to play an important role.[10]

Consideration
Tourists who are unaware of the situation and are unprepared to offer bribes risk receiving inferior care.

Bulgaria

The Bulgarian healthcare system is slowly catching up with that of Western European nations. Citizens have access to a free national health service. Medical equipment in many establishments is in poor condition, often more than 20 years old, and the healthcare system is in a critical state. Medical staff are trained to a high standard, but receive low wages and operate inadequate and outdated machinery. Hospitals and clinics may not have the equipment and facilities expected in Western Europe.

Dentists work privately and pharmacists offer affordable, unregulated treatment and medicines. Transparency International UK ranked Bulgaria the most corrupt country in the EU in 2010. There are a growing number of private hospitals and clinics, as well as state clinics and medical services in all major towns and cities. Nursing care can be sparse and knowledge of English limited.[11]

Consideration
Doctors and hospitals may expect immediate payment in cash for health services. Informal and 'gratitude' payments are often expected for simple medical and nursing attention.

Dental treatment, tattoos and injections should be avoided if possible when within the country.

Visitors should purchase comprehensive private travel medical insurance, which should include medical evacuation to Britain.

Serbia

Serbia has weathered years of political and economic turmoil, ethnic strife and civil war. The country has a well-developed network of primary/secondary care centres, but the system is inefficient and underfunded, with equipment and facilities out of date, and staff who are underpaid and demoralised. A European Health Agency study found that only a third of hospitals had functioning sterilisation equipment and 75% of the medical equipment in health facilities was more than 10 years old. Conditions are improving but vary across the country and medical care is limited. Physicians in Serbia are well trained but hospitals and clinics lack equipment and supplies; in large parts of rural Serbia ambulance services may be unavailable. In an acute emergency the best option is the Military Medical Academy in Belgrade.[12]

Consideration
Health workers routinely accept 'on-the-side' informal payments from patients and supplement income with private practice. Patients have to pay for hospital supplies – even items such as bandages and catheters – out of their own pockets.

Venous injections and acupuncture should be avoided if possible when in the country.

Croatia
Large parts of the country were devastated by war and medical facilities vary widely across the region. The best resources are along the Dalmatian coast, where medical tourism facilities are well established. Privatisation of primary healthcare (except for emergency and public health services) is underway, with about a third of primary care doctors being specialists in general medicine. GP-led primary healthcare is central to the newly organised healthcare system. Patients have a free choice of primary care doctor, who is the gatekeeper to secondary care in a polyclinic or hospital.

Those in work and their families have access to state healthcare, which is covered by government-subsidised medical insurance. Overall, facilities are good with free emergency aid available for tourists in an emergency. Major population centres have decent private healthcare facilities. Zagreb is best served with a large general hospital.[13]

Albania
Healthcare in Albania is mainly public/statutory and only partly private. The rural population – and especially those in the northeastern part of the country – have a lower standard of living and healthcare than elsewhere. There are plans to privatise parts of the healthcare system, to improve existing infrastructure and to build new institutions. Currently there are shortages of medicines, medical equipment and hospitals are dilapidated. The qualifications of medical personnel have not been carefully regulated, and nurses and doctors can still expect 'informal' payments to ensure patient attention. Three hundred healthcare centres have been refurbished, while some hospitals and polyclinics in cities have also been renovated and some modern diagnostic and treatment equipment installed.

Assistance from the EU has distributed medical equipment to 500 healthcare centres and 2,200 clinics, and there has been privatisation of pharmacies. A few private facilities are available to tourists in Tirana but quality of care for older tourists who are ill and away from the capital is problematic; emergency transportation is a further difficulty.

Consideration
Healthcare and resources vary markedly across the country and emergency aid may be delayed.

Dental treatment, tattoos and injections should be avoided when in the country. Travellers seeking medical treatment should choose their provider carefully as quality care is scarce. Tourists must tip medical personnel to guarantee that sufficient attention is given to medical conditions.

Switzerland
Although not a member of the EU, the country has reciprocal arrangements and

the EHIC card can be used in an emergency, giving access to good facilities.

Summary
Medical and nursing care resources and facilities vary greatly in countries bordering the Rivers Danube and Rhine, particularly in the Balkans. The river-based tourist may meet care as good as, or better than, that provided by the NHS, or be exposed to conditions closer to those met in an undeveloped country.

Cruise ships without a crew doctor or nurse pass through many rural areas where healthcare is limited and falls far short of that available in the big cities. Tourists should remember that they cannot wholly escape the use of local healthcare resources in an emergency. Private health insurance can only provide the best that is available locally and repatriation may be tenuous and lengthy. The public healthcare systems in Central and Eastern Europe have often been declining during the past decade; these are underfunded, lack solid infrastructure and are unable to keep professional medical staff in the country.

Mediterranean and Adriatic coasts

Older vacationers now holiday and reside for part of the year in large numbers along the Mediterranean coast, the Adriatic and on many of their offshore islands. Many of the countries along the shores are within the EU and offer good and relatively standardised healthcare to travellers who become ill or are injured.

In developing regions and those outside of the EU, standards vary and can be very poor. Tourists often only become aware of inadequacies in health facilities and support when overtaken by a medical or traumatic crisis and can suffer from delayed, or poor, intervention in an emergency. Chance can also determine whether the patient under duress is exposed to state established or private healthcare. The response to an emergency may be delivered by a private or state-sponsored ambulance, which will decant the patient into the respective healthcare sector, with each providing very different standards of provision and support. Linguistic difficulties and cultural differences can also create problems for those in medical need.

In general, the developed countries of the region operate private and state-funded medical care, with tourists protected by travel health insurance benefiting from exposure to the former. EU reciprocity ensures that the uninsured will receive emergency care equivalent to that of the countries' citizens. (Note, however, that the EHIC does not cover the cost of repatriation.) Away from mainland Italy, France and Spain, however, private healthcare may predominate and place the uninsured at risk from inadequate or a lack of care for foreign visitors.[14]

Spain, Italy, France, Portugal
British visitors are assured of good health support along the coastal fringe. Reciprocity ensures access to healthcare for all UK residents in an emergency.

Private care predominates in the south of Italy and in Adriatic resorts. There are many English-speaking and foreign doctors in resort areas and major cities. In Portugal nursing care and post-hospital assistance are below the standard expected by most northern Europeans. In mainland Greece and its islands there are variable standards of care, with patients transferred between islands and mainland by ship and air.

Morocco, Algeria, Tunisia, Libya and Egypt

There may be scant or absent universal healthcare for citizens and private healthcare predominates. State institutions may be embryonic, inadequate and offer services far below standards across the sea. The quality of resources deteriorates with distance from major population centres and may be rudimentary in rural areas. Tourists can expect good private facilities in major cities and some emergency state provision but in developing townships, in rural, small and new tourist venues, good care may be distant. Immediate first aid and casualty evacuation facilities may not exist.[15] The recent revolutions in Tunisia and Egypt bring even more uncertainty to the availability of healthcare in the country; the war in Libya has ravaged its healthcare system.

Morocco

The country has inadequate numbers of physicians and hospital beds, and poor access to water and sanitation. The healthcare system includes 122 hospitals and 2,400 health centres, which are poorly maintained and lack adequate capacity to meet demand for medical care. Tourists located far from major centres and venturing into the hinterland should be aware there are few immediate response vehicles, and access to any good hospital may be hours away. Travel health insurance can only provide what is available and local provision may be non-existent, with transfer to a unit with good facilities some time away. In an emergency, road traffic accident and bodily trauma exposes the traveller to admission to local facilities, where hygiene standards may be questionable.

Consideration

People travelling without travel health insurance may expect a modicum of emergency provision but ambulance transfer, medication and surgical intervention must be paid for, as well as the hotel element of hospitalisation. Emergency fluid and blood transfusion brings risks from contamination, HIV infection and hepatitis.

Algeria

In Algeria a system of almost free national healthcare exists. Hospitalisation, medicines and outpatient care are free to all. Most health services are provided by the public sector, although a small private sector has been expanding.

Libya
Before the civil war, Tripoli and Benghazi offered good private healthcare. There was some free health provision for the general populace providing a medium-quality healthcare system, although equipment and medicines were badly affected by the international trade embargo. A network of small hospitals serves littoral areas of Tripolitania and Cyrenaica. Small units with limited facilities exist in Derna and Tobruk which, before the war, were visited by cruise ships. The revolution has had adverse effects on the universality of healthcare in the country, has devastated facilities and has increased variation in the quality of care between east and west, and rural and city areas.

Egypt
Holiday resorts extend from El Alamein to Alexandria along the Mediterranean and up the River Nile. A good transport system brings within reach Cairo and Alexandria, and prime hospital facilities in the state and private sector. Public hospitals are open to tourists. The standard of care is good in Cairo and Alexandria but varies in other parts of the country. Healthcare provision is lacking in remote rural areas, particularly in Western Desert oases. The 2011 revolution has brought political uncertainty, with adverse impact on the healthcare scene.

Israel
Israel's healthcare system is reputed to be one of the most advanced in the world. The state maintains a system of socialised healthcare. Providers in the Israeli system consist of a mixture of private, semi-private and public entities. Cruise ships calling at Haifa can offload ill patients, who can expect good local and centralised care.

Syria
Continued civil unrest and embargo has had severe adverse effects on the provision and quality of healthcare, which was well developed in the cities. It involved state and private hospitals, as well as many public and private outpatient clinics and different sorts of health centres. The health system for rural areas is limited with few services and the country has problems with tuberculosis infection.

Turkey
Turkey has a complex healthcare system of variable quality, especially in most state hospitals. Private hospitals have raised the quality of physicians and medical equipment. Most hospitals and doctors are concentrated in cities and big towns. Private health insurance is well developed in major centres and most popular tourist resorts. A scant health service exists in rural areas with large distances between

emergency aid locations and poor transportation facilities in the hinterland.

Albania
Albania, frequently visited on coach excursions from river cruise ships, has a healthcare system in transition. It offers basic primary healthcare, but many facilities were damaged in the conflict up to 1997 and deficits are present in expertise, skills and management. Facilities remain publicly owned with the exception of licensed private pharmacies and dentists (*see 'European river cruises'*).

Croatia, Greece, Italy
See Europe.

Summary
When travelling around the Mediterranean coast, the tourist will be exposed to considerable variations in the standard and quality of care that is available in an emergency. It is important to carry the EHIC to access reciprocal services where they apply; travellers should also acquire travel health insurance for extra protection for general travel in the region. Distances to good private and state emergency care may be considerable and ambulance transportation limited.

Baltic and Black Sea cruising

Large- and small-ship cruising around the Baltic and Black Seas attracts older travellers. If illness or trauma befalls passengers, there is recourse to the ship doctor who will offload seriously ill or injured patients at the next port of call or by helicopter rescue to the nearest land hospital. Most of the shores of the Baltic belong to the EU countries of Denmark, Sweden, Germany, Lithuania, Latvia and Estonia, which have reciprocal emergency health arrangements with the UK. Travel health insurance cover will be required for repatriation if needed.

Russia
Most ships sailing the Baltic Sea call into St Petersburg and the traveller will be dependent on the Russian healthcare system. Russia has a very low standard of compulsory state-funded healthcare compared with Western standards. Healthcare is theoretically free and available to all citizens but patients say doctors, nurses and surgeons routinely demand payments – even bribes –

from those they treat.

Medical staff are adequately trained but there is a lack of funding and medical equipment. Old Soviet ways still prevail, leading to inequality. Russia has more physicians, hospitals, and healthcare workers than almost any other country in the world on a per capita basis, but since the collapse of the Soviet Union, the health of the Russian population has declined. Medical care in Russia is among the worst in the industrialised world. A 2000 WHO report ranked Russia's health system 130th out of 191 countries. There are private medical facilities in the cities.

Case history
A 70 year old lady on an inland tour from a cruise ship that was berthed in Leningrad ate ice cream and became ill. Vomiting and with diarrhoea the hotel doctor dispatched her in the middle of the night in a van to an infectious disease unit in the city. It was surrounded by high walls with an electrified fence and entry gates. Admitted to a ward and prostrated by loss of fluid and electrolytes, she was stripped, placed under a shower and hosed down with cold water. None of the staff spoke English and she had been admitted without money, passport and day clothes. A doctor prescribed a powder mixture of magnesium trisilicate given to the patient on the hand of a nurse and forced into her mouth at regular intervals. Told by signs that her group had continued on their tour, she had a dreadful few days before making a recovery. The nurses expected bribes for bed-making and the provision of bedpans. Only the intervention of the tour group leader eased her discharge.

Consideration
Adequate travel health insurance is a must for visitors but will only provide the best available care, which may be of poor quality. 'Informal' payments may be expected for basic nursing care. Health facilities vary greatly within cities and across the country.

Bulgaria, Georgia, Romania, Russia, Turkey and Ukraine
These countries border the Black Sea, with healthcare provision for tourists akin to that described previously and often of very low standard. The Crimean coast has long been renowned for its health spas and there is a thriving medical tourism industry. Travel health insurance is vital to access private facilities and ensures speedy repatriation *(see comments by country)*.

Caribbean islands

Air/cruise holidays bring many older travellers to Caribbean islands. About 20 million tourists visit the islands annually, most arriving by ship;[16] around 100 ships cruise round the islands in the European winter season. They can disgorge 12,000 passengers daily onto the quays of large and small islands and overburden medical resources. Although each ship carries medical and nursing staff, if serious medical or traumatic incident occurs on board, the patient will be disembarked at the next port of call whenever possible.[17] Local medical and onward repatriation facilities may be incapable of meeting demand.[18] Medical care can also be of variable standard. Some islands have modern hospitals with good diagnostic and investigative expertise, but there may be a dearth of nurses, doctors, infrastructure and resources.

Healthcare provision differs from island to island depending upon size, population and wealth, and is usually provided to visitors on a private basis. There is an increasing tendency for older tourists, faced with high premiums and illness exclusions for current medical problems, to travel without travel health insurance cover. They travel uninsured for conditions most likely to befall them and, in an emergency, face high medical costs if they require medical attention or hospitalisation. In an emergency, seriously ill patients may be transferred from islands to the United States for continuing treatment and be faced with exorbitant fee demands.

Disease infection risk for tourists is not high in the islands but dengue fever and malaria infections are increasing. Guadeloupe and Martinique confirm an increasing number of cases of hepatitis, which is also a special risk in the Dominican Republic. HIV/AIDS remains a problem on many islands. Malaria had been eradicated (except in Haiti and the Dominican Republic) but there has been a resurgence in tourist-frequented islands. Jamaica, Puerto Rico and Cuba have recently seen cases and deaths, with reports from the Cayman Islands, and the British and American Virgin Islands.

Cruise ship passengers particularly run the risk of norovirus infection and the older people who are affected may become dehydrated, debilitated and require island hospitalisation. Infected tourists from Dominica were quarantined on arrival in Glasgow in 2007. Badly debilitated sufferers will be disembarked en route or at departure ports in Jamaica, Puerto Rico and Barbados, where they may be quarantined and hospitalised with or without their consent.

Cruise ships carry many older passengers who have heart attacks and strokes on board and must be hospitalised at the next port of call. Cardiac medical emergencies are most likely to result in premature disembarkation. Many tourists also suffer from trauma during a sojourn in the islands. Road systems are often embryonic, poorly maintained and suffer urban congestion. The unfortunate victim may find that ambulance response may be non-existent or delayed, and accident and emergency facilities limited and short of resources.

A shortage of water and poor hygiene is evident inland from many of the ports. In island interiors and the hinterland, people may be poor and often live frugally in shanties. Local restaurant and café cuisine and ice cream can be infected. Small coastal resort eating places may offer barracuda and amberjack on the menu; there is a risk of cigatuera poisoning from a neurotoxin in fish that feed off reefs.

Older tourists sunbathe on beaches and suffer from sun overexposure, coral abrasions, and swimming and sailing accidents. Quad biking, horse riding and off-road 4x4 vehicle pastimes tempt the senior tourist into unwise activities not contemplated at home. Raft, river and rapid-running result in skin abrasions, lacerations and fractures on islands. Older people who would never consider such activity in the UK may abandon their inhibitions and, in holiday spirit, expose themselves to physical injury – a major cause of tourist morbidity.

In Barbados – a prime tour destination for Britons – 1 million tourists were studied revealing 704 emergency admissions with 26 deaths. Fourteen per cent were due to falls, 4.2% due to road accidents, and 300 injuries required emergency medical evaluation/management per million tourists/year.

Case histories
1. *In the hinterland of Grenada, two vehicles in front of a hired car were involved in head-on road accident. One passenger was knocked unconscious and had a serious head injury. Many miles and hours from the nearest hospital, emergency aid was distant and over bad roads. There was no ambulance facility. A taxi driver had to be bribed to carry him to the emergency unit in the island capital – the only route to urgent medical care.*

2. *A cruise ship reversed passage to carry a passenger with a severe myocardial infarction back to Barbados, which had better medical facilities than the nearer small island and the next destination. After a top speed six-hour sail, the patient died en route to the hospital after disembarkation. Immediate intensive care hospital attention might have saved him.*

Most islands have medical facilities where payment is expected at the time of service, but there can be delays in accessing insurers if communications are poor. The islands usually have radiographic facilities but may not have magnetic resonance imaging (MRI) scanners and laboratory services may be limited. To access these may mean a journey to another island, or to the mainland of North or South America. Serious cases in Trinidad are often transferred to Venezuela and in the American Virgin Islands, such as St Thomas, to the United States. Uninsured or inadequately insured patients may face unanticipated and very expensive hospital and medical costs. The EHIC is applicable in all French overseas departments (Martinique, Guadeloupe, and French Guiana) as they are part of the EEA, but not in Aruba.

Very ill patients who are transferred to small islands may face prolonged delay in air transfer to units with better facilities, due to a dearth of land and air transport and weather vagaries. Hurricanes, landslides, volcanic eruptions and tremors make roads impassable on many of these islands, which are mountainous or subject to flooding. The possibility of prolonged evacuation to modern medical and nursing facilities if injured or ill is not considered by British tourists, who are accustomed to prompt NHS ambulance transfer and emergency response.

Considerations
- Pre-travel consultation should bring potential healthcare shortcomings to the attention of travellers to the Caribbean.
- Hi-tech cardiac care and rehabilitative resources are unlikely to be available in many islands – a consideration for travellers with chronic ill health.
- Island pharmacies have a limited range of pharmacological products. Replacement medications may not be available in the Caribbean.
- The risk of water and food contamination should be kept in mind on small islands and in hinterlands. Tourists should anticipate infection problems and remember the adage that ingested food should be boiled, cooked, peeled or rejected if they are to avoid food and water-borne infection.
- Influenza and *Pneumococcal* immunisation, and hepatitis A vaccination is recommended; yellow fever vaccination is necessary for those calling at Venezuelan ports.
- Antimalarial prophylaxis is necessary for those travelling on ships with landfalls in Central and South America.
- Dental treatment is best avoided to decrease the risk of hepatitis.
- Safety of vehicles and the availability of seat belts should be considered.
- Local evacuation, hospital and emergency resources need consideration.

Summary
A visit to Caribbean islands is associated with low health risk, but trauma or illness can expose the tourist to lower standards of evacuation, immediate and continuing care than that expected in the UK.

Middle East

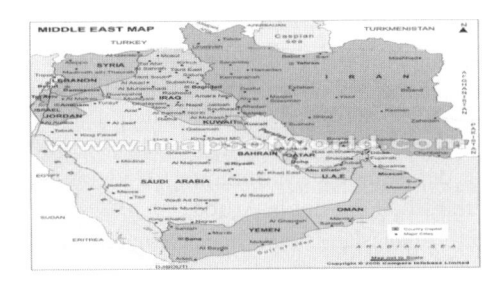

Sun, sand and antiquities attract older tourists to the Middle East. Along the eastern littoral of the Mediterranean and the Red Sea there has been a proliferation of holiday resorts. Sanitation and healthcare resources are not always commensurate with the expansion of tourist facilities. In this part of the world, access to clinics, hospitals and health professionals can be limited and the quality of resource and emergency care variable. From Sharm el Sheik to Damascus, Eilat to Dubai, older tourists embark on the cultural trail. New hotels and beach facilities are often dependent upon primitive infrastructure and the services of personnel living in squalor. The risk to Western visitors from infection and trauma is high and, when overcome by illness or injury, immediate healthcare may be unavailable or inadequate (see previous section on the Mediterranean littoral).

Facilities, resources and access can be problematic or absent in this part of the world. Recent terrorist attacks in popular resorts have exposed weaknesses in emergency response and casualty care systems. State-run hospitals and clinics are often under-resourced and of variable standard, with private establishments scarce and expensive. Sea cruisers and older people wandering historic sites are exposed to trauma on poor roads, from watersports accidents, injury from terrorist explosions and illness from ingestion of contaminated water and food. Passengers disembark for tours of the Pyramids and ancient Greek, Roman and Phoenician cities.

Daytime temperatures spiral to high extremes in the Middle East and archaeological sites become arid ovens by midday, which can desiccate the unwary. Older people are at greater risk of stroke in this situation. They can also become confused when dehydrated and may not react rationally to fluid loss and electrolyte imbalance, thereby failing to recognise the need to rehydrate.

The local population may have primitive sanitation, a scant water supply and vegetable and fruit produce may have been fertilised by 'night soil'. Water in hotels and restaurants may be contaminated and the risk of gastroenteric infection is high. River cruises along the Nile bring a high risk of enteric infection from contaminated water and older people run a greater risk from dehydration in high ambient temperatures. Tourists may forget that the on-board water may have been drawn from the river. Most passengers forget or ignore the risk of infection from salads, ice and unbottled water ingested on board ,and the attrition rate of illness is high. In high ambient temperatures dehydration and electrolyte imbalance can result from diarrhoea, with older people likely to be more severely affected. Treatment will depend on the facilities of a local hospital limited in human and equipment resources.[19]

Case histories

1. On a bus tour of Jordan only a few of the older tourists were fit to continue one day as most had developed severe gastrointestinal illness. The probable cause was chicken they eaten at a barbeque lunch, organised at an isolated scenic site perched on a hill in the desert. Hygienic preparation of the meal was difficult for the local providers in a waterless location, as there were no toilets or hand-washing facilities. The tourists ate infected poultry resulting in none of the infected being able to travel onward. Two required hospital care due to dehydration and prostration.

2. An older lady was visiting the Valley of the Queens in Egypt on a boiling hot, cloudless, day, with reflections from the amphitheatre of rocks and sand escalating ambient environmental temperature. She became dehydrated, confused and was stumbling about. When given a bottle of expensive water she squandered the fluid by pouring the contents over her overheated feet rather than down her throat.

Exploration of historic sites usually means traversing rough, unpaved locations, and manoeuvres over rocks and crudely hewn walkways. A stumble may result in a fall and fracture, with hospitalisation in those with arthritis and poor balance. Emergency aid may be distant, evacuation problematic and help from a health professional variable and limited. Cruise ships plying their trade in local waters tend to be small with very limited health facilities and doctors from the former Soviet empire. They are restricted in passenger health support and offload the ill and injured at the nearest health facility, which may not meet Western standards of care. Passengers rarely realise the limitations of small-ship cover and the likelihood of immediate disembarkation to a local health facility if a medical mishap occurs.

Exposure to the warm waters of the Red Sea and Persian Gulf can bring trauma in and out of the water, as well as from overexposure to fierce sun. If injury occurs, immediate casualty care response may be rudimentary and evacuation difficult and prolonged. Reusable needles, syringes and equipment can pose a threat of hepatitis B and HIV infection, and blood supplies may be suspect in some locations. The sporty often also fail to arrange the additional health insurance cover advisable for their physical activities. Older tourists also undertake scuba diving and paragliding, riding and other sporty pursuits at these venues, forgetting that the small print in their insurance policies is likely to exclude such activity, rendering them without cover in the event of accident.

Considerations
UK health professionals should advise travellers of potential health risks and remind them of the differences in emergency support that are likely to be encountered.

Tourists should ensure adequate health insurance protection and remember that cover only provides the best healthcare available – which may not meet their expectations. Travellers should be aware of the health hazards they might meet, take precautions (particularly against gastrointestinal infection) and seek appropriate vaccination.

Summary
In travel through the Middle East there is a high risk to health from trauma, infection – particularly gastrointestinal disease – and civil unrest. High ambient temperatures bring with them the risk of dehydration and sunburn. The quality of emergency care facilities varies from country to country, as well as within countries. Good medical aid may be distant and evacuation difficult and lengthy. There are good private facilities in the main tourist centres but these are sparse in the hinterlands and rural locations. Private travel health protection is paramount.

North and South America

United States

It is vital that visitors to the United States have health insurance protection. The need for all visitors to have comprehensive and adequate health insurance is crucial and should be emphasised at pre-travel clinic consultations. Tourists should only venture there certain of personal health insurance protection with close scrutiny of small-print clauses and exceptions to cover. Failure to secure health cover, or travel with insufficient protection or exclusions for past medical conditions, may prove disastrous. Ill tourists in the United States are exposed to very high fees inherent in the private healthcare sector.[20]

The case history illustrates a problem faced by many Americans. The United States only holds 37th place in the WHO list of top countries for quality healthcare services, despite being the highest spender. In total, 45 million US residents have no health coverage at all, and 25 million who are underinsured spend more than 10% of their income on out-of-pocket medical costs. Underinsured, they are particularly vulnerable, as are unwary tourists. Until a health catastrophe occurs, visitors are often unaware of exposure to health risk.

> *Case histories*
> *A 68 year old woman had a severe stroke on a cruise ship sailing in the Caribbean, with a home port in Florida. She had suffered a mild stroke 2 years previously and was not covered by her travel health insurance for any recurrence or symptoms of cardio and cerebrovascular disease. On admission to hospital in the United States she was very ill and required lengthy intensive healthcare and rehabilitation. The admission contract made with the family made them responsible for all financial costs. Treatment, hospital management and repatriation expenses bankrupted them.*

Canada

Healthcare in Canada is delivered through a publicly funded healthcare system, which is mostly free at the point of use and has most services provided by private entities. This system is of high quality for residents, but visitors have to make private arrangements in an emergency, with costs not dissimilar to those in the United States; adequate insurance cover is essential. Canada is a very large country with vast distances between towns and villages in the interior. Doctor's surgeries can be 100 miles apart, and distance and weather can delay immediate access to emergency healthcare for tourists in the hinterland.[21]

High-quality emergency medical care is available in North America providing the patient is insured. In the absence of this protection, there can be very long waits to access emergency units and fees can be extortionate if hospital admission is required. In rural areas, distance can delay urgent admission, especially if weather conditions prevent emergency flights.

South America

South America draws the adventurous traveller, with unique cultural and scenic attractions enticing people to Chile, Bolivia and Peru. The intrepid traveller needs to journey in robust good health to overcome the rigours of the route. Diverse geography, large distances, tenuous communications, high altitude, temperature extremes, infection and trauma can affect tourists – they should anticipate having health problems.[22]

Case histories
In an older group of travellers in Chile, a man developed a myocardial infarction and a lady a rasping cough that developed into pneumonia. In pain the man waited three hours to see the only doctor and, as the sole ambulance was in use, he had to be transported by bus back to Calambra Hospital, 3.5 hours away. After several hours' waiting to be seen there and an ECG, which confirmed the infarction, he was advised that facilities were so inadequate in the hospital that he should return to his hotel. He had travelled 3-plus hours each way to have the diagnosis confirmed but remained untreated. He was eventually repatriated back to the UK by air. The woman deteriorated despite antibiotic therapy. With poor investigative local resources, she was forced to abandon her holiday and return to Santiago. UK tour operators did not provide the ongoing support they inferred and intercontinental communication between insurance companies, tour operators and patients was desultory and anxiety provoking, adding psychological trauma to the scene.

Medical emergency and evacuation problems are likely to prevail in impoverished, undeveloped and distant tourist locations in rural parts of South America. Even with adequate health insurance cover, protection can only provide what is available. Accessibility and quality of service varies across the regions. State-of-the-art private facilities may be located in the big cities, but an embryonic health service with limited facilities is likely in the rural scene. Land evacuation is protracted and sometimes impracticable. Prompt air evacuation is not assured for cardiac and respiratory conditions as helicopter and small aeroplane transfer is rarely practicable.

A trip across the continent traverses the backbone of the Andes. Accomplishing such a journey requires pre-planning, physical stamina and endurance. It is now being undertaken by middle aged and older people some of whom are frail and chronically ill. Travel agencies do not adequately inform customers of the physical and psychological ardour of this itinerary. Most are poorly informed about the risk of prolonged travel at altitude, when much of the time spent in Bolivia and Peru will occur at altitudes of 4,000m and higher. Older, chronically ill, at-risk travellers contemplating such a trip should seek a pre-travel health consultation.

Chile and Bolivia

Geothermal areas are unguarded. Unwary visitors get scalded from superheated mud pools and fall through silica encrustment into boiling water and steam caverns. First-aid attention may be a day of car travel away. Tourists rarely appreciate the health risk of acute mountain sickness (AMS) and fail to recognise that headache and vomiting can threaten the onset of pulmonary and cerebral oedema and death. Those with chronic cardiac and respiratory problems are overchallenged and may be precipitated into cardiovascular and respiratory failure. Adverse health effects are compounded for those travelling over the border from Chile into Bolivia, with an average travel altitude of over 3,500m and passes climbing to 5,000m and more.

Onward travel in a developing country with poor hygiene facilities exposes the traveller to gastroenteritis; fluid and electrolyte loss can add to dehydration. Sanitation can be basic, hand-washing difficult and food exposed to flies and contamination. The thin air at high altitude poorly screens the sun's harmful ultraviolet light rays and solar burn is a constant risk. Roads are very bad and vehicle-related trauma is far more frequent than in the UK, with emergency aid often many hours away.

Recommendations
- Travellers should be aware that if affected by AMS in remote areas, they will face a long, rough trip to lower altitude, with evacuation taking up to 24 hours. This delay could prove fatal.
- Prophylaxis with a carbonic anhydrase inhibitor reduces the likelihood of AMS; 200mg of acetazoleamide should be taken 24 hours before exposure to an altitude of 3,000m and continued daily while at high altitude.
- Be aware that some policies from insurance companies exclude cover if one ventures above 12,000ft.
- Consider that first-aid and medical care will be delayed and limited, which may be a decisive factor in survival following infection, medical mishap or trauma.

- Precautions are required against enteric infection.
- UV light screen filters should be used.
- Tourist transport often carries oxygen in cylinders for people with AMS. It is a wise precaution to ensure there is a cylinder on board before departure.
- Big towns, such as Sucre in Bolivia, have private medical clinics and La Paz has good access to well-equipped private medical units for those who have travel health insurance protection.

Peru
A 2000 WHO report ranked Peru's health system 130th out of 191 countries. Lake Titicaca is a magnet for many tourists with an altitude of over 3,000m. AMS may prevail and its storm-tossed waters can cause motion sickness. Proceeding eastwards and down from the altiplano, mosquitos can be a problem. The tourist mecca of Cusco – at an altitude of 3,000m – is mosquito free; the train however travels down the gorge into the jungle with exposure to malaria-transmitting insects. Tourists in shorts with bare arms are often bitten at the ruins in Machu Picchu, in the local town and on the train. They fail to consider prior antimalarial medication or the use of mosquito repellents.

Considerations
At pre-travel health consultations:
Health professionals should:
- deter those with chronic conditions – e.g. chronic obstructive airways disease (COAD), frail older people, the anaemic, those with a history of deep vein thrombosis and pulmonary embolism – from setting out on such a trip.

Travellers should:
- Consider pre-travel health consultation.
- Seek prophylaxis for malaria and altitude sickness
- Carry mosquito repellent protection, anti-motion sickness medication, lip salve, first-aid kit, water-sterilising tablets and a large water bottle.
- Anticipate long, arduous land and air journeys.
- Assume water, salads and uncooked food are contaminated unless certain of the source.
- If past history includes heart attack, stroke, COAD or immunosuppression, carefully consider the wisdom of travel.

Summary
Tourists will find good healthcare in Canada and the United States. The private sector is very expensive and adequate health insurance is a vital prerequisite to North American travel. Uninsured, emergency healthcare may be delayed and of variable quality. Private South American healthcare is of variable quality and

emergency care may be inferior, limited or far distant. This is a high health risk part of the world. The older traveller and particularly those with pre-existing illness should consider the risk of gastrointestinal infection, trauma, malaria, AMS, solar irradiation and the fatigue of long-distance travel in arid, harsh environments. Medical aid may be a day away with no prospect of emergency air evacuation and land transportation is scarce.

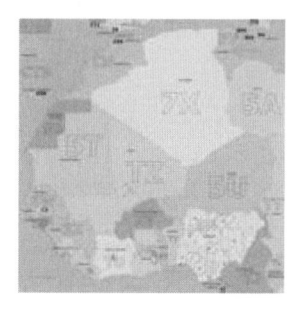

West Africa

The west coast of Africa was long known as the White Man's Grave because of the high death rate from tropical disease. Countries once shunned by Europeans are now visited in increasing numbers by those intent on accessing winter sunshine. Tourists, apparently protected by comprehensive travel health insurance, often assume that urgent healthcare needs will be met in a medical emergency overseas as speedily and efficiently as within the NHS. An adverse medical event due to trauma and disease in countries in West Africa however, may expose patients to limited resources and healthcare, and delayed treatment. Insurance companies can only provide the best locally available medical and nursing care. Evacuation and treatment may not equate with that in more developed countries. Poor communications, climatic extremes, bad roads and limited transportation can also delay hospital access in an emergency.[23]

Paucity of health professionals, hospitals and institutional resources determines poor quality of healthcare provision. Facilities are best in the cities, but up-country and small ports of call often have a rural hinterland, with difficult and distant access to major cities. Traditional medicine, dependent upon herbs and ancient and voodoo practices, often form part of the primary healthcare. Cruise ships are disgorging passengers into countries fringing the West African coast. Standards of emergency care vary considerably from country to country, are often rudimentary and may only be available in the main cities and not in ports.

Common diseases in sub-Saharan countries include cholera, typhoid, pulmonary tuberculosis, anthrax, pertussis, tetanus, chicken pox, yellow fever, measles, infectious hepatitis, trachoma, malaria and schistosomiasis.

The Gambia

A country with one of the world's lowest per capita income rates, The Gambia's healthcare system is rudimentary. There is one teaching hospital in Banjul, the capital, staffed by consultant specialists, mainly from Cuba. There is also a Medical Research Council unit in Bakau, which specialises in tropical diseases. Both of these are near coastal tourist areas but are extremely busy, crowded and sleep two patients per bed when under pressure.[24] A few private clinics with limited facilities provide emergency care for the ill or injured tourist, but have scant investigative or intensive-care capacity. The nearest treatment centres are in Dakar, Senegal; this is many hours' drive plus a ferry crossing away, with transport at a premium and roads often impassable in the wet season.[1] The alternative evacuation route is to Europe, a six-hour flight – not a viable alternative for a patient who has had a heart attack, infarction or respiratory emergency, as airlines will not fly individuals for a week or 10 days after these critical medical incidents. As in all West African countries, malaria is rife.

Senegal
This country is one of the first ports of call for ships leaving the UK on cruises to South Africa and the Far East. If passengers become ill on the Atlantic crossing, they may be disembarked here. Private clinics and a few state hospitals are under-resourced, underdoctored and medications may be difficult to acquire. Large disparities still exist in health coverage, with 70% of doctors and 80% of pharmacists and dentists living in the nation's capital city, and only 0.1 physicians and 0.4 hospital beds per 1,000 people.

Major health problems include measles and meningitis, along with water-related diseases as malaria, trypanosomiasis, onchocerciasis and schistosomiasis.

Cape Verde islands
These islands are a port of call for cruise ships on transatlantic crossings. Health facilities are very limited, and some medicines are in short supply or unavailable. There are hospitals in Praia and Mindelo, with smaller medical facilities elsewhere. Brava and Santo Antão islands no longer have functioning airports so air evacuation in a medical emergency is impossible. Malaria occurs in Cape Verde; risk is mainly limited to the island of Santiago and is highest from July to December.

Ghana
Ghana has government-funded healthcare, with hospitals and clinics also run by religious groups and a few for-profit clinics playing a role. Urban centres are well served; however, rural areas often have no modern healthcare. Patients there rely on traditional African medicine or travel great distances for care. Ghana experiences the full range of diseases endemic to the region. Private and state facilities are available to tourists in Accra, but are generally poor in the rural scene.

As with most West African countries, there is a high health risk from road traffic accidents and emergency aid may be delayed, casualty units far away, with limited resources for transfusion and surgery. Travel health insurance companies can negotiate reasonable care for patients in an emergency and there are good air connections to Europe.[25]

Sierra Leone

Sierra Leone is recovering from a vicious civil war when the infrastructure was damaged. Hospitals and clinics are decayed. Money buys access to what health support is available. Ambulance transfer is rare. This is a hazardous place for pedestrians and vehicles and the risk of accidental trauma is high. Emergency admission to a local medical unit is best avoided but air evacuation depends upon a few direct flights to Europe. Transport is scarce, the roads often dirt tracks and communication between centres fragmented. The few hospitals and clinics are grossly overburdened with the demands of a malnourished destitute population. The country suffers from epidemic outbreaks of diseases, including yellow fever, cholera, Lassa fever and meningitis.

Ivory Coast (Cote d'Ivoire)

In the Ivory Coast there are sharp regional and socioeconomic disparities in healthcare. There are 12 physicians per 100,000 people. Access to potable water and waste-disposal systems is limited in rural areas. The healthcare system is unable to meet the healthcare needs of the population, with continuing low ratios of doctors and nurses to patients. Chronic shortages of equipment and medicines contribute to overall poor service delivery. In rural areas, healthcare remains under the guidance of lineage elders and traditional healers. Malaria, yellow fever, sleeping sickness, yaws, leprosy, trachoma and meningitis are endemic.

Cameroon

Healthcare for tourists is available in big cities in Cameroon. Simple blood samples are usually analysed in the country but complex ones go to France. Healthcare activities are either run as government services or private ones managed by various churches. Modern equipment is needed with many clinics using outdated equipment. In 2004, there were seven physicians and 36 nurses, per 100,000 people. Principal diseases are malaria, HIV/AIDS, tuberculosis, sleeping sickness, cholera, dysentery and meningitis. Malaria is prevalent in the coastal region and the forests. Other serious water-borne diseases are schistosomiasis and sleeping sickness, spread by the tsetse fly. Cameroon lies in the yellow fever endemic zone.

Benin

The population depends upon traditional medical practices – voodoo doctors – when in clinical need. There are a few conventional clinics and hospitals that are accessible to tourists. There were only six physicians and 20 nurses per 100,000 people in 2004. Most serious epidemic diseases have been brought under control. Yaws has been almost totally eradicated in the north, yellow fever has almost disappeared and cholera cases are now rare.

São Tomé and Principe
These are small islands lying on the equator off the coast of Africa, an attractive port of call for cruise ships. Medical care is extremely limited. The main health facility is the Ayres Menezes Hospital, located on the island of São Tomé. Most doctors and hospitals expect payment in cash, regardless of whether the traveller has travel health insurance. Serious medical problems require air evacuation to a country with state-of-the-art medical facilities. Flights are limited and rarely fly direct to Europe. Malaria remains a health risk.

Gabon
In Gabon health facilities remain inadequate, particularly outside the Libreville area. The government provides nearly all healthcare services. The internationally known Albert Schweitzer Hospital is located in Lambaréné. Evacuation and repatriation for ill or injured tourists is likely to be delayed and emergency care is extremely limited. Malaria, sleeping sickness, tuberculosis and other infectious diseases are widespread.

Togo
Medical services include treatment centres with services free, except at the clinic at the hospital in Lomé, where patients pay a nominal fee. About 61% of the population has access to healthcare services. In recent years there have been significant decreases in mortality caused by smallpox, yellow fever and sleeping sickness. Yaws, malaria and leprosy continue to be major medical problems.

Namibia
Namibia is a country with high levels of inequality in access to healthcare resources. The main tourist centres have reasonable private health facilities but tourists safari up-country where health units and resources may be unavailable or limited and evacuation can be prolonged.[26] Drinking water outside of main cities and towns may be contaminated. Malaria risk exists in the entire northern third of the country from November to June, along the Kunene River and in the Kavango and Caprivi regions throughout the year.

Summary
Health services in West Africa:
- are poorly developed and do not meet the needs of all residents
- vary markedly from country to country
- are particularly poor in rural and coastal areas away from cities
- may not meet the needs of ill or injured tourists.
-

In the region:
- Hospitals and clinics are poorly resourced.

- Transport to hospital may be unobtainable.
- Yellow fever immunisation is mandatory.
- Maximal antimalarial precautions are required.
- Travel health insurance will not necessarily bring access to optimal emergency care.
- The risk of traffic-related trauma is very high.
- Air and land evacuation may not be possible in an emergency.

East and southern Africa

At the southern end of the African coastline is Cape Town – a port of call for many cruise ships and a place where ill passengers are offloaded. The health system consists of a large public sector and a smaller private sector. Healthcare varies from the most basic primary healthcare, offered free by the state, to highly specialised hi-tech health services available in the private sector. The public sector is under-resourced and overused. The enlarging private sector caters for foreigner visitors and medical tourists seeking top-quality surgical procedures at relatively affordable prices. The private sector also attracts most of the country's health professionals.

Kenya
Access to healthcare varies widely throughout the country, with quality and resources varying markedly between rural and urban communities. Most facilities are located in Central Province, and few in the border provinces of Western Valley and Nyanza. Prevalence of communicable disease in Kenya is a major factor with HIV, malaria and tuberculosis rife.[27] A large percentage of the population does not seek care despite being ill but 90% of the population in sub-Saharan Africa use traditional medicine as their source of primary healthcare.[28]

Stark disparities are apparent in levels of care, and between facilities in different regions. Top of the service spectrum are teaching hospitals such as Kenyatta National Hospital (KNH) in Nairobi. The next best level of care is found in provincial hospitals, with an uneven distribution of health workers between urban and rural areas. Contrast in the levels of care is seen in KNH, which offers public and private wards, attended by the same doctors. A patient in the public ward, can expect to spend long hours waiting to be seen and may be expected to share a bed with another patient. Patients are grouped in large, open, chaotic rooms and afforded no privacy, which compares badly with the private ward of the hospital.

While both public and private patients receive a reasonable level of care at KNH, the disparity between services offered there and elsewhere can be substantial. The provincial general hospital in Nyeri, for instance, demonstrates a major drop in quality of care and resources, such as morphine – a basic analgesic[29] – can be in short supply.

Zimbabwe

Zimbabwe's healthcare system is collapsing. Hospitals face dire shortages of doctors and medical supplies and are unable to undertake basic operations because of shortages of anaesthetics, sutures and essential supplies. The country is battling one of the world's highest rates of HIV/AIDS infection, estimated to be killing more than 3,000 people a week. Elective surgery has been abandoned in the central hospitals and even emergency surgery is often dependent on the ability of patients' relatives to purchase drugs, suture materials and supplies of blood from private sellers. Ambulances are grounded for want of fuel and spare parts.[29] Harare now has regular outbreaks of cholera.

Considerations
- Older people should be advised to avoid travel in the country until the healthcare system reaches minimal standards of provision.
- The healthcare and transportation systems have disintegrated and emergency aid is problematic.
- Travel health insurance cover cannot provide protection in the absence of resources.

Zambia

Services to Zambian nationals are free at rural health centres and urban hospitals. The public healthcare sector suffers from a severe shortage of doctors, medicine, medical equipment and supplies. Zambia has one of the highest rates of HIV infection, even in hard-hit sub-Saharan Africa. There are limited private facilities for tourists. Malaria and tuberculosis are major health problems and hookworm and schistosomiasis affect a large proportion of the population.

Namibia

This is a popular safari destination. The country is arid, distances between health centres can be considerable and healthcare variable (*see previous information on Namibia*).

Tanzania

Medical treatment is free or highly subsidised in company clinics and hospitals. Tanzania's national healthcare system stresses primary care at an affordable cost, but faces an acute shortage of healthcare workers. Low pay, poor working conditions and limited training programmes contribute, worsened by the burden of treating HIV/AIDS and malaria patients. Health standards in Tanzania have declined and care is poor. The public system serves the vast majority of the population but is chronically underfunded and understaffed. The wealthiest 20% of the population use the private system; this is the route followed by ill tourists who are insured.[30,31]

South Africa

Medical facilities are good in urban areas but can be limited elsewhere. Tourists on safari may find themselves distant from medical aid. Private facilities are good where they exist. Kruger National Park, Mpumalanga and northern KwaZulu-Natal are low-risk malaria areas from December until April. Swimming and paddling in stagnant or slow-moving water is not advised as there is a risk of contracting bilharzia (*see comment on West Africa*).

Considerations
- Safari travel means long hours in 4x4 vehicles in a dusty, dry wild environment, in areas where malarial mosquitos thrive.
- Safari visits depend upon early morning and late afternoon trips at a time when mosquitos are active.
- Dry and non-air-conditioned camping environs make for dehydration and water sources may be infected.

There is a high risk from infection and trauma, and emergency medical aid may be distant, of variable quality and ambulance evacuation non-existent.

Central and east African countries that offer wild-animal safaris are high-risk destinations for older travellers. Infection, trauma and dehydration are likely to befall the older person who may find that emergency medical care is distant and not of optimal quality. Ideally, safaris should only be embarked upon by those in robust health. A pre-travel health consultation is advised for those with pre-existing health conditions, and vaccine prophylaxis and antimalarial precautions should be taken.

Summary
With the exception of South Africa, the tourist will meet some of the poorest health facilities in the world if requiring emergency aid. Health professional staff are scarce, training variable and resources often basic or absent. Scarce transport and bad roads create difficulties in casualty evacuation. Blood supplies may be contaminated and emergency aid units far distant. Older travellers who are particularly vulnerable to heat and trauma should be aware of the limitations of healthcare in the region and that travel health insurance protection can only supply aid from what is locally available – it is therefore subject to severe limitations in treatment and healthcare.

Asia and the Antipodes

China
China is undertaking reform of its healthcare system to make it more affordable for the rural poor. Chinese medical schools provide training in Western medicine and also instruct in traditional medicine but relatively few physicians are competent in both areas. In urban hospitals, there may be separate departments for traditional and

Western treatment. In county hospitals, however, traditional medicine receives greater emphasis. This relies on herbal treatments, acupuncture, acupressure, moxibustion (the burning of herbs over acupuncture points) and cupping of the skin, with heated bamboo believed to be most effective in treating minor and chronic diseases. Traditional treatments may also be used for more serious conditions, particularly for such acute abdominal conditions as appendicitis, pancreatitis and gallstones – a consideration for foreign visitors who become ill far from major hospital centres.

Western-style medical facilities with international staff are available in Beijing, Shanghai, Guangzhou and a few other large cities. Hong Kong has excellent private facilities. Many other hospitals in major Chinese cities have so-called VIP wards (*gaogan bingfang*) with reasonably up-to-date medical technology and skilled physicians. They provide medical services to foreigners and have English-speaking doctors and nurses.

India
A universal healthcare system is run by the constituent states. Government hospitals, some of which are among the best hospitals in India, provide treatment for free or for a minimal charge. There is a large private sector in cities and tourist areas. Emergency transportation to hospital can prove a daunting procedure in much of rural India, a consideration older tourists should keep in mind (*see Chapter 13*).

Japan
The government provides healthcare services, with the patient accepting responsibility for 30% of the bill. Japan has excellent hospitals and clinics, and provides highly technical, state-of-the-art equipment. Patients are free to select the physicians or facilities of their choice. Due to large numbers of people visiting hospitals, emergency access is an issue in some units and a particular problem in Tokyo. In 2007, 14,000 emergency patients were rejected at least three times by Japanese hospitals before getting treatment. Some healthcare in Japan is provided free for expatriates and foreigners. The Japanese have no family-doctor system and medical ethics and bedside manners are not strong points with health professionals.

Malaysia
The country offers a comprehensive network of hospitals and clinics, with 88.5% of the population living within three miles of a public health clinic or private practitioner (*see Chapter 13*).

Nepal
The healthcare delivery network in Nepal is poorly developed. Government-operated healthcare consists of hospitals and health centres with very basic facilities. Healthcare practices in rural areas often depend upon the medicine man or shaman as well as ayurvedic treatment. Allopathic (modern) medicine and quality of care

is poor. There are private medical facilities in Kathmandu. Diarrhoeal disease is a major public-health problem and there is high risk of road accident trauma. Evacuation may be difficult and protracted, with limited air transport and tenuous road movement. In the higher valleys, patients may have to be carried to hospital on a Sherpa's back.[32-33] Infection risk is considerable, with high endemicity of malaria, food and water-borne diseases, such as typhoid and paratyphoid fever, giardiasis, amoebiasis, helminthiasis, rabies and hepatitis B. There is also a risk from the effects of high-altitude inducing AMS.

Considerations
- Think about malaria prophylaxis.
- Consider prophylaxis with acetazolamide for high-altitude exposure.
- Assume all water is contaminated and use water sterilising tablets.
- Be aware that emergency care is limited, and evacuation and hospital access may be protracted.

Southeast Asia

Indonesia
The level of healthcare in Bali – much visited by tourists – varies from local clinics and hospitals to foreign-run clinics such as International SOS. Small, urban clinics can handle simple injuries. Each district in Bali has a hospital located in the main town but Sanglah Hospital in Denpasar is the only one capable of dealing with major operations and patients are transferred here from elsewhere on the island.

Thailand
The healthcare system relies heavily on specialised medicine. The Thai government has developed a universal healthcare programme whereby everybody gets treatment at public hospitals for a standard fee per visit. If foreigners have a medical problem while in Thailand, a few hospitals of good reputation cater for foreign them; Bumrungrad Hospital is popular. Bangkok General Hospital, and its affiliates Samitivej Hospital and Bangkok Nursing Home Hospital, are also commended. Certain hospitals have been actively seeking medical tourists to visit Thailand and now up to 60% of patients at Bumrungrad Hospital and 40% at Samitivej Hospital are foreigners (*see Chapter 13*).

Summary

Large variations in healthcare occur across Southeast Asia, with some countries having excellent resources and catering for medical tourism. Congested roads and poor transportation result in high risk of road traffic accidents and trauma in many countries. Emergency transportation can be limited. Travel health insurance cover is essential. There is a high likelihood of gastrointestinal infection and malaria in many of these countries.

Antipodes

Australia
Australia has a highly commended medical care system. The Australian government has signed Reciprocal Health Care Agreements with the UK government, which entitles British visitors to limited subsidised health services for medically necessary treatment while visiting Australia. This covers any ill health or injury that occurs while in Australia and requires medical attention. The Royal Flying Doctor Service provides an excellent service to many rural areas[34] but emergency aid can be delayed due to adverse weather.[35] A UK resident is entitled to the following for any ill health or injury requiring treatment:
- free treatment as a public inpatient or outpatient in a public hospital
- subsidised medicines under the Pharmaceutical Benefits Scheme
- Medicare benefits for out-of-hospital medical treatment provided by doctors through private surgeries and community health centres.

Medical treatment can be accessed through private doctors' surgeries and community health centres. Doctors at these practices charge for their services by charging Medicare direct or presenting a bill for payment by the patient, which is then reimbursed by Medicare. If treated as a public patient in a public hospital, treatment is free on display to staff of a passport or reciprocal healthcare card. Medicare will not cover:
- medicines not subsidised under the Pharmaceutical Benefits Scheme
- dental work and allied health services
- accommodation and medical treatment in a private hospital
- accommodation and medical treatment as a private patient in a public ambulance service
- home nursing
- physiotherapy, occupational therapy, therapy, eye therapy, chiropractic services, podiatry glasses and contact lenses, hearing aids.

New Zealand
The New Zealand health system functions on the Anglo-American model of care, with emergency care in the pre-hospital setting being conducted by paramedics. There are reciprocal arrangements with the UK and WHO rates the system highly.

WHO has ranked the health systems of 191 nations: France and Italy took top spots while Australia, New Zealand, Canada, the UK and Germany rated highly on most measures of performance, including quality of care and access to it.

Arctic and Antarctica

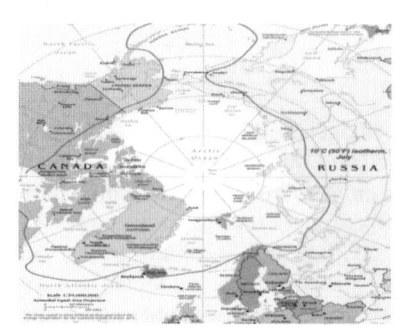

Every year 80,000 tourists visit the Falkland Islands and Antarctica. A significant number also visit the Arctic on cruise ships varying in size from small, ice-strengthened vessels to massive cruise liners. Several days are spent cruising around the Falklands with South Georgia and Antarctica, or Greenland, the Svalbard peninsula and Spitzbergen. Larger cruise ships to the region have the health facilities of modern luxury ships. Small ones may not have an on-board doctor. Irrespective of size they will offload ill or injured passengers in the Falkland Islands if cruising the southern seas and in Svalbard and the mainland in the Arctic.

Helicopter rescue is limited by range in the Arctic and patients have to be air evacuated from Svalbard to Norway and from Greenland to Denmark for intensive care. The nearest mainland countries to Greenland and Svalbard, they have good health facilities with UK reciprocation.[27]

Antarctica and the Falkland Islands

Antarctica and the Falkland Islands provide an emergency medical service for cruise ships and intrepid travellers visiting via South America. The water supply is safe and there is a reciprocal health agreement between the UK and Falkland Island governments, which allows free medical treatment for UK residents in the Falklands. This does not cover dental care. Medical services are based in the 27-bed, well-equipped King Edward VII Memorial Hospital (KEMH) in Stanley. The islands have four GPs with extended skills, two consultants, 28 nurses, a radiographer and modern digital plain x-ray equipment (excluding CT and MRI scanners). The pharmacy is stocked with UK pharmaceuticals but tourists are advised to bring enough of their regular medication to cover the duration of their visit.[36]

Given the small size of the hospital, the restricted range of diagnostic facilities available and limited ability to manage intensive-care patients, coupled with the lack of complex treatments such as kidney dialysis, it is normal to stabilise a critically ill patient and then transfer them to a larger hospital. KEMH has an agreement with the Clinica Alemana de Santiago in Santiago, Chile and every tourist must be insured to cover this potential cost. Aerocardal transport charges are in the region of US$30,000. Fees of the Clinica Alemana are comparable with a private hospital anywhere in Europe. The RAF normally will not consider transferring a tourist as a patient even if they are UK passport holders.

During the tourist season (October–March) doctors are accustomed to dealing with overseas hospitals, transfers and insurance companies. Ships leave from

Stanley to cruise the Antarctic Peninsula and islands – a four-day sail away from the nearest aid in the Falklands. Air evacuation is not practicable and emergency care will depend on ship resources.

The Arctic, Greenland and Svalbard
There are small village clinics in Greenland villages and Svalbard has a small hospital unit. Serious conditions have to be evacuated by small, fixed-wing aircraft – an expensive undertaking. Local governments are now insisting that visitors have repatriation insurance in place before arrival.

Consideration
The standard of medical care in the Falklands is broadly similar to that of the UK but tourists must bear in mind the limitations imposed by the size of the hospital, range of specialists and the limited range of diagnostic equipment available. In the Arctic resources are very limited and evacuation is often delayed and very expensive.

Case history
On a sea crossing from the North Cape of Norway to Greenland an older woman was wheelchair dependent and required help from her husband with all basic needs. The husband had a severe heart attack and had to be airlifted by helicopter, operating at its maximal range, to the nearest hospital in Norway. Bereft of assistance in daily living, the care of the wife became a major problem for crew who were not allowed to touch passengers, far less offer intimate care, and a harassed medical/nursing staff struggling to support passengers with norovirus infection. The wife had to be airlifted to the mainland by small aeroplane and, as she was uninsured, had to fund this herself. .

Summary
Older potential travellers to Antarctica and the Arctic should organise a pre-travel health consultation. Travel health insurance protection is essential with adequate cover for repatriation. They should be aware that emergency aid may be many hours – and in bad weather, days – away.

References

1 McIntosh I 1991 Travel Induced Illness Scot. Med. 11.4 14-15
2 www.nhs.uk/NHS England/www/EHIC/Pages/Introduction.aspx
3 Honor M. Medical care for visitors to France. 2008Brit.Trav.Health Assoc J.10.20-21

4 Mackay I Primary Care services with the EU. 2007. Brit.Trav.Health Assoc. IX,10-15
5 Mackay I Health care on a European river cruise.2010 Brit.Trav.Health Assoc .J 15.26-9
6 Rhisel R. Pay as you go in Romania 2010 Brit.Trav.Health Assoc. J 16.60
7 Gaál, P., Rekassy, B., and Healy, J. Health Care Systems in Transition: Hungary. Copenhagen: European Observatory on Healthcare Systems, 1999.
8 Orosz, E. and Hollo, I. 'Hospitals in Hungary: The story of stalled reforms, Eurohealth, vol. 7, num. 3, Autumn 2001.
9 Gaál, P. Study of the Hungarian Health Care System. Civitas, 2002.
10 Shannon C. Irvine F and B Analysis of Hungary' Health Care System www.civitas.org.uk/nhs/download/Hungary.
11 Popova S Feschieva, N The state of primary medical care in Bulgaria Journal of Public Health 1995 17, 1. 6-10
12 McCarthy M Serbia rebuilds and reforms its health care system The Lancet, 2007 Volume 369, I0,
13 Croatia European Observatory on Health Care Systems AMS 5001891 (CRO)CARE 04 01 02
14 Melrose A Health Care Round the Mediterranean2009 Brit.Trav.Health Assoc.J21-23
15 McIntosh I Health care and security for travellers to Middle east.2005 Brit.Trav.Health Assoc. J26-27
16 Mackay I Health Care Caribbean style Brit.Trav.Health Assoc J. 11.9-10
17 McIntosh I Cruise ship facilities 2007 Brit.Trav.Health Assoc.J10.10-12
18 McIntosh I health and safety on cruise ships2007 Brit.Trav.Health Assoc. J 10-15
19 McIntosh I Health care and security for travellers to the Middle east 2005 J Brit.Trav.Health Assoc.
20 Mackay I Health Care in the USA. 2009 Brit.Trav.Health Assoc.J13.16-17
21 Bailley R. Rural health service in north Saskatchewan 2007. X 23
22 Mackay I Travel and Health across South America.2007 J Brit Trav Health Assoc., X, 19-21
23 Melrose A. Health care for visitors and residents in west Africa.2011 Brit. Trav Health Assoc J 16 25-27
24 Dalton K Health care in the Gambia Brit. Trav Health Assoc J 2010 16.23
25 Eyob Zere, Custodia Mandlhate Equity in health care in Namibia: developing a needs-based resource allocation formula using principal components analysis Int J Equity Health. 2007; 6: 3
26 2whohgana@gha.fro.who.intUNICEF, 2008
27 Wamai, RG. (2009). "The health system in Kenya: Analysis of the situation and enduring challenges." JMAJ. 52(2): 136.
28 Kareru, PG, Kenji, GM, Gachanja, AN, Et al. (2007). "Traditional medicines among the Embu and Mbeere peoples of Kenya." Afr. J. Trad. CAM. 4(1): 75.
29 Meldrum A Zimbabwe's health-care system struggles on. 2008 Lancet, 371, 1059 - 1060
30 Mwww.world life expectancy.com/country-health-e. Tanzania health system .
31 http://www.nationsencyclopedia.com/Africa/Tanzania-HEALTH.html#ixzz1EJuipEOU
32 Mackay I Nepal, the tourist view of the health scene. 2004 J. Brit. trav. Health Assoc 5 ,35-6
33 Kharal PM Travel Medicine in Nepal 2004J Brit. Trav Health Assoc. 5.33-4
34 McIntosh I Royal flying doctor service of Australia. 2006 Brit. Trav.Health Assoc J. 7.26-7
35 Mackay I The good Samaritan response 2008 Brit. Trav Health Assoc .J. 8.14-16
36 Diggle R .Falkland's health care J Brit.Trav.Health Assoc .J XI, 2006.11-12

Index

*Note: page numbers in **bold** type refer to information in Tables or Figures.*

accidents 36, 40, 204
    adventure travel 158
    road traffic accidents 39, 41
    sea travel 67
acclimatisation 81, 162
accessibility 136, 151
acetazolamide (Diamox) 42, 82, 163, 171, 210, 220
acetylcholinesterase 102
achlorhydria 80
acid-suppressive drugs 99
acute mountain sickness (AMS) 36, 40, 42, 81–2, 162–4, 171, 210–11, 220
acute retention 27, 144
adventure travel 37, 157–9
    advice for trekkers and expeditioners 164–5
    first aid kit recommendations 166–7
    high-altitude travel 162–4
    pre-travel health consultation 164
    safari and warm region travel 159
    water activities 160–1
Advisory Committee on Malaria for UK Travellers (ACMP) 39
Age Concern 176
age discrimination 14
ageing process:
    effects of 15–16, 19–27
    impact on travel 16–17, 27–8
    psychological factors 17
    physiological function effects 17
Air Canada 149
air travel 45–6
    adverse effects of 47
    advice for older travellers 53–7
    air humidity and expansion of gases 46, 49
    anxiety about 50, 109, 110, 111–12, 113, 113–17
    advice for travellers 120–1
    phobias 116–20
    cabin air at high altitude 46–7
    cabin air quality 46, 47–9
    contraindications to 54
    disabled travellers 137, 138, 139–40, 148–50
    fly cruising 69
    in-flight immobility 50–1

    infection 49
    jet lag 52–3, 57
    limited toilet access 53
    medical fitness for 54–5
    and medication 49, 50, 56, 150
    on-board medical assistance 55
    pre-existing illness 49–50
    and risk 28
    and visual impairment 139–40
    VTE risk 51–2, **51**, 53–4, 55, 57, 84
    wheelchair travel 148–50
Airbus A319 aircraft 48
Airbus A380 aircraft 47
Albania, emergency healthcare 197, 201
alcohol, and road safety 72
aldosterone 76
Algeria, emergency healthcare 199–200
altitude:
    altitude illness 36, 40, 42, 81, 81–2, 162–4, 171, 210, 210–11, 220
    and cabin air 46–7
Alzheimer's disease 120
American Aerospace Medical Association 56
American College of Emergency Physicians (ACEP) 68
American Virgin Islands 203, 204
amiodarine 92, 127, 172
amoebiasis 220
AMS (acute mountain sickness) 36, 40, 42, 81, 81–2, 162–4, 171, 210–11, 220
analgesics 171
angina 54, 95, 124
    and altitude sickness 40
angioplasty 124
animal bites 36
    rabies 103–4
anoxia 46
    and altitude sickness 40
antacids 172
Antarctic:
    cruising 63, 160
    emergency healthcare 222–3
antiemetic medication 83
anthrax 212
antiarrhythmics, and antimalarials 92, 172
antibiotics, and diarrhoea 41, 97, 98–9, **99**
anticoagulant thromboprophylaxis 52

225

Index

antiepileptics, and antimalarials 92
antigen-driven lymphocyte proliferation 24
antihistamines 100, 101, 170, 171–2
antimalarials *see* malaria, prevention
antimotility drugs 97–8, 172
Antipodes, emergency healthcare 221
antothrombin deficiency 126
anxiety *see* flight anxiety; stress; travel anxiety
appetite, poor, and altitude sickness 82
Arctic:
    cruising 63, 160
    emergency healthcare 222–3
arginine vasopressin 76
arid environments 75–9
arrhythmia 92, 95, 124, 172
artemesinin 94
arthritis 141
Aruba, non-application of EHIC 183, 204
Asia:
    emergency healthcare 218–21
    road traffic accidents 72
aspirin, and VTE 52, 126
Association of British Insurers 179
atherosclerosis 21
atovaquone 93, 172
atrial fibrillation 95
atrophic vaginitis 146
Australia, emergency healthcare 221
autonomic response, and ageing 23
azithromycin **99**
azthromycin 173

B-GOS food supplement 41, 97
B-lymphocytes 87
Bacillus cereus 79, 99
balance 28
Baltic, emergency healthcare 201–2
Bangladesh 38
Barbados 203, 204
bed bugs (*Cimicidae*) 100
behavioural change, and travel anxiety 110–11, 113–14, 115–16, 119–20
Belize 101
Benin, emergency healthcare 214
benzodiazepines 57, 115
beta-andrenergic stimulation 21
beta-blockers 115, 127
and antimalarials 92, 172
bilharzia 218
bismuth subsalicylate 41, 98
biting midges (*Ceratopogonidae*) 101

Black Sea, emergency healthcare 201–2
bladder function 24, 53, 142–7, 144
    infections 27
    see also incontinence
blindness *see* visual impairment
blood, and ageing 23
blood pressure 21, 112
Boeing 757 aircraft 48
Boeing 787 Dreamliner aircraft 47, 48–9, 49
Bolivia, emergency healthcare 210–11
bones, and ageing 25
brain, ageing 25, 27–8
bribery, and emergency medical care 194, 195, 196, 197, 201–2
bright-light exposure 57
British Aerospace 146 aircraft 48
British Medical Association, and medical tourism 185
British Thoracic Society 56
British Virgin Islands 203
Bulgaria:
    emergency healthcare 196, 202
    medical tourism 186
BUPA 185

cabin air:
    at high altitude 46–7
    quality 46, 47–9
calcium antagonists, and antimalarials 92, 172
Cameroon, emergency healthcare 214
Campylobacteria 66, 80, 98, **99**
    Campylobacter jejuni 96, 98
Canada, emergency healthcare 208–9
cancer, deaths in world travellers **123**
Cape Verde islands, emergency healthcare 213
carbamazepine 93
carbonic acid 163
carbonic anhydrase inhibitor 82, 163, 210
cardiac drugs, and antimalarials 92
cardiac function 15, 19, 21–2, 27
cardio-pulmonary function 16
cardiovascular disease 123–7
    and air travel 46, 49–50, 54, 110
    contraindications to 124–5
    arrhythmia 92, 124, 172
    deaths in world travellers **123**
    and sea travel 63, **63**
cardiovascular system 21, 27
Caribbean islands:
    emergency healthcare 202–5
    road traffic accidents 72
cataract 139

Index

catastrophic thinking 113
Cayman Islands 203
CBT (cognitive behaviour therapy) 115–16
cell-mediated immune response 17
Ceratopogonidae (biting midges) 101
cerebral infarction 95
chemical contamination, of cabin air 48–9
chemoceptor responses 23
chest pain 124
chicken pox 212
 and sea travel 65
 see also herpes zoster
Child-Pugh classification (liver function) 93
Chile, emergency healthcare 209, 210–11, 222
China, emergency healthcare 218–19
Chironomidae 101
chloroquine 92, 93, 172
chlorpheniramine 172
cholera 212, 214, 217
chronic illness 16
 and heat exhaustion 77
Cimicidae (bed bugs) 100
cinnarizine 68, 71, 83
ciprofloxacin 41, 97, 98, **99**, 172–3
circadian-rhythm disorder 52–3
circulation, slow 28
circulatory system, and ageing 23
Civil Aviation Authority (CAA) 48
climate, and risk 28
clinical fitness 14–15
Clostridium difficile colitis 98, **99**
CO_2 levels, in air travel 48
coach travel *see* road travel
Cochrane Collaboration Database of Systematic Reviews 40, 97, 102
cognitive behaviour therapy (CBT) 115–16
cognitive function, impairment of 15, 25
cold:
 injury to skin 161
 see also hypothermia
cold-water cruising 63, 67, 160
cold-water immersion 160
colitis, *Clostridium difficile* 98, **99**
colonic flora 98
compression stockings 52, 54, 56
concentration, loss of 25
Continental Airlines 149
contraindications to air travel 54
COPD (chronic obstructive pulmonary disease), and air travel 47
coping strategies, and flight anxiety 114–15
Corynebacterium diphtheriae see diphtheria

coumarins 93
Croatia:
 emergency healthcare 197
 medical tourism 186
cruises *see* Europe, river cruises; sea travel
Cryptosporidium parvum 96
Cuba 203
Cyclospora cayetensis 96
Cyprus:
 emergency healthcare 194
 non-application of EHIC 183
cystocoele 146, 147

DAEC (diffusely adherent *E. coli*) 96
data acquisition, and pre-travel risk assessment 29
deafness *see* hearing impairment
deaths:
 aboard ship 64
 in accidents 72
 and air travel 45–6, 50
 causes of in world travellers **123**
 from dehydration 77
 from heart failure 21
 from hepatitis A 89
 from influenza and pneumonia 87–8
deep vein thrombosis (DVT) 28, 36, 50, 69, 84, 124, 141
 insurance against 181
 see also VTE (venous thromboembolism)
DEET 92, 101
defibrillators 55
dehydration 24, 76–7, 82, 95, 206
 and air travel 49, 56
 management 78
 symptoms 77–8
 and VTE 52, 126
dengue fever 35, 36, 40, 102–3
depression, and antimalarials 92
dermatological problems 36
desensitisation 116, 118, 119
destinations, risks associated with 28
detrusor function 144, 145
diabetes 26, 127–8, 172–3
 and antimalarials 92, 172
 and dehydration 78
 and diarrhoea 95
 insulin 129–30, 132–3
 patient information 131–3
 travel clinic considerations 128
Diamox 42, 82, 163, 171, 210, 220
diarrhoea 36, 37–8, 79–80, 95, 99–100, 127, 173

227

Index

and adventure travel 158
antimotility drugs 97–8, 172
causes 96–7
and diabetes 130
and Middle East travel 206
prophylaxis and treatment 41, 97–9
risk areas 79–80, 95–6
and sea travel 65, 66–7
and toilet facilities 143
diffusely adherent *E. coli* (DAEC) 96
diffusion capacity 22
digoxin levels 172, 173
diluting ability of kidney 24
dimeticone 102
diphtheria 35, 89
Diptera 101
Disability Discrimination Act (1999) 147
disabled travellers 14, 15, 16, **16**, 135–6
    advice for 141–2, 152–4
    air travel 137, 138, 139–40, 148–50
    hearing impairment 138
    incontinence problems 142–7
    medication and air travel 49, 50, 56, 150
    physical and locomotor disability 141
    pre-travel consultation 136–7
    pre-travel documentation 137
    sea travel 69
    types of disability 137
    visual impairment 138–40
    wheelchair travel 147–50, 147–52
diuretics 78, 126
dizziness 23, 47
    and altitude sickness 82
    and motion sickness 82
dogs, and rabies 103–4
Dominican Republic 203
doxycycline 41, 93, 97, 127, 172
drug toxicity, and kidney function 24
dry environments 75–9
DVT *see* deep vein thrombosis
dysentery 80, 214
dyspnoea 22, 47, 49, 54, 124

E. coli 66, 67, 80, 96
EAEC (entero-aggregative *E. coli*) 96
East Africa, emergency healthcare 216–18
EasyJet 149
Egypt, emergency healthcare 199, 200
EHIC (European Health Insurance Card) 178, 181, 182, 183–4, 186, 192, 193, 201, 204
elastic recoil 22

elastin fibres 22, 25
elderly population, statistics 11, **12**
electrolyte imbalance 24, 37, 75–9, 95
    see also diarrhoea
elevators, wheel chair access 151
Embraer 145 aircraft 48
emergencies:
    and health insurance 13
    in-flight 45–6
    and sea travel 69
emergency healthcare overseas 191–2
    Antipodes 221
    Arctic and Antarctica 222–3
    Asia 218–21
    Baltic and Black Sea cruising 201–2
    Caribbean islands 202–5
    costs of 176
    East and Southern Africa 216–18
    Europe 192–8
    Mediterranean and Adriatic coasts 198–201
    Middle East 205–7
    North America 208–9
    South America 209–12
    West Africa 212–16
emergency on-board care, sea travel 64–5
encephalitis, TBE (tick-borne encephalitis) 102
Entamoeba histolytica 80, 97
enteritis, and air travel 49
entero-aggregative *E. coli* (EAEC) 96
enterotoxic *E. coli* (ETEC) 66, 67, 96
environmental accidents 40
environmental stress, and ageing 26–8
epilepsy 125
    anti-epileptics and antimalarials 92
ETEC (enterotoxic *E. coli*) 66, 67, 96
EU:
    European Health Insurance Card (EHIC) 178, 181, 182, 186, 192, 193, 201, 204
    list of member countries 192
Europe:
    emergency healthcare 192–8
    river cruises 19–84
    road traffic accidents 39, 72
European Economic Area, and European Health Insurance Card (EHIC) 183, 192
European Health Insurance Card (EHIC) 178, 181, 182, 183–4, 186, 192, 193, 201, 204
exercise, and heat exhaustion 77, 78
exhaustion 28
exogenous melatonin 57
expansion of gases, and air travel 46, 49
expeditions *see* adventure travel

Index

Factor V Leiden 125
Falklands Islands, emergency healthcare 222–3
falls 23, 28, 40, 141
   and land travel 72
   and osteoporosis 25
Faroe Islands 184
fatigue 23, 28, 47
   and altitude sickness 82
   and dehydration 77
   and motion sickness 82
   travel fatigue 84
Federal Aviation Authority (FAA) 48
FEV1 23
filarial worms 101
fire, on ships 67
first aid kit recommendations, adventure travel 166–7
fitness:
   for air travel 54–5
   and health 157
   physical and clinical 14–15
fleas (*Siphonaptera*) 100–1
flight anxiety 50, 109, 110, 111–12, 113, 113–17
   advice for travellers 120–1
   phobias 116–20
flouroquinolones 98
fluid imbalance 24, 37, 75–9
see also kidney; water regulation
food-borne illness 28, 37, 49, 79–80
foot injuries 40, 41, 72, 128
Foreign and Commonwealth Office (FCO) 179–80, 186
frail travellers *see* disabled travellers
France, emergency healthcare 176, 192–3, 198
Frank-Starling mechanism 21
FREMEC card 125, 137
French Guiana 204
French Polynesia, non-application of EHIC 183
frostbite 161
"fume events" 48
FVC 23

Gabon, emergency healthcare 215
Gambia, emergency healthcare 212–13
gastrointestinal disorders 79–80
     acute gastroenteritis 99, 143
     sea travel 63, **63**, 66–7
   see also diarrhoea
gastrointestinal function 16
Georgia, emergency healthcare 202

Germany, emergency healthcare 193
Ghana, emergency healthcare 213
Giardia lamblia 96
giardiasis 220
giddiness, and dehydration 77
glaucoma 138, 171
glibenclamide 92, 172
glomerular function 24, 78
glucagon 128
glucose tolerance 15
Greece:
   emergency healthcare 176, 193–4
   road traffic accidents 39, 72
Greenland 184, 223
gross peripheral oedema 50
Guadeloupe 203, 204

H_2 antagonists 173
head-lice (*Pediculus humanus capitas*) 101–2
headache, and altitude sickness 82
health insurance *see* travel health insurance
health status 15
hearing impairment 26, 28, 138
heart 15, 21–2
   see also cardiovascular disease
heat exhaustion 76, 159
heatstroke 23, 28, 77, 159
helminthiasis 220
heparin, and VTE 52, 54
hepatitis 35, 203, 212
   hepatitis A (HAV) 88, 89–90
   hepatitis B 88, 90, 220
herpes zoster 88, 89
high-altitude cerebral oedema (HACE) 81
high-altitude illness 36, 40, 42, 81, 81–2, 162–4, 171, 210–11, 220
high-altitude pulmonary oedema (HAPE) 81
high-risk travellers 14
hip replacement 141
HIV/AIDS 35, 203, 214, 217
Honduras 101
Hong Kong 219
hookworm 217
hot environments 75–9
humid environments 75–9
humidity, and air travel 46, 49
Hungary, emergency healthcare 195
hyoscine 169, 171–2
hyper-coagulable states 52
hypercapnia 23, 27, 46
hyperkalaemia 76

229

Index

hyperlipidaemia 27
hypernatraemic dehydration 76
hyperprostatism 24
hyperpyrexia (heatstroke) 23, 28, 77, 159
hypertension 27, 49, 124
hyperthermia 23
hypertonic dehydration 76
hypertropia 139
hyperventilation, and air travel 47
hypnotherapy 116, 118, 119
hypocapnia 162
hypoglycaemia *see* diabetes
hyponatraemia 159
hypothermia 23, 28, 160–1
hypotonic dehydration 76
hypovolaemia 76
hypoxaemia 46
hypoxia 17, 23, 27, 28, 47, 126
    hypoxia challenge test 55–6

ICVP 103
immobilisation, and VTE 50–1, 52
immune function 15, 17, 23–4, 26, 27, 87
immunisation 87–8
    adverse reaction to 90
    antibody response to 24
    diphtheria 89
    hepatitis A 89–90
    herpes zoster 89
    influenza 24, 71, 88, 125
    malaria 90–1
    pneumonia 71, 88, 125
    poliomyelitis 90
    rabies 104
    resources 104
    and sea travel 71
    tetanus 89
    tuberculosis 90
    typhoid fever 88
    yellow fever 90
Imodium 98
    see also loperamide

implantable cardioverter defibrillator (ICD) 124
INCAD (Incapacitated Passengers Handling Advice)
    form 137, 148, 152
incontinence 24, 27, 142–4
    causes 145
    pre-travel health consultation 146–7
    treatment and management 145–6

India 38
    emergency healthcare 219
    medical tourism 185, 187
Indonesia:
    emergency healthcare 220
    malaria 91
infectious disease 24, 31, 35–6, 100–4
    and air travel 49
    deaths in world travellers **123**
    and sea travel 65–6
    see also diarrhoea; malaria
influenza 35
    and air travel 49
    immunisation 24, 71, 88, 125
    risk to older people 87, 88
    and sea travel 65, 66
information:
    patient information leaflets 41
    diabetes 131–3
    disabled travellers 152–4
    sources 42
inhalation injuries 67
injuries, and sea travel 63, **63**, 67
INR 93, 172
insect bites 36, 40, 92, 100–3
    see also malaria
insulin 129–30, 132–3
insurance *see* travel health insurance
International Society for Quality in Health Care
    (ISQua) 185
Isle of Man, non-application of EHIC 183
isotonic dehydration 76
Israel:
    emergency healthcare 200
    malaria 91
Italy, emergency healthcare 193, 199
Ivory Coast, emergency healthcare 214
Ixodidae (ticks) 102

Jamaica 203
Japan, emergency healthcare 219
Japanese encephalitis 35
Jersey, non-application of EHIC 183
jet lag 52–3, 57
Joint Commission International (JCI) 185, 187

kaolin products 172
Kenya, emergency healthcare 216
kidneys:

Index

and ageing 24, 27, 76
 see also fluid imbalance; renal function
kinetosis (motion sickness) 63, 64, 68, 71, 82–3

land travel 71–2
 and anxiety 109–10, 111
 and VTE (venous thromboembolism) 126–7
Lassa fever 214
Legionnaires' disease 35, 65, 66
leishmaniasis 35, 101
Leonard Cheshire charity 141
leprosy 214, 215
leptospirosis 35
Libya, emergency healthcare 199, 200
lice (*Pediculus humanus capitas*) 101–2
life expectancy 11–12, **12**
lifts, wheel chair access 151
lightheadedness 47
liver disease, and antimalarials 93, 94
liver function 170
LMWH (low-molecular-weight heparin), and VTE 52, 54, 126
locomotor disability *see* disabled travellers
long-distance travel 14
long-term illness, and age 16, **16**
loperamide 80, 98, 99, 182
low-molecular-weight heparin (LWMH), and VTE 52, 54, 126
low-risk travellers 14
lungs:
 ageing 22
 see also pulmonary function
Lyme disease (*Lyme borrelosis*) 35, 102

macrolides 173
macular degeneration 139
malaria 35, 36, 38–9, 40, 212, 213, 214, 215, 217, 220, 221
 Caribbean islands 203
 Peru 211
 prevention 42, 71, 90–1, 92–4, 104, 172
 vulnerability with age 91–2
malathion 102
Malaysia:
 emergency healthcare 219
 medical tourism 188
malignancy, and VTE 126
Malta, emergency healthcare 194
Martinique 203, 204
measles 212, 213
 sea travel 65

medical facilities:
 local 28
 on-board aircraft 55
 on-board ship 64–5, 68–9
medical tourism 184–8
medication 27, 169
 advice for older travellers 174
 and air travel 49, 50, 56, 150
 and diarrhoea 95, 97–8, 172
 drug carriage and purchase abroad 170
 and flight anxiety 115, 118
 interaction of antemitic medication 83
 interaction with antimalarials 92
 and motion sickness 68, 71, 83
 and older travellers 169–70
 polypharmacy 170
 and sea travel 69, 71
 travel-related prescription drugs 171–3
MEDIF form 125, 137, 148, 152
Mediterranean and Adriatic coasts, emergency healthcare 198–201
medium-risk travellers 14
MedTral New Zealand 185
mefloquine 92, 93, 172
melanocytes 25
melatonin 57
memory impairment 15, 25
men:
 and incontinence 144
 life expectancy 12, **12**
 prostate enlargement 24, 27, 53, 144, 146
meningitis 213, 214
meningococcal meningitis 35
mental impairment 15, 25
metabolic acidosis 163, 171
metabolic response 17
Middle East, emergency healthcare 205–7
midges, biting (*Ceratopogonidae*) 101
Morocco, emergency healthcare 199
mosquitos, and malaria 38
motion sickness (kinetosis) 63, 64, 68, 71, 82–3
motorbikes 72
MSU (mid-stream specimen of urine) test 146
mucociliary function 22
muscle cramps, and dehydration 77
myasthenia gravis 103
myocardial infarction 95, 124
 see also cardiovascular disease
myopia 139

Namibia, emergency healthcare 215, 217

231

Index

natriuresis 76
  see also sodium regulation
nausea 82
Nepal, emergency healthcare 219–20
neurohumoural control 76
neurological disease, and air travel 46, 55
neurological function 17
neuropsychiatric disorders, and antimalarials 92
New Zealand, emergency healthcare 221
norovirus 66, 79, 80, 96, 97, 99, 203
North Africa, emergency healthcare 199–200
North America, emergency healthcare 208–9
Norwalk virus 65, 66–7
NSAIDs (non-steroidal anti-inflammatory drugs) 171, 173

obesity, and VTE 126
oedema 50, 100
  pulmonary oedema 81, 124
oesophageal reflex 172
oligaemic shock 77
onchocerciasis 213
organophosphates 102
osteoblasts 25
osteoclasts 25
osteoporosis 25, 28
oxybutinin 145, 147
oxygen levels:
  low 27
  see also hypoxia
oxygen supplementation, in air travel 55–6, 125–6
oxyhaemoglobin dissociation curve 47

pacemaker 124, 125
painkillers 171
Pakistan 38
pappataci fever 101
parasites 101
  and diarrhoea 36, 80, 96–7
paratyphoid fever 36, 220
parenchymal elastic fibres 22
paroxysmal supraventricular tachycardia 127
partial pressure of arterial oxygen (PaO_2) 22
  and air travel 46–7
  and altitude sickness 40, 81
passenger morbidity, sea travel 62–4, **63**
passenger mortality, sea travel 64
patient information leaflets 41
  diabetes 131–3
  disabled travellers 152–4

Pediculus humanus capitas (head-lice) 101–2
pelvic floor 24, 145, 147
permethrin 102
personal health protection, for older travellers 188
personal violence 40, 41
pertussis 212
Peru, emergency healthcare 211
pharmacies, on-board ship 69
pharmacodynamic effects of drugs in older people 170
pharmacokinetic effects of drugs in older people 169–70
phenytoin 93
Phlebotominae 101
phobias, flight 116–19
photosensitivity 127
physical disability see disabled travellers
physical fitness 14–15
physiological arousal, and travel anxiety 113
physiological function effects of ageing 17
PJ Hayman (insurance) 181
placebo effect, and anti-seasickness drugs 68, 83
plasma renin 76
Plasmodium falciparum see malaria
pneumonia:
  immunisation 71, 88, 125
  risk to older people 87–8
pneumothorax 55
poliomyelitis 35, 88, 90
population trends 11, **12**
Portugal:
  emergency healthcare 199
  road traffic accidents 39, 72
post-herpetic neuralgia 89
postural hypotension 23
potassium clearance 24
pre-existing illness 15, 16, 26–7
  air travel 46, 49–50
  checklist for travellers 153–4
  travel health insurance 179–81
pre-flight assessment 55–6
pre-travel documentation, disabled travellers 137
pre-travel health consultation 16, 17, 40–1
  adventure travel 164
  assessment and management planning 29
  environmental stress 26–8
  external factors 28
  factors influencing risk 19–23
  frail and disabled travellers 136–7
  incontinence 146–7
  other systemic deterioration 23–6
  risk appraisal 29, **30–1**, 31
  risk identification **20**

Index

sea travel 70–1
summary 32
presbycusis 26
presbyopia 139
pressurisation, of aircraft cabin air 46–7
PRM (passenger with reduced mobility) teams 141
probiotics, and diarrhoea 41, 97, 172
proguanil 93, 172
prolapse 24, 27, 53
promethazine 68, 71, 83
prostate enlargement 24, 27, 53, 144, 146
proton pump inhibitors (PPIs) 99, 173
protozoa 101
pruritis 101
psychological effects of travel 83–4
   flight anxiety 109, 111–12, 114–15
   advice for travellers 120–1
   flying phobias 116–20
   other travel modes 112–14
   travel anxiety 109–11, 123
psychological factors 17
Puerto Rico 203
pulmonary embolism (PE) 50
   see also VTE (venous thromboembolism)
pulmonary function 15, 16, 17, 22, 27
   and air travel 55
pulmonary oedema 124
   high-altitude pulmonary oedema (HAPE) 81
pyrethroids 102

Qantas 149
QE2, medical facilities 69
QHA Trent 185
QT interval 92, 172
quinapril 172
quinine, hypersensitivity to 93
quinolones 173

rabies 36, 103–4, 220
rail travel:
   and anxiety 112–13
   and visual impairment 140
   wheelchair travel 150–1
reaction time, slow 28
rectal overloading 146, 148
red blood cells 23
renal function 15, 16, 17, 24, 27, 76, 77, 78, 170
renal impairment, and antimalarials 93–4
renin-angiotensin-aldosterone axis 76
repatriation 176, 177, 182–3, 203, 204

and European Health Insurance Card (EHIC) 183
respiratory alkalosis 162
respiratory conditions:
   and air travel 54–5
   and sea travel 63, **63**
rickettsia 36, 102
rifixamin 98, 99–100, **99**
risks, of travel 15, 16, 27–9, **30–1**, 31, 35
   infectious health risk 35–6
   information sources 42
   non-infectious health risk 36
   patient information leaflets 41–2
   travel-related illness 36–41
   see also pre-travel health consultation
river cruises, Europe 194–8
road traffic accidents 39, 41, 71–2
road travel:
   and VTE (venous thromboembolism) 126–7
   wheelchair travel 150
Romania, emergency healthcare 194–5, 202
rotavirus 96, 97
Royal Flying Doctor Service 221
Rubella 65
Russia, emergency healthcare 201–2

safari travel 159
safety behaviour, and travel anxiety 113
Salmonella 66, 96, 98, 99
   Salmonella typhi 103
salt depletion 76
sandflies 101
Sao Tome and Principe, emergency healthcare 215
SARS (severe acute respiratory syndrome), and air travel 49
Scandinavia 101
schistosomiasis 36, 212, 213, 214, 217
scopolamine 68, 71, 83
Scotland 101
   travel-related illness study 36–7
sea travel 61–2
   and anxiety 109–10
   deaths aboard ship 64
   and older passengers 62
   on-board medical care 64–5, 68–9
   passenger morbidity 62–4, **63**
   and passengers with disabilities 69
   risks to health 65–9
   ship pharmacy and medications 69
   wheelchair travel 69, 141–2, 151
seasickness 63, 64, 68, 71, 83

233

see also motion sickness
seasonal factors 28
Segways 72
Senegal, emergency healthcare 213
senescence 15
senile macular degeneration 139
Sensation, medical facilities 69
sensorial change in ageing 26
Serbia, emergency healthcare 196
seroconversion 87, 88
severe acute respiratory syndrome (SARS), and air travel 49
sexually-transmitted infections 35
Shigella 66, 80, 96, 98
shingles *see* herpes zoster
ship-to-shore transfers 65, 151, 160
Sierra Leone, emergency healthcare 214
sight *see* visual impairment
Simuliidae 101
Singapore, medical tourism 185, 187
Siphonaptera (fleas) 100–1
skin:
  ageing 24–5
  and sea travel 63, **63**
  and sweating ability 24, 25
sleep disturbance, and altitude sickness 82
sleeping sickness 214, 215
smallpox 215
sodium regulation 16, 17, 27, 76
  see also natriuresis
South Africa:
  emergency healthcare 218
  medical tourism 185, 187
South America:
  altitude sickness 40, 81
  emergency healthcare 209–12
Southeast Asia, emergency healthcare 220
Southern Africa, emergency healthcare 216–18
spa pools, and Legionnaires' disease 66
Spain, emergency healthcare 176, 193, 198
sphincter dysfunction 142, 144, 145
standby emergency treatment (SBET) 38
Staphylococcus aureus 66, 79, 99
stent 124, 125
stomach acid, reduced 28
Streptococcus see pneumonia
stress 17, 83–4
  and ageing 26–8
  air travel 50
  see also travel anxiety
  stress incontinence 142, 144, 145, 147
stroke 55, 110

sun damage 25
support stockings 126, 128
surgery:
  and air travel 55, 124, 125
  and VTE 126
Svalbard, emergency healthcare 223
sweating ability 17, 24, 25, 76
Switzerland:
  emergency healthcare 197–8
  and European Health Insurance Card (EHIC) 183, 192, 198
Syria, emergency healthcare 200

T-lymphocytes (T-cells) 23, 87
tachycardia:
  and air travel 47
  paroxysmal supraventricular tachycardia 127
Tanzania, emergency healthcare 217
TBE (tick-borne encephalitis) 36, 102
telemedical assistance services 55
temperature regulation 16, 23
tendonitis/tendon rupture 98, **99**, 173
terrorist attacks 84, 110
tetanus 36, 212
  immunisation 88, 89, 104
tetracyclines 93, 172
Thailand 103
  emergency healthcare 220
  medical tourism 185, 186
thiazides 127
thirst 76, 77
thrombophilia 126
thrombosis 162
  see also deep vein thrombosis; VTE (venous thromboembolism)
thymus gland 23, 103
thyroid disease, and dehydration 78
tick-borne encephalitis (TBE) 36, 102
ticks (*Ixodidae*) 102
Togo, emergency healthcare 215
toilet access 53, 142–4
  wheelchair 151
  see also incontinence
trachoma 212, 214
train travel *see* rail travel
trauma, deaths in world travellers **123**
traumatic accident 36
travel anxiety 109–11, 123
  see also flight anxiety
travel fatigue 84
travel health insurance 13, 175–9, 189

insurance provision 181–2
pre-existing conditions and exclusions 179–81
repatriation 182–3
and sea travel 62, 70
travel sickness 164
motion sickness (kinetosis) 63, 64, 68, 71, 82–3
travel-induced disorders:
high altitude illness 81–2
hot, arid, dry and humid environments 75–9
kinetosis 82–3
psychological effects of travel 83–4
water and food-borne illnesses 79–80
Treatmentabroad.net 185
trekking see adventure travel
trimethoprim/sulfamethoxazole 41, 97, 98
Trinidad 204
trypanosomiasis 36, 213
tuberculosis 36, 49, 90, 212, 214, 215, 217
Tunisia, emergency healthcare 199
Turkey:
emergency healthcare 194–5, 200–1, 202
non-application of EHIC 183
typhoid fever 36, 88, 99, 103, 212, 220

UK:
life expectancy 11–12, **12**
long-term illness/disability, and age 16, **16**
population trends 11, **12**
Ukraine:
emergency healthcare 194–5, 200–1, 202
medical tourism 188
ultraviolet light exposure 36, 68
uninsured travellers 13
United Arab Emirates 170
United States; malaria 91
United States, emergency healthcare 176, 208
upper respiratory tract infections, and air travel 49
urge incontinence 142
urinary system 24, 27
acidification 24
urinary concentration 24, 27
urinary retention 27, 144
urinary tract infections 27, 146
see also incontinence

vaccination see immunisation
vehicle sickness 83
see also motion sickness
ventilation 22, 23
ventilatory response to hypoxia 17, 27

ventricles 21–2
verapamil 127
Vietnam 103
viral gastroenteritis 79
Virgin Atlantic 149
visual impairment 26, 28, 138–40
vomiting:
and acute gastroenteritis 99
and altitude sickness 82
and dehydration 77
and gastroenteritis 79
VTE (venous thromboembolism) 45, 51–2, **51**, 84, 126–7
advice on avoidance 53–4, 55
see also deep vein thrombosis; pulmonary embolism (PE)

warfarin 126, 126–7, 172
and antimalarials 92
warm region travel 159
warm-water cruising, passenger morbidity 62–3
water:
contaminated 28
and Legionnaires' disease 66
water-borne illness 79–80
water activities 160–1
water regulation 16, 17, 27
see also fluid imbalance
West Africa:
emergency healthcare 212–16
malaria 94
wheelchair travel 147–8
air travel 148–50
fly cruising 69
road travel 150
sea travel 69, 141–2, 151
train travel 150–1
WHO ranking of national healthcare systems 221
women:
and incontinence 142, 143, 144, 146
life expectancy 12, **12**
prolapse 24, 27, 53
wound healing, slow 28

yaws 214, 215
yellow fever 36, 90, 103, 212, 214, 215

Zambia, emergency healthcare 217
Zimbabwe, emergency healthcare 217